The Best American Short Plays

2014–2015

The Best American Short Plays

2014–2015

edited by

William W. Demastes

APPLAUSE THEATRE & CINEMA BOOKS
An Imprint of Hal Leonard Corporation

The Best American Short Plays 2014–2015
Edited by William W. Demastes

Published in 2016 by Applause Theatre & Cinema Books
An Imprint of Hal Leonard Corporation
7777 West Bluemound Road
Milwaukee, WI 53213

Trade Book Division Editorial Offices
33 Plymouth St., Montclair, NJ 07042

Printed in the United States of America
Book interior by UB Communications

ISBN 978-1-4950-4648-3 [paper]
ISSN 0067 6284

www.applausebooks.com

contents

introduction

More Than Cool Reason Can Ever Comprehend

William W. Demastes

"The lunatic, the lover, and the poet / Are of imagination all compact." So says William Shakespeare in that spot-on sort of way that stops you in your tracks the first time you read his work or see his plays. There is something about a lover or a poet that does take an unconventional turn, and at their deepest or most profound, the lover and the poet actually slip into a sort of lunacy, with feelings and senses "that apprehend more than cool reason ever comprehends." The implication here is that these lunatic visionaries take us deeper into the depths of truth than logic, science, reason or any of those other cool, objective tools of thought are ever able to do. And so it is that midsummer madness can be a good thing. But it's probably only good in relatively small doses.

Theater in general offers us those doses of the lunatic's/poet's/lover's apprehending imagination. There's something really mesmerizing about walking into a theater and entering the strange, unfamiliar world of someone else's imaginings, trying on a different set of eyes and ears, and experiencing a world that doesn't quite correspond to our own day-to-day experiences.

Sometimes it's a matter of entering into a past that we'll never actually experience. What was life like in this city a hundred or two hundred years ago? What was it like during the waning days of World War II?

Or we can head over to the other side of the tracks into neighborhoods that we may drive through or even walk through, but that we'll never be part of and therefore will never "know" its inner workings. Theater can take us inside these worlds and share with us the struggles but also the joys of living in a world that is not our world. What's it like living in a halfway house? What's it like living in a hardscrabble Southern town? What's it like living in war-torn Iraq?

Or we can get into the minds of people whose experiences lie at the edges of our own experiences. What's it like to have cancer? What's it like to have no idea where your next meal will come from? What's it like to suffer from unrequited love?

What's it like to have it all, or to be spoiled rotten, or to be incredibly physically attractive? If these are things we all dream about, maybe we need to ask whether we are wishing for or aspiring to achieve the right things in life. Maybe dreaming of wealth is a misguided notion. Maybe we shouldn't worry so much about becoming one of the beautiful people because true beauty really is more than skin deep. Or is it?

Theater lets us dream.

I personally am constantly surprised by what I don't know and have never thought about when I read plays in this *Best American Short Plays* series. Plays as short as ten minutes can sweep me into a world I'll never actually experience, introduce me to characters I'll never actually meet, and alter my view of my own life I've never really considered. Sometimes the plays humble me when I meet characters who have so little and see them embrace life so completely. Sometimes they anger me when I see injustice laid out before me. I feel emotions of joy or sadness, and sometimes both intermingled. And I wonder: How do these writers do this?

The playwrights in this series, and in this volume in particular, are truly exceptional observers of life, capable of distilling a world of experiences into vignettes that capture the essence of so much that for the rest of us goes unnoticed. When it is brought to our attention, we are the better for it. They truly do apprehend more than cool reason comprehends, and their plays work to nudge the world just a little closer to the kind of world we'd all like to live in.

That's what happens when people spend time with lunatics, lovers, and poets: the world nudges a little closer to "better." Though I might be making a libelous observation, I believe that spending time with lunatics, lovers, and poets is exactly what you'll be doing when you settle down and read the works of those seething brains who have produced the following catalog of very fine short plays. "Cool reason" finds its match in this volume with works of imagination, vision, whimsy, humor, and poignancy. Together they each teach us a little about beauty, love, insanity, and so many of the other things—good and bad—that make life worth living.

This volume's first offering, *B'hoys Do* Macbeth by Jonathon Ward, takes us back to the bustling immigrant world of nineteenth-century New York City. We're at Five Points in particular, where gangs, bars, and theaters generate a world where dreamers hope for lives that include something more than the day-to-day hurly-burly of mere existence.

Losing Sight by Kevin D. Ferguson takes a young artist who is losing his sight and has him confront his past as he paves his way into an uncertain future. Haunted by the ghost of his dead grandfather, the onset of blindness reminds the character—and us—that "sometimes we lose sight of what matters the most."

Long Time Coming by David Rusiecki presents a fairly commonplace city scene: two young and struggling male stand-up comics in a coffee shop discussing women. The unusual twist is that one particular woman of interest works in the sex market, which causes a good deal of confusion about how to move forward. What unfolds would horrify any young, aspiring performer of any stripe, but not in the manner one might expect.

Petra by John Yarbrough tests the bounds of memory between a reminiscing elderly couple who do their best to recall certain events of a long-ago vacation to the Middle East that may or may not have happened. How to deal with faded memories and long-lived lives?

The Secret Keeper by David Meyers is firmly set in the Middle East and, sad to say, involves an event that definitely has happened far too often and in far too many places: needless slaughter caused by suicide bombings. With great dignity, though, Meyers introduces decent humanity into the equation and, with it, a glimmer of hope. He presents a haunting encounter in a war-ravaged village graveyard, where only the dead seem able to rest in peace. Into this desolate scene, however, grace blesses the suffering and consolation comes to two people hardly likely to make peace under any but the most unusual circumstances.

Super Hot Raven and Raven II: The Ravening by Megan Gogerty update what can only be thought of as an unusual symbiotic relationship between a bird-brained muse and an under-talented poet. Domestic squabbles ensue, but love continues to grow, demonstrating the odd truth that "nobody really understands a relationship except the people in it."

Norma's Rest by Jordan Morille introduces us to a poor but proud woman willing to dedicate her life to the least among us—the addicted and abandoned—opening her home to them and encouraging them as they try to recover their lives in a world filled with deceptive temptations.

It should be apparent by this point that the plays in this volume encourage the reader to view the world through a variety of visual prisms, emotional and intellectual foundations, time warps, and other viewpoints not typically part of our daily existences. *The Hour* by Susan Goodell puts a comic twist on such matters by taking a sort of film noir police-room interrogation and very nearly turning it into a "who's on first" comedy spiel. So much so often depends on so little that laughing is often the only response to life and living.

Then there are times when the response needs to be far more muted. *The Lilac Ticket* by C. J. Ehrlich visits a couple married for over fifty years, suffering through a mortal crisis at the moment and coming upon a decades-old emotional betrayal at the same time. Recovery requires a sense of humor, though perhaps not the kind of humor that sparks laughter.

Relationships make drama, of course. While the long-lived lives of aging adults may have more material to organize in their life stories, youthfulness has its own drama, though the young have less to bring to the table. *The Subterraneans* by Adam Kraar takes a look into the secret world of two siblings, brother and sister, including the brother's fantasy woman brought to life. Judd Lear Silverman's *Feathers* looks at empty-nest syndrome—losing one's child to adulthood—from an intriguingly literal perspective. And *The Gulf* by Audrey Cefaly engagingly presents two women fishing in the shallows of southern Alabama and confronting pasts and presents in ways that unify and strengthen the future. Then there are the tales of lives too soon cut short, as in *Winning* by Mercilee Jenkins, where vitality and living engage in a noble struggle against an insidious invasion by cancer with an inevitable outcome. In *Winning*, it's not heroism that is celebrated but the straightforward act of just living with fortitude and sober defiance that is honored.

The Grass Is Greenest at the Huston Astrodome by Michael Ross Albert brings living, love, and art together in an ensemble study of the fears and insecurities that come attached to pursuing the uncertainties that attend "success." Angst-filled young artists struggle to come to some understanding of the world around them. Maybe the closing speech shows the greatest sign of understanding: "They'll come across this photograph and they'll think to themselves . . . 'Wow. That person understands.' And it'll change them a little bit. Or it'll change them a lot." Connection is the first step. And so it happens in *Sword Play* by Charlene A. Donaghy, which takes us to 1960s New Orleans, a city caught up in a time of double-dealing Jim Crow segregationism that finds support and opposition from some unlikely sources. An unlikely relationship blossoms in a world that clearly discourages unlikely relationships. It's a place filled with obstacles working to prevent the most innocent and important of human bonds. But hope for the future begins in these unlikeliest of circumstances.

Quoting Clive Barker prior to the play's opening—"Any fool can be happy. It takes a man with real heart to make beauty out of the stuff that makes us weep"—Hal Corley introduces the fragile though imaginative lives of a creative but dysfunctional couple in *Dolor*. What is it, one wonders, that makes relationships "work"? *Dolor* suggests that perhaps "authenticity" is a key ingredient.

There are of course no rules to follow as we pursue love, understanding, or "the good life," whatever that may be. But rules do govern a good deal of our lives, sometimes to an absurd extreme. *Gonna Need to See Some ID* by Donna Latham is a comic assault on a world gone crazy with rules and regulations designed to make us all feel safe and secure. It's the kind of comedy that has the serious intent of asking us all to wonder what ever happened to good old common sense.

Confronting our pasts as we look forward to the future occurs frequently in literature and theater. Craig Pospisil takes us into this sort of time-bending in *There's No Here Here* by creating a different kind of ghost story, involving a lively engagement between the living and the dead. Included in the play is an extended resurrection of Gertrude Stein, which leads into an engaging discussion between the living and the dead of art, love, and the waiting class.

Vertical Constellation with Bomb by Gwydion Suilebhan takes us back to the latter days of World War II, in New York City, where three strangers discuss war, death, art, shooting stars, and other matters of greater or lesser import. The evening's discussion finally leads to a special bonding and a moment of sharing that includes recounting the loss of a child due to a freak accident. Can pain become meaning? Can pain become something beautiful?

With a Bullet (Or, Surprise Me) by John Patrick Bray is set in a Hudson River Valley bar on New Year's Eve 1999. But it could be any small bar in any place in the USA: the Midwest, South, Northwest. In the bar are denizens pretty easily found in any bar, all talking life, liberty, and the pursuit of happiness, and all enduring the threat of karaoke.

These special talents speak with different voices and see through different eyes than most of us possess. Labeling them poets, lovers, or madmen (and madwomen) recognizes their special outlooks on the world that surrounds us all. Having them in our midst helps us all to see our surroundings in ways that we haven't quite seen even just a few moments ago. And that, to my mind, is a good thing.

B'Hoys Do *Macbeth*

Jonathon Ward

Jonathon Ward

Jonathon Ward is a playwright who has written the following: *The Artist of the Beautiful*, an adaptation of a Nathaniel Hawthorne story (Metropolitan Playhouse 2016); *Life Passing By* (Lama Theatre at Dixon Place Reading 2015); *Dexter and Lewellyn* (Barter Theater Appalachian Festival Reading 2015); *Room to Roam* (InspiraTO 2015 Toronto); *B'Hoys Do* Macbeth (Metropolitan Playhouse NYC 2015); *Burbopolis Play* (Commission 2015 NYSCA Huntington Arts Council); *Shakespeare in America* (accepted FringeNYC Festival 2015); *Memorial Night* (NYSCA Individual Artist Commission presented at Open Eye Theater 2014); *Hip and Lip Get a Grip* (10by10 in Raleigh, semi-finalist 2015); *Murderous Caduceus* (TACT Development 2015); *Pension Check* and *Man of Zoo* (Riant Theatre); *Atalanta, Wolf!, Minotaur, The Little Lame Prince*, and *Raksha's Child* (Abrons Arts Center and Great Small Works); *Little Love Child, Desperate Flippancies, Reverence and Romance*, and *Damnation of Theron Ware* (Community Free Theater NYSCA grants). He was artist-in-residence at Catskills Center Platte Clove Cabin in 2013. He retired from the NYU Graduate Acting Program in 2014.

···production history···

World premiere produced by Metropolitan Playhouse, New York City, April 2015. Artistic director, Alex Roe. Directed by Michael Durkin. Alex Roe, set design; Sidney Fortner, costumes; Christopher Weston, lights; Michael Hardart, sound; Samantha Davis, stage manager.

PETE WILLIAMS   Ian Eaton

SEAN KERRY   Sean Michael Buckley

NED BLUNT   David Perez-Ribada

MAGGIE DARCY   Emerald Rose Sullivan

OFFICER DUNCAN   Seth McNeill

RIOTERS and OFFICERS (offstage)   The company

cast

PETE WILLIAMS   African American, 38, owner of Almack's Dance Hall in Five Points

SEAN KERRY   Irish unemployed dockworker recently immigrated from Galway, 23, who recites Shakespeare and wants to be an actor

NED BLUNT   English nativist gang leader in the Bowery, 25, fireman and an up-and-coming ward leader

MAGGIE DARCY   a saloon worker and dancer and illegitimate daughter of Pete Williams, 19, mixed race

OFFICER DUNCAN   a bulldog American cop, 30, who controls his beat

scene 1

[*New York City. Five Points. Almack's Dance Hall. May 1849. Late afternoon before opening time.* MAGGIE *is teaching* SEAN *a juba step and song.*]

MAGGIE   *Juba dis and Juba dat,*
and Juba killed da yellow cat,
You sift the meal and ya gimme the husk,
you bake the bread and ya gimme the crust,
you eat the meat and ya gimme the skin,

and that's the way,
all da trouble begin.

[*At the end, they swing around and laugh at their play.* PETE WILLIAMS *enters from the basement with a box of liquor bottles.*]

SEAN Thank you for seeing me.

MAGGIE I already taught him the new steps.

SEAN It's brilliant. You got the best minstrel show in town!

MAGGIE He can swing me around. He'd love to dance in Master Juba's number.

PETE I'm not interested in your dancing anything other than the jig right now.

SEAN Yes, sir.

PETE Are you willing to be in blackface?

SEAN I'll do anything to get a speaking part.

PETE Can you read?

SEAN I didn't come all the way from Galway—

PETE Can you?

SEAN I learned at my mother's knee. She taught me all of *Macbeth* 'cause he stood up to the English—

MAGGIE I can help with his accent.

PETE This is the script. You're reading Tambo. Maggie, please stock for opening?

MAGGIE I can read the other part.

PETE My part?

MAGGIE Dad, I'm just offering to help.

PETE You can help by stocking.

[MAGGIE *goes behind the bar to work and reacts to audition.*]

PETE From the top.

SEAN [*With Irish brogue.*] "Man, I'm hungry. I want somethin' to eat."

PETE "That's all you talk about. Somethin' to eat."

SEAN "Well, that's all I can do. I don't ever get nothin'."

PETE You'll be in blackface and you need to say the line, the whole line, in exaggerated Negro dialect.

SEAN Make fun of him?

PETE No. My minstrel show doesn't make fun of anyone. Tambo is smarter than the audience, and he's Negro and he's poking fun at them. Let's try it again.

SEAN [*Putting on caricatured Negro manner but still with brogue.*] "Man, I'm hungry. I want somethin' to eat."

PETE "That's all you talk about. Somethin' to eat."

SEAN "Well, that's all I can do is talk about it. I don't ever get nothin'. You tol' me you'd stick by me through thick and thin?"

PETE "Yeah."

SEAN "The longer you stick the thinner I git."

PETE Thank you.

SEAN I could do it as an Irishman and get the crowds laughing.

PETE My crowds are American and they don't want to be outsmarted by a Negro and an Irishman. The script.

MAGGIE [*Taking SEAN's arm.*] Maybe we could do a night of Shakespeare. He can recite very well.

SEAN I auditioned for Edwin Forrest's *Macbeth* at the Bowery Theater.

PETE Were you called back?

SEAN Not yet.

PETE The first performance is tonight.

SEAN They said they might cast me as a soldier at the last minute. I know when to enter and my lines.

PETE And you speak with a Scottish accent?

SEAN They weren't so particular. I promise if you cast me in your show, I'll bring the Irish in.

PETE I want the Irish with money in my saloon. Not the out-of-work roustabouts.

MAGGIE Dad.

SEAN I'll be getting work next week.

PETE You'll be lucky to find it.

SEAN Just because the Whigs are voted in, Tammany Hall will fight back. Maggie told me you favor Macready's English style of acting.

MAGGIE Daddy, all he needs is a chance.

SEAN "If chance will have me king, why, chance may crown me."

PETE Chance only crowns fools.

SEAN [*Starting to exit.*] "Come what come may, / Time and the hour runs through the roughest day."

MAGGIE Don't go.

[*To* PETE.]

He knows his Shakespeare.

PETE And his brogue.

SEAN Listen to the hoity-toity.

MAGGIE This is America.

SEAN I have as much right to speak the way I—

PETE No, you don't. If you want to work on the stage, you need to learn to suit the action to the word and the word to the action. And that means learning English and American dialects.

MAGGIE Not everyone can afford a ticket to hear Macready at the Astor Place Opera House.

SEAN You're going to see Macready's Macbeth?

MAGGIE   Ever since Charles Dickens wrote about Pete Williams's Almack's Dance Hall, he has friends in the Upper Ten Percent of society.

PETE   They are customers.

MAGGIE   He even sits downstairs in the orchestra instead of the galleries.

PETE   We have work to do.

MAGGIE   Just because you can afford a ticket and dress up for a night at the Opera House.

PETE   Maggie.

SEAN   You should go to see Edwin Forrest and support America's greatest living actor. He plays Macbeth as a rugged individualist.

PETE   I would describe him as a vast animal bewildered by a grain of genius.

SEAN   And Macready's style is dainty as English lace, if you ask me.

[*Knock at the door.*]

PETE   Tell them we're not open yet.

[*To* SEAN.]

Your call is at nine for the jig.

NED   It's Ned Blunt. From the Sixth Ward in Five Points.

MAGGIE   A Bowery B'hoy.

[*To* PETE.]

What is he doing here?

PETE   Making trouble. What else?

MAGGIE   [*To* SEAN.] You better go.

SEAN   I'm not afraid of him.

PETE   [*To* SEAN.] Are you a member of the Dead Rabbits?

SEAN   No.

PETE   I don't want any trouble from them or the Bowery B'hoys.

SEAN I'm not in a gang.

[*Knocking.*]

NED I'm here to talk to you. I come alone.

PETE Let him in.

[*MAGGIE lets* NED *enter.*]

What do you want?

NED Is that a way to greet a friend?

[*Taking in the saloon.*]

My fire station was the first to come to your saloon when it was burning down.

PETE What did you come for?

NED "Heat not a furnace for your foe so hot that it do singe yourself."

PETE From *King Henry the Eighth.* You're Norfolk of Tammany Hall.

NED That's right.

[NED *sits at the bar.*]

Are you open for business?

[PETE *takes out a bottle and pours.* NED *puts down his money.*]

You always ran a first-rate saloon. I see you built a bigger and better establishment since the fire.

[PETE *slides his money back.* NED *drinks.*]

Ha! Thank you. I'm here because Macready's daring to perform Macbeth again at the Opera House. Only the Upper Ten can afford to attend, but I have tickets from Tammany Hall.

[*To* SEAN.]

They sent me round to gather up supporters so we can show the Whigs and their English actor friends that they can't push workingmen out of the Sixth Ward by excluding us from their Opera House and gentrifying Five Points. We're pulling everyone in the neighborhood together, even your friends in the Dead Rabbits.

SEAN I'm not a Dead Rabbit.

NED Okay, but you're Irish and on their side and the gangs need to come together for once. The English workingman, the Germans, and now the Irish are being pushed out of their homes—

PETE First were the Indians and don't forget the Africans and the Jews and the Italians.

NED That's right. All of us are trying to get ahead. It's the Whigs that are pushing us down. We got to show them like Andrew Jackson, a Democrat, did. Tonight there will be three hundred of us in the audience showing Macready what Macbeth is about and how he ought to be acted. Do you want to join us?

[NED *holds out the tickets.* SEAN *starts to reach for them.*]

MAGGIE We have a show tonight.

NED You may want to cancel it. There are people from all over New York City who are angry with the insults Macready leveled at Mr. Forrest. There are troops gathering in Washington Square Park. The cops might close the saloons.

[*To* SEAN.]

So how about it?

SEAN I'm doing the minstrel show here.

NED An actor in blackface. Ain't that a step down for an Irishman?

PETE He dances the jig, a damn good one.

SEAN But if we're closed.

PETE I thought you were hoping to be a soldier in Forrest's *Macbeth* tonight, if you don't have to dance the jig.

NED Tonight we need soldiers from Five Points to take the stage at the Opera House. I'll leave these tickets for you and a friend, in case you change your mind. I'll go out the back. Is this the way?

PETE [*To* SEAN.] Go with him. Show him out and lock up.

[NED *and* SEAN *exit.*]

MAGGIE Won't you give Sean another chance?

PETE   He has fresh energy, but he's got a lot to learn.

MAGGIE   I can work on his accent.

PETE   I put you in charge of producing my show, but you can't get carried away by your emotions.

MAGGIE   I see his potential.

PETE   Of course, you do.

MAGGIE   Are you going to the Opera House?

PETE   Of course. Do you think the Upper Ten Percent is going to let the rabble decide who can appear on American stages?

MAGGIE   What if there's a riot?

PETE   I can take care of myself, and I'll be with the young Mr. Astor. I'm trusting you to keep an eye on the saloon.

MAGGIE   What do I do if there's trouble?

PETE   Close the shutters and lock the door. Don't worry. The police and the army will preserve order.

[SEAN *enters and takes the tickets.*]

You need to get ready to open. The show goes on. I'll take the tickets.

SEAN   No. I can use them when I've done my dance.

PETE   [*To* MAGGIE.] You're not going with him.

MAGGIE   If we're closed—

PETE   You're not to go.

[*To* SEAN.]

As for you, if you go, you need to listen to Macready speak and learn instead of being one of those heckling rabble-rousers.

[PETE *exits.*]

SEAN   Will you go?

MAGGIE   We have a show.

SEAN   I'm needed there. This is the first time the Bowery B'hoys want to work with an Irishman instead of bashing his brains out.

MAGGIE You're needed here.

SEAN Doing what? A jig?

MAGGIE My father will never hire you again.

SEAN I can do the dance and leave. Your dad thinks I'm worse than a nigger.

MAGGIE What?

SEAN He won't hire an Irishman to talk.

MAGGIE He won't hire someone who can't play a part.

SEAN Why can't I play an Irishman?

MAGGIE Because that's not the part. There are no black Irishmen in his minstrel show.

SEAN There are black Irish women.

MAGGIE Listen to me, Sean Kerry, I can suit the words to the action and the action to the words.
[*Putting on a brogue.*]
I'm as Irish as you, and my da loves the Irish as much as anyone 'cause he loved my ma.

SEAN Then why don't he take me brogue and all.

MAGGIE That's not his show. He's got more things to think about than your being Irish. He's a nigger to every white man that comes in, including you, it seems.

SEAN I'm not saying—

MAGGIE And his show is meant to teach white people that they are just as dumb as they think black people are, if they act that way. It would be dumb to cast someone with a brogue as thick as yours who's too dumb to know that.

SEAN I can act.

MAGGIE You didn't show it in your audition.

SEAN I need a chance!

MAGGIE Ask him for another.

SEAN What am I going to do if he says no?

MAGGIE Work on the docks if that's all you can do, until you learn.

SEAN Now the Whigs are in, they'll be no jobs. When I left Ireland, I was going to be like Macbeth, "Thou shalt be / What thou art promised." America promised me a chance and I'll be damned if an Englishman will set foot on an American stage when I can't even be in a minstrel show.

MAGGIE You'll get your break.

SEAN Yeah. When!?

MAGGIE My dad said you were a fresh talent.

SEAN He did?

MAGGIE Yes. He's fair.

[*She goes to console him.*]

He wouldn't let my mom onstage until she could speak American. He taught her so well, she got into a vaudeville show and went out west. I'll help you.

[*They start to embrace. A knock on the front door with a billy club.*]

DUNCAN It's the police. Open up. I know you're in there, Pete Williams.

SEAN What's he want?

MAGGIE He comes once a month, but not until next week.

SEAN I bet he's looking for Ned.

DUNCAN [*Pounding.*] I'll take the door off its hinges if you don't answer me.

[PETE *enters. More knocking.*]

PETE I'm coming. No need to keep knocking.

[PETE *goes to open the door.*]

You're early.

[DUNCAN *and* PETE *enter.*]

DUNCAN   I don't like waiting. Who's this?

PETE   A dancer.

DUNCAN   Where from?

PETE   The neighborhood.

DUNCAN   What street?

SEAN   Cross Street.

DUNCAN   What are you doing up here?

PETE   We have a show tonight.

DUNCAN   [*To* PETE.] We need to talk in private.

[PETE *indicates to* MAGGIE *and* SEAN. *They exit.*]

I'll have a whiskey. There's going to be trouble tonight.

PETE   What sort of trouble?

DUNCAN   Ned Blunt has been going around giving out tickets to the Opera House. There's talk on the streets of the scum gathering outside the theater. I arrested an Irishman in the park orating about housing and jobs like the communists in Germany. We need to get the scum back to where they came from. It's going to be a difficult week. That's why I'm coming early.

PETE   [*Pulling out an envelope of money.*] It catches me up short, but I scraped it together.

DUNCAN   [*Taking the envelope.*] You're smart for thinking ahead.

PETE   "'Tis the plague of great ones / Prerogatived are they less than the base."

DUNCAN   Shakespeare?

PETE   Yes.

DUNCAN   *Macbeth*?

PETE   No.

DUNCAN   What play?

PETE *Othello.*

DUNCAN You're a cultured one, ain't you?

PETE I try to be. I hope you'll keep the peace at the Opera House tonight. I'm looking forward to hearing Macready do Macbeth.

DUNCAN Where'd you get a ticket?

PETE I have a friend.

DUNCAN Ned Blunt?

PETE No. Mr. Astor, the younger. He was in my saloon last week rubbing shoulders with the common people on his night out with his mistress.

DUNCAN You let me know if you see any of the Bowery Boys around.

[DUNCAN *gets up to leave.*]

Are you sure you don't know nothin' about tonight?

PETE I know *Macbeth* fairly well and I've seen Macready perform several times.

DUNCAN I'll keep an eye out for you at the Opera House and make sure you're enjoying the play.

PETE I appreciate that. I'll be in the orchestra. Row three.

DUNCAN I don't want to see any heckling from that section.

PETE Not on your life.

DUNCAN It's your life you should be concerned about. The way you mix things up in your saloon is not what they want in the Opera House.

[DUNCAN *exits.* SEAN *and* MAGGIE *enter.*]

PETE [*To* MAGGIE.] After Macbeth starts at eight, lock up everything and go home. The gun is loaded behind the bar. I'm going home to dress.

MAGGIE Are you going to be all right?

PETE Yes. Lock the door behind me. I'll see you at home later.

[PETE *exits.*]

SEAN   He threatened him.

MAGGIE   What else is new?

SEAN   That's what the Whigs are doing. We have to go.

MAGGIE   What if my dad sees me?

SEAN   We'll be in the gallery. He'll be in the orchestra.

MAGGIE   It could be dangerous.

SEAN   What's there to worry about. I'll be with you to make sure you're safe.

[*He starts to kiss her.*]

MAGGIE   Sean Kerry, that's enough of that.

[*She pecks him on the cheek.*]

We'll go out the back and close the shutters on the way.

[SEAN *and* MAGGIE *exit. Lights to black. The sound of an angry crowd crescendoes.*]

scene 2

[*Later that night. The sound of a crowd continues.* SEAN *and* MAGGIE *enter from the back holding up* NED, *who is wounded in his side.*]

MAGGIE   Sit and don't move.

NED   Is the bleeding stopped?

MAGGIE   I'll clean it and see.

[*To* SEAN.]

Get some of the whiskey and a cloth. Behind the bar.

NED   [*To* SEAN.] You saved my life.

MAGGIE   We're not safe yet.

NED   Did you reach them?

MAGGIE   They said they'd come before daybreak.

SEAN   Did they give you any trouble?

MAGGIE   No. I told them Ned sent me and they were sweet as can be.

NED They'd better be.

MAGGIE They escorted me back across Houston. I told the soldiers at the barricade I had children at home and they let me through.
[*With cloth.*]
It's going to sting.

NED Worse than now?

MAGGIE Hold him.

SEAN [*With a rag.*] Bite on this. And hold my hands.

NED I don't want to hurt you. You got that copper son of a bitch. Aaa. A cobblestone to the head taught him. Aaaaa.

[*A knock on the door.*]

COP This is the police. Pete Williams!?
[*Pushing against the door.*]
We need a place to rest. I don't want to break in, 'cause you're a friend. We know where you live, Pete. We'll go to his house. Let's go.

[*Silence.*]

MAGGIE It went right through, and it's not bleeding.

SEAN Take a drink. To numb the pain.

NED I got to get back to Bleecker.

MAGGIE No. Not until your friends come. There are troops on Bleecker barricading Five Points. Your friends are taking a boat up the East River to get here. I saw three bodies on Lafayette Street.

NED Were they in uniform?

MAGGIE No.

NED Bowery Boys?

MAGGIE [*Looking at SEAN.*] They had the colors of the Dead Rabbits.

NED The Whigs will pay for it! I promise you that. The Irish were heroes. You should have seen your boyfriend going down to the orchestra taking some hoity-toity's seat.

MAGGIE   Is that where you went?

SEAN   It was your dad's seat.

MAGGIE   He better not have seen you.

SEAN   He didn't. He left probably 'cause he couldn't hear a word out of Macready's mouth.

NED   Your boy landed a tomato right on Macready's forehead.

SEAN   Macready started his speech: "To be thus is nothing, / But to be safely thus."

NED   Sploosh!

SEAN   The rich people started pushing me, and I smashed their top hats!

NED   It started the whole riot! Chairs were thrown from the balcony!

SEAN   A cop got hold of me and tried to lock me up in the basement, but I slipped away.

NED   I saw you beam that copper!

MAGGIE   I couldn't find my dad. They may have caught him and locked him up.

SEAN   We'll find him.

NED   I promise we will.

[*Knocking on the door.*]

RIOTER   [*With a brogue.*] Is anyone there?

MAGGIE   Shhh.

ANOTHER RIOTER   [*German accent.*] They brought the cannons up and the cavalry.

MAGGIE   We can't take any more in.

SEAN   They'll be caught.

MAGGIE   And so will we.

RIOTER   There's no place that's safe!

[*In the distance, a sound of a cannon discharge.*]

NED If we're found together, they'll hang us all. They saw you with me.

[*Silence. Sound of someone in the back.*]

MAGGIE They got in the back. The gun.

[SEAN *tosses the gun to* MAGGIE. PETE *enters. His coat is torn.*]

PETE What are you doing here?

MAGGIE We had no place to go.

PETE I told you to go home.

    [*Seeing* NED.]

    What is he doing here!?

MAGGIE He's hurt.

PETE You were at the theater!

MAGGIE I was worried.

PETE [*To* SEAN.] Get him out of here.

MAGGIE Dad.

PETE The both of you. Get out!

SEAN They're looking for him.

PETE They're not going to find him in my saloon. Get out!

MAGGIE They'll hang him!

SEAN And I'll go with him!

MAGGIE And I will, too!

PETE He started this riot.

NED The Upper Ten—

PETE And I'm not going to lose everything to save him!

    [*Grabbing his gun and aiming it at* NED.]

    Get the hell out. As far as I know, your boys burned my last saloon and I'll be damned if you destroy my business again.

NED We didn't burn it.

PETE For protection money.

NED It was the coppers. We need you on the side of the Democrats.

PETE I've got all the protection I need.

NED From Duncan?

PETE That's right.

NED The Whigs won't be in power forever. Twenty thousand people are on the streets. That's the protection you need. If they hang me, the Bowery Boys and the Dead Rabbits will know who did it and then you'll see how long your saloon stays open. The Upper Ten will stop coming and no one in the neighborhood will either.

MAGGIE His friends are coming for him.

[*Knock on the door.*]

DUNCAN [*Off.*] Pete Williams! It's Officer Duncan. Open up. I need to talk with you. I sent my men around back.

[*There's banging on the back door.*]

PETE I'll turn you in.

MAGGIE They'll find out we brought him here.

SEAN We've got to fight.

NED [*To* PETE.] Whose side are you on?

MAGGIE They'll arrest you. They'll hang us. You know they will.

DUNCAN [*Pounding.*] We'll force our way in!

PETE [*Lowering the gun.*] Hide in the dressing room downstairs. There's a door behind the costume rack. Quick!

[*To* DUNCAN, *putting the gun away.*]

I'm coming! No need to break the door.

[MAGGIE, NED *and* SEAN *exit with gun and coats, etc.* PETE *lets* DUNCAN *in.*]

DUNCAN What took you so long?

PETE I was in the basement checking my storage room, making sure rioters didn't get in.

DUNCAN Did they?

PETE No. Thanks for looking out for me.

DUNCAN [*Shouting to the back door.*] It's all right! Check down the street while I talk to the proprietor.

[*The banging at the back door stops.*]

The troops scattered the crowd, but the scum is showing up on the side streets. We're rounding up the organizers. What do you have to drink?

[PETE *takes a bottle.*]

Is that the best you got? After tonight, I think I deserve a little higher quality. How about that Balblair's malt whiskey? I'll take a bottle for the boys outside, too. How'd your coat get torn?

PETE Pushing through the crowd.

DUNCAN You were among them?

PETE I left early.

DUNCAN You were in the third row orchestra.

PETE That's right. I thought you'd be able to control the hecklers in the gallery. I couldn't hear a word.

DUNCAN The crowd outside was out of control, and there were collaborators downstairs.

PETE You assured me that there'd be peace.

DUNCAN When there are people inside helping the agitators, the authorities have a difficult time. This is a very fine whiskey. Where have you been hiding this? I'll have another shot.

PETE I need to save some for my customers who pay for it so I can stay in business.

DUNCAN There are a lot of ways to lose your business. Fires. Theft. Riots. Acts of God. A Higher Authority decides you're out of business and you're gone. Do you pray a lot to da Lawd? Do you make offerings?

PETE I'm tithed by my church.

DUNCAN Did you pray to stop the riots? Or make burnt offerings to a Higher Authority?

PETE What do you want?

DUNCAN The riots made my job very difficult and your business is still standing. I think that in itself is reason enough to give a Higher Authority an offer of thanksgiving.

PETE You came a week early and took cash I use for running my business.

DUNCAN I'm not paid enough to know how much cash you have, but I have information that's worth something to you.

PETE What?

DUNCAN I saw you leave your seat at the Opera House and then that Mick from Cross Street, your dancer, took it. He threw a tomato at Macready and started fighting with the gentleman around him. You gave him your seat.

PETE I didn't give him my seat. I left because I couldn't hear.

DUNCAN How did he get in?

PETE You let him in the theater!

DUNCAN We didn't let in anyone without a ticket! You can explain this in court or come to a little understanding with me. My men's throats are very dry from the smoke and fires that have been set. Do you want me to let them in? Or do you want to take care of this here and now.

[SEAN *enters in blackface, followed by* NED *in blackface and* MAGGIE.]

SEAN [*With dialect.*] Boss. We dun finished rehearsin' for the new minstrel show and cleanin' up the dressin' room to your satisfaction. Is there sumpin' the matter?

DUNCAN Who are they?

PETE Well, we're always developing new material for our shows.

MAGGIE We've been rehearsing all night and I think you'll like what we've done. Is the officer going to come to our opening? He could be our honored guest.

SEAN Yes, sir. That's the troof.

[*Taking out the gun.*]

We goin' to shoot the moon wif dis one and we'se wants to honor our guests wif our bes' shot.

DUNCAN Does he know how to handle one of them?

SEAN I never did learn how. Is this the way you point it?

DUNCAN Put that down.

SEAN I'm jus' tryin' to protect you. I'm keepin' an eye on you and not letting you out of my sight.

PETE You have to aim it at the floor to be safe.

SEAN I'm jus' makin' sure he's real safe.

DUNCAN You get that nigger away from me. He's going to do something stupid.

SEAN I'm stupid? So stupid I could kill someone wif dis? I bes' turn da switch off. Is dis da switch?

PETE No. That's the trigger.

DUNCAN Don't pull that.

MAGGIE He doesn't mean you're stupid. He's just saying it'd be smart not to kill him.

NED, SEAN, MAGGIE, and PETE Ohhhh.

NED [*Awkward dialect.*] Hahah. Dat's funny. I never seen no one killed befo.

PETE [*Concerned* NED *will give them away.*] Ahem. You have to understand. Officer Duncan is here to protect us. He was inquiring how my business was doing. And I let him know I'm a little short now, but for his trouble I can give him a bottle of scotch for his men.

[*Gives the less expensive bottle to* DUNCAN.]

Thank you for stopping by.

SEAN Don't you worry.

DUNCAN Get him away.

SEAN I'll protect you all the way to da door.

DUNCAN Put that down.

PETE [*Taking gun from* SEAN.] He means no harm. He's jess learnin' how to be a cultured man.

DUNCAN I'll be back next month.

PETE I'm sure you will, and I'll introduce you to Mr. Astor.

SEAN He a fine man who stand by us tru tick and tin.

MAGGIE, NED, and PETE Yeah, he do.

PETE And we'd hate to see his father's opera house burn to the ground through neglect of duty.

SEAN, MAGGIE, and NED No no no. Uh-uh.

SEAN May I show you to da door, Masta?

[SEAN *bows and scrapes.* NED *bows and* MAGGIE *curtsies.* DUNCAN *and* SEAN *exit.* PETE *starts to laugh with all.*]

NED Damn, he's good.

MAGGIE [*To* PETE.] I've been working with him.

[SEAN *enters.*]

PETE All right, son, you've earned yourself a speakin' part.

SEAN [*With brogue.*] Faith and begorah! I have!?

PETE [*In brogue.*] Aye, me lad, you most certainly have.

MAGGIE *Juba dis*

[PETE *starts clapping a rhythm.* SEAN *crosses to* MAGGIE *to start the Juba dance.* NED *pounds the rhythm on the bar and drinks the Balblair's.*]

SEAN *and Juba dat,*

PETE [*Joining dance.*] *and Juba killed*

MAGGIE and SEAN *da yellow cat,*

PETE *You sift the meal*

MAGGIE and SEAN *and ya gimme the husk,*

PETE *you bake the bread*

MAGGIE and SEAN *and ya gimme the crust,*

PETE *you eat the meat*

MAGGIE and SEAN *and ya gimme the skin,*

ALL *and that's the way,*
all da trouble begins

[*When the dance finishes, the lights hit black.*]

• • •

Losing Sight

Kevin D. Ferguson

Kevin D. Ferguson

Kevin D. Ferguson is playwright-in-residence at Atlantic Stage in Myrtle Beach, South Carolina, where his plays *Child's Play* and *Spinning Jenny* premiered. He is also the resident dramaturge and literary manager at Atlantic Stage, administrating the annual New Voices Playfest there. He is a teaching associate in the Theatre Department at Coastal Carolina University. Ferguson is also a former national playwright-in-residence at The Tesseract Theatre Company in St. Louis, Missouri, where his plays *A Thing with Feathers* and *Orders* were both workshopped. He has won several playwriting awards, including a Kennedy Center Award for his one-act play *Losing Sight*. Ferguson received an MFA in playwriting with a concentration in dramaturgy from Hollins University's Playwrights Lab. He is a member of the Dramatists Guild of America and the Literary Managers and Dramaturgs of the Americas.

··· production history ···

Losing Sight received a staged reading at the Kennedy Center in April 2013.

BARRY   Jon Hudson Odom

NOLAN   Stephen Patrick Martin

AMY   JjanaValentiner

Stage directions read by Heather Howard

Directed by Michael Dove

Losing Sight was performed in Americus, Georgia, at Georgia Southwestern State University Theatre in January 2014 and then in Roanoke, Virginia, at Mill Mountain Theatre in February 2014.

BARRY   Jason Ryan Wallace

NOLAN   William C. Searcy

AMY   Sara Sellers

Directed by Jason Ryan Wallace, stage-managed by Christopher Gilstrap

Awards include: John Cauble Award for Outstanding Short Play National Finalist, April 2013; Kennedy Center ACTF Region IV One-Act Play Award, February 2013; Georgia Theatre Conference One-Act Play Competition Winner, October 2012

characters

BARRY CAUSEY   an artist losing his sight

NOLAN CAUSEY   his deceased grandfather

AMY JACKSON   owner of an art supply store

synopsis

Sometimes we lose sight of what matters the most.
An artist races the clock to finish a painting before going blind. Haunted by the ghost of his grandfather, he must confront the lost relationships of his past before he can face his future.

[*A one-room beach cottage transformed into a simple artist's studio. Messy. Soda bottles and pizza boxes. Canvas on an easel, tables littered with tubes of paint, brushes in jars and out of jars. Several different strengths of reading glasses sprawled about, and a large magnifying glass. Possibly the sounds of waves and windows with an ocean view. Lots of light.* BARRY, *a man in his late twenties to early thirties, stands at the easel, brush in hand, trying different glasses and squinting at the canvas.* BARRY *throws his paintbrush across the room.*]

BARRY Shit!

[*He picks up the paintbrush, cleans it, returns to the easel. He paints, continuing his ritual of squinting, painting, and alternating glasses.* NOLAN, *a man in his late fifties to early sixties, enters.*]

NOLAN Painting not going well?

BARRY No, damn it.

NOLAN Sorry to hear it.

BARRY Why are you here, Nolan?

NOLAN Can't a man drop in on his grandson?

BARRY Not if that man is dead.

NOLAN Well, there is that.

[BARRY *continues to paint in silence.*]

Monet went blind doing *Water Lilies.*

BARRY His last major work. Never painted again. Died right after.

NOLAN Well, that's depressing.

[BARRY *shows* NOLAN *a tube of paint.*]

BARRY What color is this?

NOLAN Magenta.

[BARRY *rummages around for a different tube.*]

BARRY Shit.

NOLAN How come you haven't opened up the main house yet? Been a month.

BARRY You see any phthalo blue?

NOLAN Why didn't you visit?

BARRY   I need phthalo blue.

NOLAN   You were busy. Making a name for yourself. But you couldn't visit?

BARRY   Maybe cerulean?

NOLAN   You know the cliché, a blind man hears better than a sighted man? Not true. Blind man just listens more, that's all. You need to listen more, Barry.

BARRY   I'm listening, Grandpa. It's just you're not really saying anything. You're dead.

NOLAN   You still need to listen.

BARRY   I can't face the house yet, okay? Happy? I can't face the house. I know I ordered phthalo blue.

NOLAN   So you're hiding out in the studio?

BARRY   Not hiding out.

NOLAN   Hid out in my studio after your parents died, too. You were ten, remember? Scared to death of me, angry as hell. Sarah brought you down here and you just pounded and pounded the clay. She told me my own studio was off-limits. Until you were ready to quit hiding.

BARRY   Not hiding. Working. Working, damn it!

NOLAN   I can see that.

BARRY   Very funny.

NOLAN   See a lot of things clearly now that I'm dead.

[BARRY *resumes painting in silence.*]

Folks take sight for granted.

BARRY   I didn't. Don't.

NOLAN   Didn't you? Don't you?

BARRY   No. Saw everything while I had the chance. Van Gogh. Munch. Chagal. Picasso. Mattise. Dali. Gaugin. Studied them. Memorized them.

NOLAN   Visited all your expressionist friends, did you?

BARRY Yep. Had a face-to-face with them all.

NOLAN Might have made time to visit a living artist. While he was still living.

BARRY You don't understand.

NOLAN I understand better than anyone.

BARRY My career is ruined. My life is my career.

NOLAN The best thing that ever happened to me was losing my sight.

BARRY Right.

NOLAN It's true. When I lost my sight I had to find a new medium. And it wasn't easy. Sculpture hadn't been my focus before. Your grandmother, Sarah, was one of my first models. Of course, being blind, I had to touch her. It was 1956, and I can tell you, touching Sarah was worth going blind.

BARRY I don't want to hear this.

NOLAN Touching Sarah brought back my passion, and my passion brought life to my art. Took me past going blind, took me to a way of seeing things I never had before.

BARRY Quit talking about touching Grandma!

NOLAN She wasn't always your grandma. How do you think your dad came along? By stork? We weren't always old. We used to make love right here. . . .

[BARRY *sticks his fingers in his ears or some such.*]

BARRY I can't hear you! LA LA LA LA . . .

NOLAN Sarah was my muse. My sexy, passionate muse. And she was curvy in all the right ways.

BARRY For the love of God!

NOLAN The legs your grandma had . . .

BARRY Nolan, I'm begging you. Stop. Just stop.

NOLAN You need to find some passion in your life, boy. Like I did.

BARRY You're too old to be talking like this. Not to mention being dead.

NOLAN And you're too young not to be talking like this. Not to mention being alive. You need to loosen up. You should call Amy.

BARRY I'm not calling Amy. I broke up with Amy ten years ago. I'm not calling Amy. I'm not you, Nolan.

NOLAN You've got my blood. You've got my talent. You've got my . . .

BARRY . . . eyes.

NOLAN We finally gonna talk about it? How you blame me?

BARRY . . . No. Yes. No. I couldn't look at you. Once I realized I . . . I couldn't look at you. I'm sorry.

NOLAN I understand.

BARRY You say that! Wish I believed it was true, and not just what I want to hear. Don't you blame me for not coming home?

NOLAN Maybe I was hurt. Maybe I was angry. Maybe I thought you were a selfish little shit who only thought about himself.

BARRY Thought you said you understood.

NOLAN Being dead gives you some perspective. Now I know you were just a scared little shit.

BARRY Thanks, Nolan.

NOLAN Either way, you're still a shit.

BARRY Where is the damn phthalo blue! Should have been delivered by now.

NOLAN You're lucky the art supply store delivers at all. Delivery was set up just for me. Special. Because I know the owner.

BARRY The kid mentioned when I placed the order.

NOLAN You really ought to call Amy. Sweet girl. Pretty.

BARRY I'm not calling her. She probably doesn't live in town anymore, anyway. Probably married and fat with a ton of kids. Probably forgotten all about me.

NOLAN Probably. Although she was quite the fan of a certain young art student.

BARRY I don't remember.

NOLAN Liar. You ate it up. Her admiration. Your first fan. Your first love.

BARRY Doesn't matter. Didn't want her admiration then. Don't want her pity now.

NOLAN Don't worry. That girl's not going to pity you.

[AMY *enters as if she's used to coming in and out, catches herself, and "knocks" while inside. She neither sees nor hears* NOLAN. *She is of an age with* BARRY, *and dressed the way a woman dresses when she wants to make an old boyfriend regret losing her. She carries a bag with fresh paint and brushes.*]

AMY Knock, knock.

BARRY Took you long enough. Did you bring the phthalo blue?

[AMY, *taken aback, sweeps the trash off a table with one hand and dumps the bag onto the table with the other. She speaks with a dangerous sweetness.*]

AMY Phthalo blue? You didn't order it. You ordered cerulean, phthalo red rose, and cadmium yellow light. That's what I brought. And the brushes.

BARRY Amy?

AMY Barry.

NOLAN Surprise!

BARRY Didn't know you worked at the art supply store. . . .

AMY I don't. I own it.

NOLAN Told you I had a special arrangement with the owner.

[BARRY *replies to* NOLAN.]

BARRY Why is the owner making deliveries?

AMY Better question would be: Why is the owner selling to you at all?

NOLAN Told you the girl wouldn't pity you.

BARRY Uh. Okay. Why?

AMY Because it wouldn't look good for the local art supply store to refuse to sell to the leading local artist.

NOLAN Ouch.

BARRY That what I am now? The leading local artist?

AMY Apparently.

[NOLAN *speaks to* AMY, *who can't hear him.*]

NOLAN I'm barely dead and gone and already you've replaced me as the "leading local artist"?

BARRY You're still mad that we broke up. . . .

AMY Are you kidding me?

BARRY What?

AMY Do you honestly think I would care about a high school break-up at this point in my life? Who carries that kind of baggage around?

[NOLAN *points at* BARRY.]

NOLAN He does.

AMY And we didn't break up.

BARRY We didn't?

AMY No, we didn't. Saying that we broke up implies that we actually had a conversation in which we officially broke up. We didn't. You just went off to college and quit returning my phone calls.

[NOLAN *loses his temper with* BARRY.]

NOLAN You didn't have the guts to break it off face-to-face? Of course not. What am I saying?

BARRY Nolan!

AMY What's your grandpa got to do with this?

NOLAN You didn't have the guts to come see me, so it's no big surprise you didn't have the guts to talk to Amy. . . .

[BARRY *replies to* NOLAN.]

BARRY I can't believe that's what makes you angry.

NOLAN You don't treat a lady that way, Barry. I taught you better than that.

AMY Of course that makes me angry. I'm mad as hell about what you put your grandparents through.

BARRY Excuse me?

AMY Do you think for a minute that I dropped your grandparents because you dropped me?

BARRY I never really thought . . .

AMY Because I didn't. We were close.

NOLAN Yep. Thick as thieves.

BARRY I didn't know . . .

AMY No, you didn't know, did you? You broke your grandmother's heart, Barry. Broke Sarah's heart.

BARRY I thought she . . .

AMY It was inexcusable.

BARRY I'm not making excuses.

NOLAN Well, why the hell not?

AMY Have you even been in the main house at all?

BARRY Not yet. Too busy trying to finish this.

[*Despite herself,* AMY *is drawn to the easel.*]

AMY May I see it?

[BARRY *quickly covers the easel.*]

BARRY No! Don't like to show my work until it's done.

AMY Nolan liked to show his work in progress. I was glad to know him. And Sarah. Have them as friends, as well as customers. Nolan left me a sculpture, you know.

[BARRY *responds to* AMY, *but aims his answer at* NOLAN.]

BARRY He did?

NOLAN Yep. Should have read the will more closely, Barry. *Laughing Girl.* She was the model.

BARRY Really.

NOLAN Not like that, you ass! Kid, your grandma Sarah was it for me. Amy was like . . .

AMY Yes, really. Why is that so hard to believe? I was like a . . .

[BARRY *responds to both of them.*]

BARRY Like a grandchild.

[NOLAN *emphasizes daughter.*]

NOLAN Yes. Like the grand*daughter* I never had.

AMY Like a granddaughter, maybe.

BARRY Sorry I was such a disappointment.

AMY Why haven't you been in the main house yet?

BARRY Been too busy.

AMY If you'd gone inside, you'd know you weren't a disappointment. How proud they were of you.

BARRY How?

AMY I created a private gallery. Reproduced all your work. Special lights. Enlargements. Sarah's idea. Nolan wanted to see as much of it as he could.

BARRY Didn't know.

AMY They were so proud of you. Sarah kept every notice you ever got. Nolan called you the greatest work of art he'd ever produced.

BARRY God, Nolan . . .

NOLAN Gonna get a sno-cone. On the beach.

[NOLAN *exits.*]

AMY Been documenting your career for them. It's how we got so close.

BARRY Are you so close to all your customers?

AMY You really are an ass, Barry. Nolan and Sarah were friends. Most of my customers are students. Hobbyists. People who think anyone can paint. Which is true, actually. Almost anyone can paint a "couch painting."

BARRY "Couch painting"?

AMY Painting that matches your couch. A lot of customers come into my gallery looking for a painting to match the couch. Complement the drapes. The rug. Some of them buy several paintings. Switch them out according to the season. It's not about art for them. Just decorating and color coordination.

BARRY I think I'd rather give up art.

AMY Yeah. Well, it's my living. Here, I've got to go.

[AMY *holds out a tube of paint.* BARRY *neither reaches for it nor reacts. She drops the tube on the table. He starts a bit. She realizes his condition.*]

It's at your three o'clock.

[BARRY *reaches for the tube.*]

Retinitis pigmentosa?

BARRY Yep.

AMY Came on a little late, didn't it?

BARRY Yep.

AMY Hit Nolan when he was a lot younger.

BARRY Yep.

AMY When Nolan's sight got bad, he switched to sculpting.

BARRY Sounds familiar.

AMY Maybe you could change mediums.

BARRY You and Nolan. I'm a painter. Not a sculptor. A painter!

AMY So was Nolan.

BARRY Yeah. Well.

AMY He swore by vitamin A. And fresh fruit—oranges.

BARRY Did he?

[AMY *takes a good look around.*]

AMY Artist cannot live on pizza alone.

BARRY What do you want to do, document the end of my career too? The last painting.

AMY God, you are an unbelievable ass. The last painting. Doesn't have to be the end of your career. I could bring some clay.

BARRY Yeah. I'm not my grandfather.

AMY No, you're not. Not even close.

BARRY Glad we finally agree.

AMY You were actually even better. Are actually better. Sorry.

[BARRY *is stung to the core by her accidental use of the past tense.*]

BARRY I don't need fucking clay. I don't need fucking fruit. I don't need fucking pity. I do need phthalo blue. Bring me the goddamned phthalo blue.

[AMY *slaps* BARRY—*hard*—*across the face.*]

What the fu—

AMY That's for feeling sorry for yourself.

[BARRY *regains his equilibrium.* AMY *slaps him again.*]

BARRY The hell?

AMY That's for not visiting Nolan and Sarah. Next time it'll be for dumping me. Be right back.

[AMY *exits.* BARRY *again regains his composure, uncovers the easel, and studies his canvas.*]

BARRY The last painting. Going to be the "unfinished last painting" if I don't get some phthalo blue.

[NOLAN *enters.*]

NOLAN Got a sno-cone on the beach. Rainbow. Didn't remember how vibrant the colors were. Red, yellow, blue, green. Melting together. Wonderful!

BARRY You didn't get a sno-cone on the beach, Grandpa. You're dead.

NOLAN You're in a mood.

BARRY Think?

NOLAN Clear the air with Amy?

BARRY Really don't know.

NOLAN Screwed it up, didn't you, kiddo?

BARRY Probably.

NOLAN Didn't I teach you anything?

BARRY You were always smoother with the ladies than I was, Grandpa.

NOLAN That's true. I cut quite the figure in my day. The roguish artist. How do you manage to screw that up?

BARRY How come you didn't tell me about the gallery?

NOLAN What gallery?

BARRY "What gallery"? The gallery. Of my work. Amy created. In the main house.

NOLAN Oh, that gallery. Your grandmother wanted it. Would have preferred an indoor sculpture garden myself.

BARRY I'm honored.

NOLAN Wanted to see my grandson's work. That's all. What I could of it.

BARRY Still honored, Nolan.

NOLAN Speaking of my grandson's work, can I see his latest?

[NOLAN *indicates the easel.*]

BARRY Never show my work until it's finished.

[BARRY *prepares to paint again.*]

NOLAN   But I'm your grandfather.

BARRY   No.

NOLAN   But I'm dead.

BARRY   Still no.

NOLAN   You always were a moody pain-in-the ass, kiddo.

[NOLAN *picks up discarded items on the surfaces of tables, maneuvering closer to the canvas to steal a peek.*]

BARRY   Quit trying to peek. You'll see when it's finished.

NOLAN   When will that be?

BARRY   When I get some phthalo blue.

NOLAN   Really? All you need is the right paint?

BARRY   Yep. The right paint.

NOLAN   Phthalo blue?

BARRY   Phthalo blue.

[NOLAN *holds up a tube of paint he's found on the table.*]

NOLAN   The phthalo blue is right here, Barry.

BARRY   I know.

NOLAN   What's the holdup, kiddo?

BARRY   Might be my last painting.

NOLAN   Might be. Might not be. But probably.

BARRY   Finish that last stroke, it's . . . over.

NOLAN   What is?

BARRY   The painting. My career. My life.

NOLAN   Bullshit.

BARRY   Christ.

NOLAN   Don't take the Lord's name in vain.

BARRY Why not? He hasn't answered my prayers lately.

NOLAN Don't think so? Why am I here?

BARRY God sent you?

NOLAN Not saying yes. Not saying no. You are talking to your dead grandpa. You decide.

BARRY Decided awhile ago that you're part mental breakdown, part guilty conscience.

NOLAN That's flattering. I offer you a messenger of God, you take mental illness.

BARRY What do you want from me, Nolan?

NOLAN Question is, what do you want from me?

BARRY I want my sight back.

NOLAN Not mine to give, kiddo. Wish it was.

BARRY That's all I want.

NOLAN Liar.

BARRY I want you to make it all better.

NOLAN That why I look the way I did when you were ten?

BARRY Forgive me. I just need to hear it, Grandpa.

NOLAN I forgive you.

BARRY Thank you.

NOLAN You sure that's all?

BARRY Hand me the phthalo blue.

[NOLAN *hands* BARRY *the phthalo blue. He squeezes it onto his palate and mixes it a little. He prepares his brush, then lifts it to the canvas.*]

BARRY Can't see it, Nolan.

NOLAN Your sight that bad now?

BARRY Yes. No. I mean, the tunnel vision is bad. But that's not it. I mean, I can't see it. In my head. My vision. My vision of the painting. It's gone.

NOLAN It's still there.

BARRY Don't tell me it's still there, Nolan. I'm empty, I tell you.

[NOLAN *stands behind* BARRY *and looks at the canvas.*]

NOLAN It's your best work.

BARRY Sorry I can't finish it.

[NOLAN *takes* BARRY's *hand and guides it to the canvas.* BARRY *finishes the painting with* NOLAN's *hand over his.*]

BARRY How is it? I can't tell anymore.

NOLAN It captures . . . the loss.

BARRY I'll hang it in the main house. In the gallery. Gonna come see it?

NOLAN You've gotten too used to being haunted. So . . .

BARRY So.

NOLAN You finished.

BARRY Yeah. I did. Thanks, Nolan.

NOLAN Anytime, kiddo.

BARRY Nolan, the tunnel's getting smaller. I can barely see you.

[NOLAN *starts to exit.*]

NOLAN You're going blind, Barry. Don't lose sight of what's important.

[AMY *enters with a bag of oranges, vitamins, trash bags, a tube of phthalo blue, and clay.* NOLAN *exits.*]

AMY Knock, knock.

BARRY Come on in.

[AMY *pulls the tube of paint from the bag.*]

AMY Got the phthalo blue.

BARRY Found some. Sorry you went back for nothing.

AMY No problem.

[BARRY *hoarsely shoves ten years of regret into one word.*]

BARRY Sorry . . .

[AMY *graciously does not call him on it.*]

AMY So, that mean you finished?

BARRY Yeah.

AMY Mind if I . . .

BARRY No. Take a look.

[AMY *moves to the easel and looks at the painting.*]

AMY My.

BARRY Is that a good "my" or a bad "my"?

AMY That's a very good "my." Plans for it?

BARRY Yeah. Gonna hang it in the main house. In the gallery.

AMY They'd have liked that.

BARRY You handle it for me?

AMY Sure. My pleasure.

BARRY I'd offer to show you the house, but I think you're gonna have to show me.

AMY I can do that. Planning to stay?

BARRY Don't know. Maybe. Don't have any plans, really.

AMY Gonna start another painting?

BARRY No.

AMY Oh.

BARRY Yeah.

AMY What about . . . ?

[AMY *takes a lump of clay and thumps it onto the table.*]

BARRY Not sure. Maybe art just isn't an option anymore.

AMY You have too much talent to say that.

BARRY Talent's pretty useless if I can't see.

AMY How bad is it now?

BARRY Pretty bad.

AMY Told you Nolan swore by vitamin A. And oranges. Brought both.

BARRY Don't think vitamins and oranges are gonna fix things.

AMY Talent shouldn't be wasted.

BARRY Amy . . .

AMY Remember high school art class? Third place, sometimes. Honorable mention, mostly. You always took first prize. When I couldn't get into art school with you, I thought—just work harder. At college I realized I was as good as I was ever gonna get. I have some talent—but not enough. Me, I'm ordinary. But you? You're extraordinary.

BARRY Don't feel extraordinary.

AMY I understand how frustrating it is. To have something inside you. To have something inside you, but not quite be able to express it. Not the way it needs to be expressed.

BARRY I'm sorry.

[AMY *responds ironically and slightly mockingly.*]

AMY Don't need your pity. I found my way. Figured out my niche. I'm very good at recognizing talent. Nurturing it. Making it grow. Think about it.

[AMY *picks up the clay and places it in* BARRY'*s hands.*]

BARRY I will. I am. Thinking about things.

[BARRY *works the clay, warming it up.* AMY *pulls out a trash bag and picks up in companionable silence. He pounds the clay on the table. The pounding becomes an angry echo of the ten-year-old boy hiding in the studio pounding out his grief.*

Guttural cries keep time with the pounding. Not self-pitying or dramatic cries; true grieving. As his cries subside, AMY *holds him from behind. They rock together awhile.*]

If I did start sculpting, would you model for me?

[AMY *laughs deeply and richly, showing why* NOLAN *named his sculpture of her* Laughing Girl.]

AMY   You and Nolan!

BARRY   *Laughing Girl.* Maybe you could let me come over and see it. Touch it. Nolan's sculpture.

AMY   Maybe.

BARRY   Maybe?

AMY   Maybe.

BARRY   I'd like that.

AMY   Me too.

[BARRY *reaches up but stops short of touching her face. She takes his hands in hers and guides them the rest of the way.* BARRY *touches her face very gently. They look at each other intently.*]

BARRY   I see you.

• • •

Long Time Coming

David Rusiecki

David Rusiecki

David Rusiecki is the president of the New Voices Playwrights Theatre based in Orange County, California. He has served as head of the New Works Festival Literary Committee and Board of Trustees with the Long Beach Playhouse. His full-length plays and one-acts have been given staged readings and produced in California at STAGES Theatre, Stage Door Repertory, and Theatre Out. His full-length play *Sides* was selected for the Long Beach Playhouse New Works table-read series while in the same year . . . *Prep* . . . received honorable mention with Panndora Productions' annual festival of new play readings. His one-act play *Kid Gloves* (originally entitled *Have a Nice Day*) was published in *The Best American Short Plays 2012–2013* (Applause Books) as well as in *Best Monologues from Best American Short Plays* (Applause Books). He is a graduate of Loyola College in Baltimore, Maryland, and holds an MBA.

···production history···

Long Time Coming was first performed as part of Summer Voices 2015: Eight One-Act Plays produced by New Voices Playwrights Theatre from August 1 to August 16 at Stage Door Repertory Theatre in Anaheim, California, featuring Brandon Kasper and Simerjeet Singh. It was directed by David Rusiecki.

characters

> KEITH   male, 30s
>
> LEE   male, 30s

place and time

Coffee shop lounge in the present.

scene 1

[KEITH *and* LEE *fist-pump, then sit on a couch.*]

KEITH   Hey, Lee.

LEE   Keith, good to see you. How are things?

KEITH   Can't complain. And you?

LEE   Oh, you know.

KEITH   No, I don't know. That's why I asked.

LEE   Sorry, sorry. I have . . . you know, a bit of news.

KEITH   Well, don't keep me in suspense.

LEE   I started seeing someone.

KEITH   That's great. You guys meet online?

LEE   Actually an open mic.

KEITH   She does standup? Lee, come on. You know better than to date another comic. That's a no-go right off the bat.

LEE   Theoretically speaking, she's not a comic. Look, she just started out. I'm helping her build up material.

KEITH   Which open mic?

LEE   Sal's . . . over on Melrose.

KEITH   She a Latina?

LEE   No, her name's Vickie. She's a teacher. She also does hand modeling on the side.

[*Lowers his voice.*]

She's . . . unbelievable.

KEITH   You mean, unbelievable, in the bedroom?

LEE   No, dude. We haven't done any of that . . . no way.

KEITH   All-right, didn't mean to imply.

LEE   Nah, I'm just . . . you know.

KEITH   No, I don't know.

LEE   I'm very deliberate about these things.

KEITH   Hey, I understand. Been a long time coming for you. Seriously, talk about a dry patch. So, what's she like?

LEE   God, she's . . . smart. Real smart. A redhead.

KEITH   Hold up, she's a ginger?

[LEE *smiles and nods his head.*]

You dog, you. How old?

LEE   Thirty-two.

KEITH   Okay, we can work with that. Where's she from?

LEE   Canada. I tell ya, she's something else.

KEITH   Boy, you're really . . .

LEE   What?

KEITH   Now don't take this the wrong way. But, to me, sounds like . . . you're in love.

LEE   Stop. You think? Tell me what to do, you're better than me at these things.

KEITH What are you freaking out over?

LEE It's just . . . usually every girl I go out with becomes my mother in the end. I mean, I hit my ceiling with women back in the eighth grade. That was as good as it got.

KEITH Look, take a deep, cleansing breath.

LEE I know, I know.

KEITH It's all good. You'll be fine. So, Vickie, you said?

LEE Yes.

KEITH Great job, my man.

[KEITH *and* LEE *high-five each other.*]

scene 2

[KEITH *and* LEE *fist-pump, then sit on the same couch. A week later.*]

LEE You look good. Lose some weight?

KEITH Nah, still the same. Damn carbs. So, how are things with you and . . . what's her name again?

LEE Vickie.

KEITH The Filipina?

LEE The ginger . . . from Canada.

KEITH You told me she was coming.

LEE Yeah, but she had to feed her boa constrictor tonight, so I left. I don't like being around dead rats, especially if they're kept stored in the freezer.

KEITH Right, so what's going on?

LEE Oh, you know.

KEITH No, I don't know. That's why I asked.

LEE Well, to be quite frank with you, it's taken a turn.

KEITH With Vickie? Last week you were smitten like a schoolgirl.

LEE Well, we're sort of at an impasse.

KEITH How so?

LEE She's really ingratiated herself to me. Telling me how nice I am to her. How polite I act around her. What a gentleman I am . . . all of which is true.

KEITH Stay on topic.

LEE And we've been attending a number of comedy shows together. We walk up and down Sunset arm in arm. People stop and look at us, like what is *she* doing with *him?*

KEITH Have the two of you . . .

[KEITH *makes a discreet but suggestive gesture.*]

LEE That's where things get dicey.

KEITH Oh, boy. She's married.

LEE No.

KEITH Kids?

[LEE *shakes his head.*]

She has a penis.

LEE Uh-uh.

KEITH Used to be a man? Like some Caitlyn Jenner transformational kind of thing.

LEE Nope, nothing like that.

KEITH Okay then, what's the problem?

LEE She . . . oh God . . . she confided in me something. And she made me promise not to share this with anyone.

[KEITH *motions to his lips, turning a key.*]

KEITH Steel trap. Locked in the vault.

LEE [*Sighs.*] She used to do . . . adult entertainment.

[KEITH *stares at LEE for a moment.*]

KEITH Porn. You're saying she did porn.

LEE She prefers the term "adult films."

KEITH Like, straight porn? Girl-on-girl action?

LEE Does that matter?

KEITH To me it does.

LEE I don't know where to begin.

KEITH Is this a joke? Are you putting me on?

LEE I wish. No, I mean . . . no, this is not a joke.

KEITH Again, I ask, what's the problem?

LEE So, I mean . . . Jesus, what do I do?

KEITH You could role-play.

LEE Come again?

KEITH Check this out. Pretend you're the casting director, she's the hungry actress. You have her come in and give you a very private audition, if you're thinking what I'm thinking. Along with multiple callbacks in your casting office on your plush leather sofa. Use your imagination.

LEE No, no . . . I really can't.

KEITH Why not?

LEE Because she's . . . she's not at all like that anymore. She told me that part of her life is way behind her.

KEITH You don't seem to realize, this is a gift. This is the greatest opportunity you'll ever have fall into your lap.

LEE What are you saying?

KEITH Do you know how much you'll have for your routine by dating a former porn star?

LEE Exotic film actress.

KEITH That's a gold mine of material. I don't want to see you blow this chance.

LEE No, absolutely not. Vickie's totally off-limits. She told me, and these are her exact words, every boyfriend she's ever had treated her like shit. I'm the first guy to come along with who's, like, normal.

[KEITH *takes out his phone.*]

KEITH What's her porn star name, do you know?

LEE She used to go under Norma Wray.

[KEITH *types in his phone.*]

KEITH I don't see her listed.

LEE What website are you looking at?

[KEITH *brings the phone for* LEE *to look at.*]

KEITH Doctor Skin.Com.

LEE Here, type W-R-A-Y, not R-A-Y. She's a huge fan of Marilyn Monroe and King Kong.

[KEITH *types in his phone.*]

KEITH Norma Wray. Ah, man . . . impressive resume.

LEE What does it say?

KEITH You mean you never looked her up?

LEE I told you before, my laptop is on the fritz.

KEITH Check it out *Hotter Than Hell . . . Climb Every Virgin . . . Third Time's a Charm.* You know, I think I downloaded *Springtime in the Rockies.*

LEE Seriously, Keith . . . and I've cogitated this over for some time . . . this girl is special, she's far more intelligent that I'll ever be. And far more . . . experienced that I can ever imagine. It's daunting enough to think somewhere, someplace her movies are occupying a shelf of some stranger who's getting the same satisfaction as I should be getting. And there's not a damn thing I can do to get that visual out of my head. I feel totally inadequate.

KEITH Look, I told you from the start it was wrong to date another comic, did I not?

LEE Yes, you said that.

KEITH Did you listen to me?

LEE No, I didn't.

KEITH Remember when I told you not to send a friend request to your old high school prom date. But you decided to do it anyway. Which backfired, because she denied your request and reported you to security. You couldn't send a friend request for at least a month.

LEE I was drunk at the time.

KEITH I need to know this won't fall on deaf ears. I'm looking out for you. I'm the Love Doctor, remember?

LEE Got it, I'm all ears.

KEITH Now, here's what you do. Hold out as long as you can. Stay cool, keep your poise, don't do anything irrational. The longer you hold out, the crazier she'll be. Before you know it, you'll have her eating from the palm of your hand. She'll be under your thumb completely. That sense of inadequacy will erode in no time.

LEE Again, the Love Doctor comes through in the clutch.

KEITH If there's anything I know, it's women.

[KEITH *and* LEE *high-five each other.* KEITH *gets up from his chair.*]

Look, I gotta split. Oh, one last thing.

LEE What's up?

KEITH I'm doing five-minutes at the Laugh Factory next Tuesday and need three peeps in attendance . . . think the two of you can make it?

scene 3

[KEITH *and* LEE *fist-pump, then sit on the same couch. A week later.*]

LEE Hey, sorry about missing your showcase. How'd it go at the Factory?

KEITH It went fine. Never mind that, what's up with you?

LEE Oh, you know.

KEITH No, I don't know.

LEE Well . . . I did what you told me.

KEITH And?

LEE It's off, it's over. We're done, through.

KEITH What?

LEE Finished, finito.

KEITH Tell me.

LEE So, yeah . . . well, things were going well for a while. I held out as much as I could.

KEITH But?

LEE We wound up having . . .

KEITH No, you didn't.

LEE Yeah, it was pretty . . . *memorable* would be a good word. At least, on my end, don't know about hers.

KEITH You never listen to me. Why do I even bother?

LEE I did listen, but then things took another turn. Instead of sloppy seconds, she wanted to do standup at this midnight open mic. You know, the one on LaBrea.

KEITH Wait a sec, you're telling me instead of any post-coital bliss, she went up and performed a three-minute set?

LEE Oddly enough, she did.

KEITH And? How'd it go?

LEE She's been asked to do a showcase there next week.

KEITH Wow.

LEE Only, there's a caveat.

KEITH Which is?

LEE She's doing my material.

KEITH Say that again?

LEE My routine, she stole it.

KEITH Seriously?

LEE Verbatim. Plagiarism to the nth degree.

KEITH Are you sure?

LEE Everything . . . you name it. From my jokes on finding used Q-Tips to Tarzan . . . even my take on Bill Cosby.

KEITH How is that possible? I've known you longer and I couldn't do any of your jokes.

LEE Here's the kicker, she gets laughs. Really strong laughs I never imagined getting on my own.

KEITH So, what are you going to do?

LEE I was thinking about quitting standup altogether.

KEITH Really? And do what?

LEE Perhaps, continue writing for her.

KEITH After what she did to you?

LEE I've come to the conclusion, she's made it to my level in such a short span of time . . . I figure, why bother.

KEITH Okay, you're taking all this pretty . . . sound, I guess.

LEE Yes, I am very much at ease with my decision.

KEITH Do the two of you still talk?

LEE Yeah.

KEITH But you're no longer an item?

LEE Correct.

KEITH So, you wouldn't mind if I . . . you know, got together with Vickie? I have a weakness for dirty girls.

LEE Be my guest.

KEITH Because that showcase you mentioned.

LEE Yes.

KEITH I'm on it too.

LEE Oh, fabulous.

KEITH And I was thinking, since you missed last week, and if you're not busy . . . any chance you'd like to come see the two of us perform?

• • •

Petra

John Yarbrough

John Yarbrough

John Yarbrough is a playwright and writer in New York City. *Petra* won top prize at the Strawberry One-Act Festival in New York in February 2015. Along with plays developed for the stage, his work has been selected for staged readings by the Writers Guild of America East and the Screen Actors Guild Foundation. Previously, he took a happy detour to Washington, D.C., where he served as press secretary to Congresswoman Nancy Pelosi. A former artist-in-residence with Hudson Warehouse in New York, he is a member of the Dramatists Guild and the Writers Guild of America East, and is a professional member of PEN America.

···production history···

Petra had its world premiere at the Manhattan Repertory Theatre on September 23, 2014.

> **CONRAD** Larry Gutman
>
> **JANICE** Yvonne "Bonnie" Cole
>
> **AVERY** Olivia Mell
>
> **DAVID** Michael Gibson

Directed by Jesse Michael Mothershed, stage-managed by Stephanie Connors

It subsequently won top prize at the Strawberry One-Act Festival in New York in February 2015, performed at the Hudson Guild.

> **CONRAD** Larry Gutman
>
> **JANICE** Sarah Giller
>
> **AVERY** Tressa Preston
>
> **DAVID** Eric Kirchberger

Directed by Drew Rosene

Song "Caterwaulin' Sunday" © 2014 John Yarbrough.

characters

> **CONRAD** male, 60s
>
> **JANICE** female, 60s, wife to Conrad
>
> **AVERY** female, 30s/40s, daughter to Conrad and Janice
>
> **DAVID** male, 30s/40s, Avery's husband

time

Present day. Father's Day and the following morning.

place

A home in suburban Westchester County, New York. Present day.

[The living room of a home. CONRAD, 60s, walks in. In a bathrobe and pajamas, oxygen tubes in his nose, he walks with a cane. In one hand he holds a glass of white

wine, in the other the cane and a urinal, a third full. He pushes a portable oxygen concentrator forward with his foot, as he sings.]

CONRAD "Ah, sweet mystery of life at last I've found thee! Ah, I know at last the secret of it all" . . .

[CONRAD's *wife, JANICE, 60s, sits off to the side, talking on the phone as she works on a crossword puzzle.*]

JANICE You're ten minutes away?

CONRAD "All the longing, seeking, striving, waiting, yearning! The burning hopes, the joy and idle tears that fall" . . .

JANICE "Close overlap of fugue voices." Seven letters. Starts with an "s."

[*Into phone.*]

Sorry. You're on the Metro North? Dobbs Ferry station. Well, get here as soon as you can.

[CONRAD *sits on a couch next to a table and two chairs, puts the glass and urinal on the table.*]

CONRAD Eh.

[CONRAD *tosses the tubing on the oxygen concentrator. He takes a remote and turns on a TV, watches with the sound down.*]

This batter couldn't hit a parked bus! Square up and bunt, dammit!

JANICE He's already had one glass of wine. "Close overlap of fugue voices"? I hate you, Will Shortz.

CONRAD Why did you swing at that!

JANICE [*Into phone.*] Hurry.

[JANICE *gets off the phone, walks over to* CONRAD.]

Why aren't you dressed, Conrad?

CONRAD Exactly, honey. A guy with a .250 OBP batting below the Mendoza Line should not swing at a 3-0 cutter. And he should have known that!

JANICE Yes, dear. I agree. Why aren't you dressed?

CONRAD Where am I going?

JANICE Avery and David are coming up from the city.

CONRAD Why?

JANICE It's Father's Day. And you're a father.

CONRAD I am, aren't I. Okay.
[*Beat.*]
Oh. Janice. What was that Yankee's name?

JANICE What Yankee?

CONRAD You know, Janice. That Yankee that said that thing.

JANICE That Yankee that said that thing. I need a little help.

CONRAD You know. They just put his picture up.

JANICE Derek Jeter?

CONRAD No. Way before.

JANICE Yogi Berra?

CONRAD No.

JANICE Stretto!

[JANICE *writes "stretto" in the puzzle.*]

CONRAD No, that wasn't it.

JANICE Was he a manager?

CONRAD I don't know.

JANICE Was he a pitcher?

CONRAD I don't know.

JANICE Did he play first base?

CONRAD Maybe.

JANICE [*Frustrated.*] Did he have Lou Gehrig's disease?

CONRAD Yes! That's it! Lou Gehrig.

JANICE And?

CONRAD What?

JANICE What about Lou Gehrig?

CONRAD What *about* Lou Gehrig?

JANICE You—never mind. You always watch with the sound down. You should turn it up, sweetie.

[CONRAD *finishes his glass of wine.*]

CONRAD Oh. There's something I want to talk to you about.

[CONRAD *pats the couch.* JANICE *sits down next to him.*]

JANICE Yes?

CONRAD Janice, I was just thinking about Petra.

JANICE Petra?

CONRAD Yes, that summer day in Petra.

JANICE What summer day in Petra?

CONRAD You remember. Our traveling year abroad, before the kids. What a year that was. Ah, that glorious summer day in Petra.

JANICE I remember the trip. I don't remember Petra.

CONRAD Of course you do. The Rose-Red City, half as old as time.

JANICE Yes, the Rose-Red City. But I'm telling you, we never went to Petra.

CONRAD Of course we did.

JANICE Egypt, yes. Turkey, yes. Greece, yes. Jordan, no. Petra, no. I left you in Cairo to get back to finish my PhD. And you came back the next week. Remember?

CONRAD Oh, we went to Petra. The narrow passageways, the tombs . . .

JANICE We didn't go to Petra.

CONRAD The temples, the silk, the spices. That beautiful summer day in Petra, with you and me and Walter the whistling dog.

JANICE   [*Astonished.*] Walter the whistling dog?

CONRAD   That's the name we gave him. Remember? I don't know what his Arabic name was.

JANICE   There was no Petra, and no Walter the whistling dog.

CONRAD   Of course there was.

JANICE   You seem a little light-headed.

CONRAD   [*With great import.*] "From rock as if by magic grown, eternal, silent, beautiful, alone!" Ah, Petra.

JANICE   Ah, Petra. Isn't it time for another hit of oxygen?

CONRAD   I just had some. I'm going to have tube prints on my cheeks for the rest of my life. Promise me I'll have a closed-casket funeral. No viewing, please.

JANICE   You're not dying. Not if I have anything to do with it. And the prints will go away. But if you keep wearing the tubes so tight, they won't.

CONRAD   I love you.

   [*Beat.*]

   Come here.

[JANICE *cuddles up next to him.*]

JANICE   I love you.

CONRAD   Sometimes life ain't easy, is it?

JANICE   No, it sure isn't.

CONRAD   If only it could be. Like that summer day in Petra.

JANICE   We never went to Petra.

CONRAD   It was you and me and —

JANICE   Walter the whistling dog. Yes.

CONRAD   You do remember!

JANICE   No!

CONRAD   It was you and me and Walter the whistling dog.

JANICE   Okay. Fine. It was you and me and Walter the whistling dog.

CONRAD   I lost my train of thought.

JANICE   It was you and me and Walter the whistling dog.

CONRAD   You have such a good memory! It was you and me and Walter the whistling dog. Our senses were enveloped by the sheer grandeur of the ancient Nabataean caravan city.

JANICE   Nabataean? What have you been smoking?

CONRAD   Don't play dumb. You know this better than I do.

JANICE   Yes. Of course.

  [CONRAD *picks up the urinal, starts to pour it into the wineglass.*]
  Conrad! Give me that!

  [JANICE *snatches the urinal away, puts it on the floor. Frustrated.*]
  You were saying?

CONRAD   The vast sandstone landscape that spans from the Assyrians to the Nabataean.

JANICE   There's that word again.

CONRAD   The arching, narrow passageways that welcome the world like glorious rose vaginas.

JANICE   Conrad!

CONRAD   And that's when Walter kissed your hand.

JANICE   Kissed my hand?

CONRAD   He kissed your hand, then took us to his Bedouin master.

JANICE   Bedouin master?

CONRAD   The Bedouin offered us spices, candies, clove cigarettes, and warm Coke. You had a warm Coke, but didn't let me have a clove cigarette.

JANICE   Well, that was probably the right thing to do.

CONRAD   And then we began to argue.

JANICE   Over a clove cigarette?

CONRAD   Not you and I. Me and the Bedouin. And Walter didn't like that.

JANICE   Why were you arguing?

CONRAD   I told him that we were going to Aqaba by land, and that we would cross the Nefud Desert. But he said the Nefud could not be crossed. I assured him it could. And he raised his voice and said,

[CONRAD *shakes fist.*]

"You will not be at Aqaba, English!"

JANICE   That's Peter O'Toole and Omar Sharif in *Lawrence of Arabia*. And we never went to Aqaba, either. You crazy fool.

CONRAD   Oh yes, we did.

[*The doorbell rings.*]

JANICE   At last!

[*Stage goes dark.*]

[*Lights up. That afternoon.*]

[CONRAD *and* JANICE *sit together on the couch across from* DAVID *and* AVERY, *who sit in the chairs. A shopping bag sits next to* AVERY. CONRAD, *still in his pajamas and bathrobe, has* AVERY *and* DAVID *in tears, laughing, as* JANICE *sits quietly.*]

CONRAD   And that's when Walter the whistling dog kissed your mother's hand!

AVERY   Mom, you never told me you all went to Petra!

JANICE   We never went to Petra.

AVERY   The silk! The spices!

DAVID   The sheer grandeur of the ancient Nabataean caravan city!

AVERY   Petra, the Rose-Red city!

CONRAD   The lost city of stone!

JANICE We never went to Petra.

DAVID [*Shaking his fist.*] "You will not be at Aqaba, English!" Ha, ha!

CONRAD The narrow passageways that welcome the world like glorious—

JANICE Conrad, no! Now. How was the trip, Avery?

AVERY Oh, it was wonderful. The kids had so much fun.

DAVID Yes! We were beguiled by the staggering allure of the new and the *basso profundo* of the old!

JANICE [*Annoyed.*] Wonderful.

CONRAD Like Petra! Now, about Walter —

DAVID Oh, how travel opens the mind!

AVERY How are you feeling, Dad?

CONRAD I've been better, and I've been worse, but for today, grave digger . . .

CONRAD and AVERY Put the hearse in reverse!

[AVERY *touches* CONRAD'*s arm. He touches her hand.*]

CONRAD Back to Petra, and Walter . . .

DAVID Oh, to laugh at pale death!

CONRAD About Walter . . .

DAVID Let us smirk at the worms that await us all! Dark horseman—do not call!

CONRAD Let's get back to Walter!

JANICE Yes. Let's get back to Walter.

AVERY Yes, Dad. Walter . . . What was it? Walter . . .

JANICE Walter the whistling dog.

CONRAD Yes! Janice, you are amazing.

DAVID Who was Walter?

JANICE   Some dog we met in Petra. Allegedly.

CONRAD   Oh, he was more than just "some" dog we met in Petra. "Allegedly."

JANICE   Conrad thinks we went to Petra. But we never went to Petra.

DAVID   The lost jewel in the Arabian desert!

JANICE   We never went to Petra.

DAVID   It seems no work of man's creative hand! But from rock as if by magic grown!

[DAVID *nudges* AVERY *to join in.*]

AVERY   Eternal, silent, beautiful, alone!

CONRAD   Our glorious day in Petra! Ah, Petra!

[CONRAD *encourages* AVERY *and* DAVID *to join in.*]

AVERY, DAVID, and CONRAD   Ah, Petra! Ah, Petra! Ah—

JANICE   Ah, Petra! Now let's open some goddamn Father's Day presents!

AVERY   Okay, Mom. Jeez.

　　[AVERY *puts the shopping bag on the table.*]

　　Sorry we didn't have time to wrap, Dad. The trip and all.

　　[AVERY *pulls out a scarf.*]

　　This one's from Lilly and Jenny. They made it at eco-camp.

　　They're there today, cutting up six-pack rings so dolphins won't drown. Otherwise they'd be here. It's a reclaimed hemp scarf dyed with cranberries, beets, and crab-apple bark.

CONRAD   Lovely.

[AVERY *puts the scarf around* CONRAD's *neck. Playing with it,* CONRAD *pulls it over his head and covers up his face with it as if he were in a sandstorm. He then lets it fall back over his shoulders. He takes a whiff of the beet-dyed scarf, grimaces.* AVERY *pulls out a bottle of wine.*]

AVERY   This is from David.

DAVID A client introduced it to me. It's an upstate cab that blends the piquant hint of the abattoir with the fruity vigor of a sad bordello. I would describe it as—

AVERY Shut up, David.

JANICE So, Conrad. Did they sell hemp scarves and upstate cabs in Petra? To go with the warm Coke and clove cigarettes?

AVERY Mother! Don't be mean.

JANICE Sorry. Yes, that was mean.

CONRAD Why would a country on the ancient Silk Road make scarves out of hemp? Of course not, Susanne. You were there. You know.

JANICE Susanne? That glass of wine has already done you in.

CONRAD Whatever, Susanne.

[CONRAD *starts to shake, slightly.*]

JANICE Conrad, you've got to stop drinking.

[JANICE *puts her hand on* CONRAD*'s shoulder, he brushes her away.*]

CONRAD Leave me alone, Susanne! I told you not to worry. Janice will never find out!

JANICE Susanne? Janice will never find out? Janice will never find out what?

CONRAD What?

JANICE What won't Janice find out?

CONRAD What are you talking about, Susanne?

JANICE Susanne?

CONRAD Yes, Susanne?

JANICE Susanne *Isringhausen? Sunny* Isringhausen?

AVERY Sunny Isringhausen?

DAVID Who is Sunny Isringhausen?

CONRAD Yes, Sunny?

JANICE   Sunny Isringhausen? I can't believe you! That's when it started? On our year abroad?

CONRAD   What started?

DAVID   Who is Sunny Isringhausen?

JANICE   You went to Petra with Sunny Isringhausen? After I left?

CONRAD   I was in Petra with *you*.

JANICE   You said it had been only one night. A stupid, one-night mistake, you said. It would never happen again, you said. But apparently it had already been going on for years!

DAVID   Who's Sunny Isringhausen?

JANICE   Did you fuck her in Petra?

CONRAD   Janice!

AVERY   Mother!

JANICE   Did she blow you in Petra?

AVERY   Mother!

CONRAD   Janice!

JANICE   Was the Bedouin master there with you? Did he fuck Sunny Isringhausen too?

AVERY   Dad?

DAVID   Who is Sunny Isringhausen?

JANICE   So walk me through it, Conrad! Did you take Sunny Isringhausen by land?

AVERY   Please, Mother.

JANICE   Did you cross her Nefud Desert?

AVERY   MOTHER!

CONRAD   I don't know what you're talking about. I'm an ill man. Very ill.

JANICE   Oh, I'm sorry. I forgot! The bedouin master said the Nefud could not be crossed!

AVERY   Please, Mother! He's an ill man. Very ill.

JANICE   The bedouin master said,

[JANICE *shakes a fist*]

"You will not be at Aqaba, English!"

DAVID   Who is this Sunny Isringhausen? This wicked seductress, this femme fatale who—

AVERY   Shut up, David.

JANICE   Who needs Aqaba anyway, when you have glorious rose vaginas!

CONRAD   Janice!

JANICE   [*Hands raised in air.*] Ahhh, Petra!

DAVID   Who is—

JANICE   Shut up, David! She's nobody. She's dead. Bitch! Poor Walter's probably dead, too.

CONRAD   Who's Walter?

JANICE   Walter the—stop it, Conrad! What other lies have you told me over the years? How many other Petras were there?

CONRAD   We went to Petra?

JANICE   Bastard.

AVERY   Mom, I think we should go. Will you be okay if we go?

JANICE   Yes. Just go.

AVERY   I'll call you later.

JANICE   Okay.

[AVERY *walks over to* CONRAD.]

AVERY   There's another present in the bag, Dad. From me.

[AVERY *kisses* CONRAD'*s head; she and* DAVID *leave.* JANICE *walks over to a corner, her back to* CONRAD.]

JANICE [*With anger, then frustration, then sadness.*] Ah, Petra. Ah, Petra. Ah, Petra. Ah, Petra!

[*Stage goes dark.*]

[*Lights up. The next morning.*]

[JANICE *walks into the room.* CONRAD *lies on the couch, singing.*]

CONRAD "Ah, sweet mystery of life, at last I've found thee! Ah, I know at last the secret of it all. All the longing, seeking"—

JANICE Good morning.

CONRAD Oh. Good morning.

[*Beat.*]

I don't feel well.

JANICE Well, you shouldn't have had that extra glass of wine yesterday. And you need an Ensure, and more water. You get dehydrated.

CONRAD I know I am supposed to be sorry about something. But I don't know what it is. I heard you crying last night.

JANICE Well. It was long ago.

CONRAD What was it?

JANICE It was long ago.

CONRAD Was it bad?

JANICE It was long ago.

CONRAD Oh. Well.

JANICE Yes. Oh, well.

CONRAD I love you, Janice.

JANICE [*Flat.*] I love you.

CONRAD The Yankees lost.

JANICE Well, they should have bunted more.

CONRAD Yes. I suppose.

JANICE Yes.

CONRAD I don't feel well.

JANICE Drink some water.

CONRAD I had a dream about Petra.

JANICE Seriously? You've got to be kidding me.

CONRAD Why would I dream about Petra?

JANICE I don't know.

CONRAD I don't feel well.

JANICE Just breathe. Drink some water.

CONRAD No. I mean I really don't feel well.

JANICE What is it?

CONRAD I don't . . .

[JANICE *sits down at his side.*]

JANICE Just breathe in. And drink some water.

CONRAD Breathe in! Drink some water! I can't do both!

JANICE Be still!

    [CONRAD *slumps on the couch.*]

    Conrad!

    [JANICE *grabs a bottle of water, sits down beside him.*]

    Sit up. Breathe in. That's good. Now drink some water.

[CONRAD *drinks.*]

CONRAD Doesn't help.

[JANICE *grabs an inhaler.*]

JANICE Suck on it. Hard.

[CONRAD *sucks, it doesn't help. He grimaces in pain.*]

CONRAD This isn't helping.

[JANICE *pulls the oxygen concentrator closer, puts the tubing around* CONRAD*'s head and in his nose. She flips a switch on the generator.*]

JANICE   It won't work. It won't work!

CONRAD   Oh no, oh no.

JANICE   What happened? It wasn't plugged in! The battery's dead!

CONRAD   Janice?

JANICE   I have to get help.

[JANICE *stands up, starts to walk away.*]

CONRAD   Don't leave me.

JANICE   I have to, Conrad!

[CONRAD *grabs her arm.*]

CONRAD   Don't leave me! I think the end is near.

[JANICE *sits down next to him.*]

JANICE   No, it's not.

CONRAD   I can feel it.

JANICE   Just breathe!

CONRAD   Janice?

JANICE   Don't speak. Just breathe.

CONRAD   Janice? Talk to me. I want to hear the sound of your voice.

JANICE   I'm right here.

[JANICE *cradles him.*]

CONRAD   I'm dying.

JANICE   You're not dying. You're going to be okay.

CONRAD   [*In pain.*] It hurts. Talk to me.

[CONRAD *sighs, drops his chin to his chest.*]

JANICE   Conrad? Conrad? Conrad!

CONRAD What?

JANICE Listen to me. Stay with me.

[CONRAD *drops his chin again.* JANICE *lifts it up.*]

Let me tell you . . .

CONRAD Yes?

JANICE I'll tell you . . .

CONRAD Yes?

JANICE I'll tell you about Petra.

CONRAD Petra?

JANICE Yes. Our glorious summer day in Petra.

CONRAD Our glorious summer day in Petra?

JANICE On our trip abroad. Before the kids.

CONRAD I remember the trip. I don't remember Petra.

JANICE Of course you do. The Rose-Red City, half as old as time. The narrow passageways, the tombs.

CONRAD The silk? The spices?

JANICE Yes!

CONRAD No. I don't remember. I don't remember Petra.

JANICE Of course you do.

CONRAD Can you tell me about it? Please. Please tell me about it.

JANICE [*Trying to remember* CONRAD's *story.*] Uh . . . well . . . it . . . it was a glorious summer day in Petra.

CONRAD It was?

JANICE And it was you, me and . . .

CONRAD Yes?

JANICE It was you, me, and Walter.

CONRAD Walter?

JANICE   Walter the singing dog. Uh, Walter the whistling dog.

CONRAD   Fascinating.

[CONRAD *begins to cough.* JANICE *holds him tight.*]

JANICE   Easy, easy. Breathe easy.

CONRAD   Go on.

JANICE   Our senses were enveloped by the sheer grandeur of the ancient Nabataean caravan city.

CONRAD   Nabataean? What have you been smoking?

JANICE   The vast sandstone landscape that spans from the Assyrians to the Nabataean.

CONRAD   There's that word again.

JANICE   The narrow passageways like glorious rose vaginas.

CONRAD   Janice!

JANICE   [*Holding* CONRAD *tighter.*] It was you and me and Walter the whistling dog. And Walter kissed my hand. And he took us over to his Bedouin master.

CONRAD   Bedouin master?

JANICE   Yes. Just listen. The Bedouin offered us spices, candies, clove cigarettes, and warm Coke. I had a warm Coke, but I didn't let you have a clove cigarette.

CONRAD   That was probably the right thing to do.

JANICE   And then you began to argue.

CONRAD   Over a clove cigarette?

JANICE   Not you and I. You and the Bedouin. You told him we were going to Aqaba by land, and would cross the Nefud Desert.
[CONRAD *coughs.*]
Conrad?

CONRAD   Yes?

JANICE   Listen to me.

CONRAD   Yes?

JANICE   The Bedouin said the Nefud could not be crossed. And you assured him it could. And he raised his voice and said,

[*Shaking her fist.*]

"You will not be at Aqaba, English!"

CONRAD   That's Peter O'Toole and Omar Sharif in *Lawrence of Arabia.*

JANICE   Oh, sorry. You're right.

[CONRAD *breathes easier.*]

CONRAD   I think I'm going to be okay now.

JANICE   Are you sure?

CONRAD   Yes.

JANICE   Thank goodness.

CONRAD   I love you, Janice.

[*A long beat.*]

JANICE   I love you.

CONRAD   So it really was a glorious day in Petra?

JANICE   Yes.

CONRAD   I wish I could remember it. Can you tell me about it?

JANICE   I just told you about it.

CONRAD   You did? Can you tell me again?

JANICE   Yes. Of course. It was a glorious summer day in Petra, the Rose-Red City. And it was you and me and Walter the whistling dog . . .

[*Lights out.*]

• • •

The Secret Keeper

David Meyers

David Meyers

David Meyers is an actor and playwright based in New York. His plays have been read and performed Off-Broadway and at professional theaters around the country. His play *Broken*—about a mass shooter who kills nineteen people at a shopping mall—had its world premiere in 2015 and is published online by Indie Theater Now. Meyers previously worked as a communications aide in the White House and as a writer in the U.S. Senate. Visit www.DavidActs.com.

···production history···

World Premiere: FUSION Theatre Company, Albuquerque, New Mexico. Directed by Danny Kovacs.

AHMAD Matt Andrade

FARIBA Kate Costello

New York Premiere: Nylon Fusion Theatre Company, New York, NY. Directed by Ivette Dumeng.

AHMAD Al Nazemian

FARIBA Bianca Nejat

characters

AHMAD 50s

FARIBA late 30s

setting

A barren graveyard in Afghanistan. The present.

[*A barren graveyard. Afghanistan. No headstones or plaques. Mounds of dirt serve as unmarked graves. Silence. Stillness. After a few beats,* FARIBA *(late 30s) enters, wearing a black burqa. She's tentative, nervous. She looks around cautiously to make sure no one else is present. Then she drops to her knees and begins examining the graves.* AHMAD *(50s—calm, serene) enters and observes her for a few moments. Then . . .*]

AHMAD Can I help you?

[FARIBA *falls back, surprised.*]

I'm sorry, I didn't mean to / frighten—

FARIBA Get away from me.

AHMAD I'm sorry. I . . .

FARIBA Get away!

AHMAD [*Pause.*] You don't even know me.

FARIBA Anyone who visits this place, I don't want to know.

[AHMAD *looks at her calmly.*]

AHMAD You are here.

FARIBA That's different. I . . .

[*She stops herself. Then she gets up and begins to leave.*]

AHMAD I'm not a visitor. I work here.

[*She stops. Pause.*]

FARIBA You bury them?

[AHMAD *nods.*]

AHMAD Yes.

FARIBA That's horrible.

AHMAD . . . It can be.

FARIBA Even when they're in pieces, you . . . ?

AHMAD Yes.

FARIBA And you cleanse the body? The pieces?
[AHMAD *nods. Pause.* FARIBA *looks at him.*]
Why?

AHMAD Because it is my job.
[*Pause.*]
No one claims the bodies. Many don't have families.

FARIBA They don't have families? Or their families are too ashamed?
[AHMAD *doesn't answer; it's probably the latter.*]
They don't deserve this.

AHMAD Every child of Allah deserves to be buried.

FARIBA They're not children. They're monsters.

AHMAD He makes us all. The good and the bad.

FARIBA I disagree.

AHMAD [*Friendly.*] Then we can agree to disagree.

[*He smiles. She looks at him. Pause.* AHMAD *gestures to the pile of dirt where* FARIBA *was digging.*]

Are you looking for something?

FARIBA The graves—they're not marked.

AHMAD Yes, they are.

FARIBA Where?

[AHMAD *points to his head.*]

AHMAD Here.

FARIBA You? You remember where they're buried?

[AHMAD *nods.* FARIBA *balks.*]

There must be hundreds.

AHMAD One hundred twelve since I started. Eight years ago.

[*Pause.*]

Are you looking for someone?

FARIBA No—no.

AHMAD So you just came to browse?

FARIBA Yes.

AHMAD Strange for someone who thinks they don't deserve to be buried.

[*Pause.* FARIBA *looks at him, decides to engage.*]

FARIBA Anwar Maradi.

[AHMAD *processes it in his brain for a second, then he gestures to a nearby grave.*]

AHMAD He is there.

[FARIBA *looks at* AHMAD. *Then she reluctantly brings herself to Maradi's grave. She looks at it for a moment, a pained expression on her face.*]

FARIBA You know what he did?

AHMAD Of course. That's why he's buried here.

FARIBA No—I mean his attack, what *he* did.

[AHMAD *pauses, processes it for a second.*]

AHMAD The market? Two years ago?

FARIBA Yes.

AHMAD Twenty-eight victims.

FARIBA [*Correcting him.*] Twenty-three.

AHMAD Ah.

[*Pause.* FARIBA *looks at the grave.* AHMAD *watches her.*]

FARIBA Didn't it bother you to bury him? Knowing what he did?

AHMAD I don't think about what they do.

FARIBA How can you not?

AHMAD It's how I manage. I become sad when people cut down a tree, let alone kill each other.

FARIBA Then how can you bury them?

AHMAD I look at them as people. People who were full of hope.

FARIBA Someone who blows up a market, or children playing soccer— they are full of hope?

AHMAD Yes—once.

FARIBA When?

AHMAD When they were children, perhaps. When their parents loved them.

FARIBA The victims—they have parents, too. Parents who loved them—who raised them better than this. . . .

[*Pause.* AHMAD *looks at her compassionately.*]

AHMAD Your child? He was victim?

FARIBA *She.* Habiza. She was eleven. I sent her to the market for spices. Cardamom, salt . . .

AHMAD I am sorry for your loss.

FARIBA Thank you.

[*An awkward pause.*]

AHMAD   May I ask . . .

[FARIBA *nods.*]

If you feel so strongly about these men, the bombers—why did you come?

FARIBA   I don't know. I wanted to see.

AHMAD   And your husband—he allows . . . ?

FARIBA   He doesn't know.

[*Pause.*]

Ever since she died, I'm so angry. All the time. At my husband, my children. The world.

[*She stops herself.*]

Do you have children?

AHMAD   . . . No.

[FARIBA *stands up, goes to him.*]

FARIBA   To lose them, is the worst thing on earth . . .

[*Gesturing to the grave.*]

I thought that maybe if I came, if I saw him, it might make a difference.

AHMAD   Has it?

FARIBA   No. She's still gone . . .

[*Pause. They stay with each other for a moment.*]

How do you bear this? The pain, the suffering?

AHMAD   It's very calm. And it makes me live my life better.

[*Gesturing to the dirt.*]

To realize, in the end, this is all we are.

FARIBA   Isn't it depressing?

AHMAD   No. There are many jokes.

[FARIBA *almost laughs.*]

FARIBA Jokes? Here?

AHMAD Yes—whenever there is an attack, my coworkers come to my desk. They say:

[*Trying to deliver a joke.*]

"Ahmad, get ready, there is another attack!"

[*Pause.*]

FARIBA That doesn't sound funny.

AHMAD We've been at war thirty years. Humor is how I survive.

FARIBA No. I mean, what you described—it doesn't sound funny. "Get ready, there is another attack"?

AHMAD For the Afghan government, this is high humor.

[*They share a smile. A beat. Then* FARIBA *begins to leave.*]

FARIBA I'm sorry I wasted your time. . . .

AHMAD Oh, not a waste. It is nice to spend time with the living.

FARIBA Yes. I don't suppose you get much of that here.

AHMAD *As-salam alaykum.*

FARIBA *Wa alaykum asalam.*

[FARIBA *starts to exit, but then she turns back to* AHMAD.]

Can I invite you for tea?

AHMAD I don't think that would be appropriate.

FARIBA With my husband, of course. And my family.

AHMAD I would not be welcome at your home.

FARIBA Don't be silly. I insist.

AHMAD No, you—you wouldn't want me.

[FARIBA *looks at him.*]

FARIBA Why not?

AHMAD Nothing. *As-salam alaykum.*

FARIBA No—tell me.

AHMAD I don't think that would be a / good idea—

FARIBA Why? Why wouldn't I want you?

[*Pause.* AHMAD *looks at her, decides to tell her.*]

AHMAD If you knew why I am here. Why I do this.

FARIBA You told me—because everyone deserves to be buried.

AHMAD No.

[*Pause.*]

Because my son deserved to be buried.

[FARIBA *looks at him, confused.*]

FARIBA You said you didn't have any children.

AHMAD I don't. Not since that day—eight years ago.

[FARIBA's *eyes grow wide as she pieces it together.*]

FARIBA Your son. He . . . ?

AHMAD No one would bury him. They wanted him to rot.

[*Pause.*]

But I raised him. Well. And I loved him. Still. Even after what he did.

[*Pause.*]

So now I bury the bombers for their parents. For the ones who can't bear to acknowledge, to forgive . . .

[*A beat.*]

So: would you still like to invite me for tea?

[*Pause.* FARIBA *and* AHMAD *look at each other. For the first time, the anger begins to drain from her eyes.*]

FARIBA Yes.

[*A beat.*]

• • •

Super Hot
Raven
and
Raven II:
The Ravening

Megan Gogerty

Megan Gogerty

Megan Gogerty is a playwright and comedian. Her solo work *Save Me, Dolly Parton* and her comedy *Bad Panda* are both available from Original Works Publishing. Megan's musical drama *Love Jerry* was produced in the New York Musical Theatre Festival, where it won three Talkin' Broadway Citations and four NYMF Excellence Awards including Excellence in Writing (Book). Her ten-minute play *Rumple Schmumple* (Dramatic Pub.) was a Kennedy Center/National ACTF honoree. Her comic tribute album to the TV show *Buffy the Vampire Slayer* is widely available online. Megan was a Playwrights' Center Jerome Fellow, a WordBRIDGE alum, and she earned her MFA in Playwriting from the University of Texas at Austin. She currently teaches playwriting at the University of Iowa's Playwrights Workshop. Find her online at MeganGogerty.com.

··· **production history** ···

Super Hot Raven and Raven II: The Ravening had its world premiere in 2014, produced by Iron Crow Theatre at the Baltimore Theatre Project, Baltimore, Maryland. The original production was directed by Ryan Clark as part of *The Homo Poe Show*, conceived by Steven J. Satta.

POET   Meggie Twible

RAVEN   Maddie Hicks

characters

POET   A Stevie Nicks–esque poet in the feminist neo-pagan bookstore tradition.

RAVEN   A fix-it woman in a Baltimore Ravens jersey. Super hot.

Super Hot Raven

[*A dark and rainy night. An old Victorian that's been chopped up into apartments; we're in the turret that's been converted to a studio/1BR. It's a cluttered, gothic space with candles stuck into wine bottles and heavy tomes. A small radio plays NPR, but we don't really notice it.*]

[POET *enters all aflutter—she's wearing something drapey and Stevie Nicks–like. She's having a bad night. A thunder clap illuminates* RAVEN, *who perches near the radiator. She wears a Baltimore Ravens jersey and is super hot. She holds a heavy wrench.* POET *screams.*]

POET   Ahh! What are—what do you want? What are you doing here? Who let you in here? Did you break in, is this a break-in?

RAVEN   Hey . . .

POET   I'm going to scream! I took a self-defense class!

RAVEN   Landlord.

POET   What are you holding? What? Landlord? You're not my landlord. My landlord is a Pakistani gentleman who wears sandals.

RAVEN   No—

POET Even in the wintertime he wears sandals. Don't tell me you're my landlord.

RAVEN Your landlord . . .

POET . . . is a Pakistani gentleman . . .

RAVEN . . . Let me in.

POET Why? I'm not behind on my rent. How dare he.

[RAVEN *lifts the wrench. She's pointing at the radiator, but* POET *doesn't get it.*]

Are you threatening me? Are you trying to intimidate me? I will not go quietly into that good night!

RAVEN Look. Where I'm pointing. The radiator.

POET Oh. You're here to fix the radiator. Of course. I'm sorry. I got a little spooked. I just made that service request so long ago, I forgot. I didn't think he was ever going to . . . Thank God. It's freezing in here.

[*Small rest.*]

You're going to fix the radiator?

[RAVEN, *without shrugging exactly, communicates: "Obviously. So?"*]

I just . . . didn't know we had a lady . . . handy . . . person.

RAVEN I'm not a lady.

POET Oh! Forgive me, I made a gender assumption. How essentialist of me, I'm so embarrassed.

RAVEN I'm just kidding.

POET Oh.

RAVEN Y'know, I meant . . ."Not a lady." Like fancy.

POET Oh. I'm sorry. You must think I'm stupid. I'm not. I mean, I do own a couple Adam Sandler movies.

[RAVEN: *a slow, sly grin.*]

I don't know what I'm saying. I find you . . . I wasn't expecting to find you.

RAVEN Sure. You come home, somebody's in your bedroom. Got a big wrench.

POET   It's not the wrench.

RAVEN   What is it?

[*A little pause. Is it getting hot in here?*]

POET   Um. Do you want some tea? I was going to make some. It's so cold in here, how can you even do anything. Tea?

RAVEN   Sure.

POET   Oolong? Chamomile? What are you in the mood for?

RAVEN   Surprise me.

POET   Okie-dokie.

    [*She plugs in the electric kettle, readies the tea.*]

    How long have you been a radiator-fixer?

RAVEN   About forty minutes.

POET   No, I mean in life. I mean, do you fix radiators often?

    [*Pause. Noticing her jersey.*]

    Aren't you cold?

    [RAVEN *shrugs.*]

    When I was a girl I had a cat named Whiskers, who would disappear anytime it got cold, which what is the point of having a cat then? Who wants a cat in the summertime? Nobody. Don't you want to cuddle up?

RAVEN   What?

POET   With a cat. I'm just prattling. I get rattled, then I prattle. I'm a rattled prattler. Actually, I'm a poet.

RAVEN   I know.

POET   You do?

    [RAVEN *points to a sign/art project on the wall that says, "I am a poet!"*]

    Oh. That. I was having a self-esteem . . . I'm a student, really. A graduate student. In poetry. Oop, here's the tea!

[*Hands her the mug. They're close.*]

RAVEN It's hot.

POET Yeah . . . Oolong. I long for Oolong . . .

[RAVEN *takes the tea and breaks the spell.* POET *chastises herself for her stupid Oolong joke.*]

So, uh . . . all right. Don't let me get in your way. You want me to leave, or . . . ?

RAVEN Why would you leave your own house?

POET I wouldn't. Okay then. Good. I'll just, uh, busy myself with whatever while you . . . get down to business.

[RAVEN *starts working on the radiator.* POET *attempts not to look at her.*]

So do you . . . uh . . . know much about poetry?

RAVEN Some.

POET I do a lot of readings. Around town. Of my work.

RAVEN Who's Lenore?

POET [*Maybe not a spit-take, but something with the tea.*] What? How do you know about that? Have you been going through my things? How dare you. You have no right. Those are my private papers.

RAVEN Relax.

POET Don't you tell me to relax.

RAVEN Radio.

[*Small beat.*]

The radio. That was you, wasn't it? On the radio? Just now?

POET Oh. You heard that? Of course. That was me on "Live from the Blessed Bookstore." I did a reading . . . I wish you hadn't heard it, actually. It didn't go well.

RAVEN They seemed to like it.

POET They clap at anything. Did you . . . ? What did you think?

RAVEN Of your poems? I don't know.

POET You hated them.

RAVEN They don't rhyme.

POET [*A bit condescendingly.*] Well, no. Not all poems have to rhyme. There's a style called blank verse. It's about imagery, metaphor, cadence. How it sounds.

RAVEN I know what blank verse is.

POET Oh.

RAVEN I like poems that rhyme.

POET Everybody likes poems that rhyme.

RAVEN So?

POET Well, it's a little elementary, don't you think?

RAVEN You think I'm stupid?

POET No. I value the working class.

[*Off* RAVEN's *reaction.*]

I just meant, what you do. I value what you do. You don't need an education to have worth.

RAVEN You think because I'm here to fix the radiator, I don't have an education? Or that education is the same as smart?

POET I was born with my foot in my mouth. I just meant I don't like to label things.

RAVEN Sure you do. You're a poet. That's all you do. My sadness is the ocean. The winter is like a cat.

POET You're right. Forgive me. That was terrible.

RAVEN No, it's . . . I shouldn't have said anything about your poems.

POET No, please. I want to hear your thoughts. I'm so used to talking to other poets, we get boxed in. I'm interested.

RAVEN [*Small beat.*] Well, they're depressing.

POET Yes.

RAVEN Don't you want people to like your poems?

POET I don't write poems for people to like them. I'm participating in a feminist neo-pagan choral tradition.

RAVEN Oh.

POET I'm using my poems to ameliorate my feelings.

RAVEN Your depressed feelings.

POET Yes.

RAVEN So all that stuff about the Goddess . . . that's Lenore?

POET No. The Goddess is Gaia, the earth mother. Lenore is my ex.

RAVEN She dumped you.

POET She left me.

RAVEN And now you're writing poems about her.

POET Yes.

RAVEN Okay.

POET [*Justifying.*] When she left me, I thought about killing myself, but then I thought I would probably definitely lose my security deposit. And I didn't want to give her the satisfaction. So now I go out. I go out all the time. I do readings, I attend lectures. Drum circles. Coffees. I shop. I protest the commercialization of whatever holiday it is. I do everything. When all I really want to do is curl up in the bed and not move.

RAVEN And you write poems about her. The one who dumped you.

POET Yes.

RAVEN See, that's where I think you're making a mistake. If you keep writing about her, she's never going to leave you alone.

[*Beat.*]

POET That is an excellent point. I'm sorry I called you stupid.

RAVEN Nah. Sometimes I do dumb things.

POET Like what?

[*Beat. They fall in love a little bit across the distance.*]

RAVEN   Impulsive things.

[*Beat.* POET *gives a little accidental giggle/snort.*]

POET   I wish I knew how to fix a radiator. I mean. I'm glad I don't.

RAVEN   So she dumped you. Why?

POET   She had things she wanted to do. People, really.

RAVEN   No, I mean, how? How could she dump you?

POET   Well, you know, I'm so eloquent. I'm so good with words and not insulting people. I don't always . . . see the other person. You know?

RAVEN   I could write a poem about Lenore. And it would be better than your poems because it would rhyme.

POET   You don't even know her.

RAVEN   I know enough. Let's see. Lenore. Is a whore. And a bore. And she snores.

POET   That's an imperfect rhyme.

RAVEN   It's an imperfect world. She's feeling sore because you showed her the door and now she's making war on whatever came before. It's causing an uproar galore. Send a message semaphore: Lenore is no more worth setting store by than a poor four-leaf clover that's missing the four.

POET   Those are good rhymes.

RAVEN   You want to cuddle up in bed all day? What's the matter with that? You could just stay here, get warm, drink tea. Just stay in bed. Never leave. It could be relaxing.

POET   I have things to do.

RAVEN   Like what?

POET   [*Small beat.*] I can't think of anything while you're looking at me.

RAVEN   Am I?

POET Who are you?

RAVEN I'm the one that's looking at you. Hasn't anybody ever looked at you before?

POET So you're an angel from dyke heaven? You just go around from apartment to apartment, fixing people? Their problems? Seducing them? What do you want from me?

[RAVEN *removes the mug of tea from* POET's *hands.*]

RAVEN I fixed your radiator.

POET I noticed.

[RAVEN *kisses* POET. *They kiss more. It's super hot. It might be the hottest kiss in this whole play so far.*]

Never leave my bedroom.

RAVEN Okay.

[*End.*]

[*Optional/transitional voice-over.*]

[*Use this voice-over text to cover a transition, or don't.*]

[*Local NPR–ish station. The host of the* Live from the Blessed Bookstore, *who is a sleepy Terry Gross type.*]

POET [*Voice-over, reciting poetry.*] And that is why the earth doth spin and spin. That is why the earth doth spin. Some people believe it spins because of space. Those people are incorrect. It spins not for thee but for thouest and for the other things. Anon, and thither, and again I say space.

HOST [*Voice-over.*] Thank you, beautiful. What I love about your poetry is how poetical it is.

POET I bring a poetical intentionality to my work.

HOST That's obvious.

POET Thank you for noticing.

HOST That's all the time we have today, for time is a patriarchal structure we have yet to subvert. I want to thank the fearless women and androgynines who shared their verse with us today. Coming up next on Maryland Public Radio: *Birds of Maryland*, followed by *Lens on Maryland*, *All Maryland Things Considered*, then *Maryland Maryland Maryland*, and finishing things off with *Who Cares About Delaware*. I'm your host, Sky Morningwater. Please join us again next week as we hear more poetry on *Live from the Blessed Bookstore*. Now the weather, which continues to be portentous. . . .

· · ·

Raven II: The Ravening

[*The same apartment, sometime later.* POET *brushes in cheerfully, wind in her sleeves.* RAVEN *spins around in a chair, waiting for her. This surprises* POET. RAVEN *is pissed.* POET *doesn't notice, or pretends not to.*]

POET Oh. You're here.

RAVEN Obviously. I'm always here. That's my thing.

POET Guess how many copies of my chapbook have sold on Amazon? Digital downloads plus real copies, the whole thing, total. Guess. Do you want to know? Fifty-six!

[POET *thinks this is great.*]

Isn't that fabulous? And most of those people are strangers! I don't have fifty-six friends, you know what I'm saying?

RAVEN I believe it.

POET I'm just giddy from the success. You know, it was suggested to me that I write a follow-up essay. Sort of an inner workings, discussing how I wrote various sections. My approach, etcetera. I mean, of course such a thing wouldn't sell nearly as well, it's strictly inside baseball, but I think there's a certain limited audience that might appreciate some thoughts as to my process. Strike whilst the iron's hot!

RAVEN Where were you?

POET Out. Sometimes I go out. Sometimes I have to leave the bedroom.

RAVEN I bet.

POET Are you feeling neglected? I will dedicate the essay to you.

RAVEN Damn straight you'll dedicate the essay to me.

POET Isn't there a game of some sort you're supposed to be watching?

RAVEN You were with her.

[*Pause.*]

Thanks for not bothering to lie.

POET I didn't tell you because I knew it would upset you.

RAVEN Correct. I am upset.

POET Honey. We have a history. It is fraught, but it is real.

RAVEN I don't care about your history. I care about your present.

POET My present is you.

RAVEN Damn straight.

POET How come every time you say "damn straight" I think of Garth Brooks?

RAVEN Don't change the subject.

POET Whatever happened to him anyway?

[*Pause.*]

RAVEN You think of Garth Brooks because you're ignorant. I say "damn straight" and that makes you think of George Strait, but you don't quite remember George Strait, so your mind goes to Garth Brooks. Because you know, like, three country songs in your whole life, and they're all horrible. And what happened to him was, his hair fell out and he tried to reinvent himself as something other than Garth Brooks, and he failed. And everybody stopped liking him.

[*Pause.*]

POET Lenore . . .

RAVEN Lenore? I never want to hear that name again. Never. Never.

POET Sometimes . . .

RAVEN What's the name of your chapbook?

POET [*Small beat.*] *The Raven.*

RAVEN That's right. Your big success. I think you owe me.

POET It's not like I can't see her. Even if I wanted to. This is a very small community, we run in the same circles.

RAVEN So don't run anymore. Stay here.

POET Locked in this room with you?

RAVEN Yes.

POET That is not remotely feasible.

RAVEN Why not?

POET I have a life! I have obligations. I am part of the world! You drive me crazy.

RAVEN You drive me crazy.

POET No. No, I don't. You drive me crazy.

RAVEN Never leave my bedroom, you said. Never.

POET I didn't mean it literally.

RAVEN Yes, you did. You love her so much, why don't you marry her?

POET Are you kidding? I'd rather marry my thirteen-year-old cousin.

RAVEN I'm the one who's looking at you!

POET You think I don't think about you all the time? You think you're not on my brain, in my brain, every second of the day? It's unnerving how much I think of you. I feel your eyes on me every second. When I'm making breakfast, when I'm knitting a prayer shawl. Even when I'm masturbating, I'm thinking of you. Shouldn't I be thinking of someone else? If I'm with you, shouldn't I be fantasizing about somebody else? It's not normal.

RAVEN I think about you, too.

POET I have to go out sometimes. I will occasionally cross paths—

RAVEN You don't cross paths. Call it what it is.

POET I don't know what you think.

RAVEN You drink coffee. You show her your poems. Whose idea was it to write this essay thing you're gonna write now? Whose idea was it?

POET How do you know that?

RAVEN Because I have eyes. You think I'm stupid. I'm not.

[*Pause.*]

POET I'm afraid it's not healthy, what we have. Locked in here together. Always alone together. I don't know if I love you or if I'm enthralled by you. Or if that's the same thing, or different. The books say a healthy relationship needs balance. This is not balanced.

RAVEN Do you want me to go?

POET [*A grim laugh.*] You can't go. Even if you were to walk out this room, you would still be here. I would still feel you sitting and staring. Do you get me? Do you understand? If you were to leave me, I would never write another word.

[*Pause.*]

RAVEN Oh.

POET Yes. "Oh." It's terrifying. The power you have over me is terrifying.

[RAVEN *scratches herself or does some other non-terrifying thing.*]

RAVEN So you're not getting back together with her?

POET No. God, no.

RAVEN Never?

POET   Never.

RAVEN   Never . . . ever?

POET   Never ever. I am with you.

[*Pause.*]

RAVEN   Good.

POET   We have a problem, though. I can't get you to leave the bedroom. Why don't you go out?

RAVEN   I don't like to go out.

POET   You can come out with me.

RAVEN   Your friends treat me like I'm your pet.

POET   My friends are jealous. Nobody really understands a relationship except the people in it.

RAVEN   So . . . You want room to breathe.

POET   If that's possible.

RAVEN   You want me to go out with you.

POET   Yes, please.

RAVEN   Okay. I'll go out. And then we're going to watch an Adam Sandler movie. A real one.

POET   You don't like *Punch-Drunk Love?*

RAVEN   It's not an Adam Sandler movie. He's in it, but that's not the same thing.

POET   [*Regarding their relationship.*] I can't decide if this is a good or bad thing.

[RAVEN *kisses her hand.*]

RAVEN   Me, neither.

[RAVEN *travels up* POET'*s arm. Gettin' steamy.*]

POET   I just know I don't want it to end.

RAVEN It will never end. Never.

POET Say it again.

RAVEN Never.

POET Once more.

RAVEN Never. Never. Nevermore.

[*Fast blackout like a thunderclap.*]

• • •

Norma's Rest

Jordan Morille

Jordan Morille

Jordan Morille is from Katy, Texas, and earned an MFA in dramatic writing at Texas State University. He was awarded the 2015 John Cauble National Award for Outstanding Short Play at the Kennedy Center in Washington, D.C., for *Norma's Rest*. He was also a national finalist for the Gary Garrison Ten-Minute Play Award for his play *Jars*. Previous accolades include: The 2014 Ken Ludwig Award for best body of work (including the plays *Love, Norman*; *Thirty Deep*; *Jackalope*; and *Speedball*), second place for the National Partners of American Theatre Award (*Love, Norman*), and national finalist for the John Cauble Award (Speedball in 2014, and *Thirty Deep* in 2013). Other plays include *The Ballad of Zipfiled* and *Gus, Kilo Promise, The Thieves of Santa Muerte*, and *Liza Does Alaska*. He currently lives in Austin, Texas, with his wife and daughter.

···production history···

Staged Reading at the KCACTF Regional Festival: San Angelo, Texas, Spring 2015

NORMA   Ana Uzele

TENNESSEE   Gino Chaviano

SHAE   Shelby Acosta

TILLY   Drake Shrader

FERRET   Brianna Ripkowski

MARSHALL   Neil Patrick Stewart

Staged Reading at the KCACTF National Festival: Washington, D.C., Spring 2015

NORMA   Dawn Ursula

TENNESSEE   Chris Dinolfo

SHAE   Jessica Frances Dukes

TILLY   Delany Williams

FERRET   Jenna Sokolowski

MARSHALL   Sasha Olinik

characters

NORMA   Sixties. African American female. Caretaker/owner of Norma's Rest and mother to all. Dying of cancer.

TENNESSEE   Thirties. Transsexual male-female. Resident of Norma's Rest. Drug addict.

SHAE   Thirties. African American female. Norma's daughter.

TILLY   Forties. Caucasian male. Resident of Norma's Rest. Ex-felon and former member of the Aryan Brotherhood. The biggest man you've ever seen.

FERRET   Eighteen. Female. Resident of Norma's Rest. Vandal and thief.

PASTOR MARSHALL   Fifties. Male. Calculated man behind a big, white smile.

setting

Norma's Rest, a sober house that sits on a lake in Mineola, Texas.

time

Present.

[*Lights up. The front yard of Norma's Rest. It's the morning after a violent and terrible storm. Debris and garbage now litter what was a calm and beautiful garden. The myriad colors from many flowers are now splattered all over the front of the house and lawn. The porch furniture, consisting of two chairs, small table, and porch swing, now lie on the ground. A birdbath has toppled over near the flower beds. Above the front door, a sign reading* Norma's Rest *hangs by only one side. A tree lies to one side of the porch, having been ripped from the earth and smashed into the side of the house.* NORMA *kneels in one of the flower beds, digging with a spade. She hums to herself as she does this.* TILLY *enters from inside the house, holding a tray of seedlings. He walks over to* NORMA *and sets them down next to her without a word. She glances at the tray.*]

NORMA Thank you, Tilly.

[TILLY *places his hands on* NORMA's *shoulders. She reaches up with one hand and takes his.*]

Storm done took just about everything out here.

[*Looks up at the tree.*]

Just glad nobody hurt.

[*She resumes her work as* TILLY *walks away and exits around the house. She starts humming again.* TENNESSEE *enters from inside the house, wearing a cooking apron over sundress.*]

TENNESSEE Breakfast's almost one.

[*Sees* NORMA.]

Man alive, Norma . . .

[*She walks over to the flower bed.*]

You shouldn't be down in the weeds like that.

NORMA What I tell you 'bout callin' my children weeds?

TENNESSEE Get up, now. Got no place gardenin'.

NORMA Why come?

TENNESSEE A woman your age should be sittin' right up on this porch sippin' lemonade and spillin' tea.

NORMA My grandmomma climbed mountains 'til she was eighty-seven. Had a good twenty-five years on me doin' that, so my gardenin' ain't hurtin' nothin'. Not with these genes.

[*She goes back to the flower bed.*]

TENNESSEE Crotchety old coot.

NORMA Uppity lil' nag.

TENNESSEE Should make Shae do this dirty work for you. Her bein' the "heir to the throne" and all.

NORMA Gotta wake up 'fore the sun to be doin' this. That girl liable sleep through her own weddin'.

TENNESSEE Gotta get a man first.

NORMA Watch it now, that's my daughter you jawin' on about.

TENNESSEE Shall I bring your pancakes out to you, then?

NORMA That'd be fine.

[TENNESSEE *heads back into the house with a smile.*]

Tennessee.

[TENNESSEE *turns back.*]

Don't be scrimpin' on that syrup, now. It ain't diabetes I'm leavin' this world on.

[TENNESSEE's *smile fades as she exits inside the house.* NORMA *resumes working. She starts placing the seedlings in the garden. Her humming continues.* FERRET *enters from the side of the porch opposite* NORMA, *wearing a hoodie and carrying her large purse. She sees* NORMA *and creeps around her, trying to make it to the front door.*]

Where you been at, Ferret?

[FERRET *stops.*]

FERRET Uh, nowhere really just . . . out, you know?

NORMA Uh-uh, I don't. Out where?

FERRET Nowhere. Just met up with some friends—

NORMA Who they were?

FERRET Jodie and Liz. Saw a movie—

NORMA What you see?

FERRET *Handmaidens of Death Part Two.*

NORMA That don't come out 'til next Friday.

[*Beat.*]

I read the paper, girl. I know what pictures be happenin' when.

FERRET Uhh—

NORMA Awfully big purse for someone your size. Whatchu got in it?

FERRET My stuff.

NORMA Stolen stuff?

FERRET No, ma'am.

NORMA Gotta clear it with Tennessee first, you gonna be headin' out.

FERRET He was asleep.

NORMA *She's* an insomniac. Why you think I make her the one you gotta clear things with?

[*Looks at* FERRET.]

Ain't you wear that yesterday?

[FERRET *looks down at her clothes, then back up to* NORMA, *who flashes a smile.*]

What's his name?

FERRET Avery.

NORMA Good to see you child. Breakfast be ready soon.

FERRET Pancakes?

NORMA You know it. Go get cleaned up.

[FERRET *heads up to the porch, she sees the tree.*]

FERRET   Holy shit!

NORMA   Language, girl.

FERRET   This is . . .

NORMA   A tree.

FERRET   How did . . . ?

NORMA   Storm done smashed it right on through. Everyone's okay, though. Just a lil' bit more breezy in there. Tilly gonna trim it off today.

FERRET   I'm sorry.

NORMA   Why you apologizin' to me? Your house, too.

[*Beat.*]

Go on inside, now.

[FERRET *opens her mouth about to speak, but* SHAE *enters from inside the house wearing a big sweatshirt and holding a coffee mug.* FERRET *glares at her.*]

SHAE   Good morning.

FERRET   Whatever.

[FERRET *exits inside the house.* SHAE *makes her way down the porch and sits on the edge.*]

SHAE   Morning, Momma. How are you?

NORMA   Mornin' done came and went, girl. Damn near afternoon, now.

SHAE   It's ten-thirty.

NORMA   Mornin' must be different over in Austin. Here in Mineola it's over at nine. Ten-thirty just be the waitin' time. Saturday's no different. Best get used to that.

SHAE   Or what? You gonna kick me out?

NORMA   Maybe.

[SHAE *watches her mother work a bit.*]

SHAE Hey, so I was thinking. Maybe you can take the week off. After tomorrow.

NORMA Week off? What I need a week off for?

SHAE Just take it easy for a while. Let me take over. Get used to how things go around here. . . .

NORMA Ain't you learn enough 'bout how things go this past month?

SHAE Takes more than that if I'm gonna be taking this place over after . . .

NORMA I don't need no week off. Wouldn't know what to do with myself, anyhow. Got to keep movin', baby. Like a shark. You know sharks die when they quit movin'. Bet no shark never took a week off.

SHAE Sharks don't run halfway houses.

[*Beat.*]

You ever think you'd be living in a place like this?

NORMA Not at first. But when your grandfolks left me this place, and 'specially after your daddy passed, I found my calling, I suppose. Must be from all them days spent at the shelter.

SHAE Hard to imagine. Woman like you. Alone. Sharing a house with people . . . knowing what they've done.

NORMA Don't matter the what. Only matters the who.

SHAE Huh?

NORMA Someone can be an alcoholic who don't drink. Tennessee can be an addict who don't use, and Ferret can be a thief who don't steal. The who, girl. That's what's important. Folks always gonna need to find who they is after what they done.

[*Pause.*]

SHAE And Tilly? He find out who he is yet?

NORMA Don't worry 'bout Tilly.

SHAE I've seen the way he looks at me. Man's got hate in his eyes.

NORMA That's just his face. Always looks like that.

SHAE Those tattoos . . .

NORMA You talk to him enough times, you won't even notice 'em.

SHAE He doesn't say a word.

NORMA Don't have to say things to talk to somebody.

SHAE How can you be so comfortable around that man?

NORMA Somebody's gotta be.

SHAE Doesn't have to be you. Sure as hell not going to be me. When I take over, the first thing I'm gonna do is kick that evil man to the curb.

[NORMA *stops working and turns to her daughter.*]

NORMA You'll do no such thing! That man lives here, now. Belongs here. You set him loose, he liable to start runnin' with the same folks done turned him that way. You won't be doin' a lick a' good.

[*She turns back to the garden.*]

Talkin' 'bout sendin' people away. That ain't the kinda talk of a girl gonna run things around here. That's the talk a' one who got a lot left to learn.

[*Pause.*]

SHAE Sent me samples to the newspaper the other day.

NORMA *Mineola Monitor?*

SHAE Yeah.

NORMA What they say?

SHAE Haven't heard back.

NORMA My baby the writer. You speak to Jerry?

SHAE Yeah.

NORMA You tell him who you were?

SHAE I did. Said he wants me to bring him some of your lemon bars. If they hire me, anyway. Might be good. Have some extra money coming in for this place. Barely stay afloat with everyone's income.

NORMA Outside world don't see these folk for who they really is yet. One day, maybe. But 'til then, it's minimum wage for them.

[SHAE *stands.*]

SHAE I'm going for breakfast.

NORMA Alright, then. Tennessee's got them pancakes goin'.

SHAE I saw. Wheat pancakes or buttermilk?

NORMA The good kind.

[SHAE *heads for the door.*]

SHAE Got to start getting that wheat, Momma. Better for you.

[NORMA *waves this off.* SHAE *goes to exit, but turns back.*]

I want to be here, Momma. This is my life now.

NORMA I know you do, baby.

[SHAE *exits inside the house.* TILLY *re-enters from around the porch, carrying a chain saw.*]

Where them goggles, boy?

[TILLY *stops.*]

Best go find 'em. Can't have you losin' an eye, now. This a sober house, not no damn hospital.

[TILLY *turns and exits back the way he came.* NORMA *resumes her work.* PASTOR MARSHALL *enters from across the yard, carrying a fruit basket. He walks up to* NORMA.]

MARSHALL How you doin' this fine Saturday mornin', Miss Norma?

NORMA Fair to middlin'. You, Pastor Marshall?

MARSHALL God is good, I tell ya.

[NORMA *looks up at the tree, then back to* PASTOR MARSHALL.]

NORMA Is he now?

MARSHALL Mighty storm we had last night, huh? Hope you and yours are safe and healthy.

NORMA   We fine. How'd you make out?

MARSHALL   Few broken windows, nothin' major.

NORMA   Good to hear.

[*Pointing off.*]

McMeans' damn near lost they roof.

MARSHALL   No kidding?! They alright?

NORMA   They wasn't there. Use that place to spend their summers.

MARSHALL   Praise God for that.

NORMA   Sure makes my little tree seem like just that. A little tree.

MARSHALL   Well, no matter how little it is, I brought this.

[*He holds out the fruit basket for her. NORMA looks at it.*]

NORMA   Boy, you church people are all the same. Thinkin' you can fix everything with fruit and a smile.

[*Takes the basket.*]

Thank you, kindly.

MARSHALL   You're in our thoughts and prayers.

NORMA   Why?

[TENNESSEE *enters from inside the house, holding* NORMA's *plate of pancakes. She stops as she sees* PASTOR MARSHALL. *The two lock eyes.*]

Back inside, Tennessee.

TENNESSEE   What—

NORMA   Go on, now. I'm handlin' it.

[TENNESSEE *exits back inside.* PASTOR MARSHALL *watches her.*]

Still with us, Pastor?

[PASTOR MARSHALL *turns back to* NORMA.]

MARSHALL   I have something I'd like to talk with you about.

NORMA   I'm busy.

[*She resumes working.*]

MARSHALL I'll be quick.

[*He heads for the porch.*]

NORMA Hey—

[PASTOR MARSHALL *stops.*]

"Quick" don't sit.

MARSHALL Okay.

[*He moves back from the porch.*]

My drive out here to this lake got me thinkin' about a few things.

NORMA More than a few, I'm sure.

MARSHALL And walkin' up to your lovely home an seein' this tree just lyin' on top of it only reaffirms my thoughts.

NORMA How'd it do that?

MARSHALL I want to buy this place.

[NORMA *stops.*]

NORMA That right?

MARSHALL Hear me out, now. I'll start by paying for all the storm repairs, and then you and I can draft up a little agreement. Nothing's gonna change for you and yours at all. Think of it as an outreach project.

NORMA Outreach?

MARSHALL A subsidiary of the church. Make this place a holy house of repentance.

[*Pause.*]

NORMA Nah.

[*She resumes gardening.*]

MARSHALL We pray for you, Miss Norma. Every Sunday we bow our heads and ask that you be and your people are met with love and good fortune now, and in the sweet hereafter. I think those prayers have been answered. The Good Lord saw fit to bless you with this here tree.

NORMA Oh, he went and blessed me, huh?

MARSHALL Yes, ma'am.

NORMA How you call it a blessing?

MARSHALL Led me to your doorstep, didn't it? Let me help you turn this House of Sin into a House of God.

NORMA Your God don't belong here, Pastor.

MARSHALL Why's that now?

NORMA 'Cause your God is one of judgment. Ours is one of repentance.

MARSHALL My God forgives plenty.

NORMA That why he saw fit to smash my roof in with a tree?

MARSHALL Works in mysterious ways, Miss Norma.

[*Extending his hand.*]

You take my hand in yours and I can start moving pieces on it today.

[*Pause.*]

NORMA Why this place, huh?

MARSHALL Pardon?

NORMA Why not some other spot? Why not go on and build you up a sober house of your own? Do whatever you want with it then.

MARSHALL Easier this way.

NORMA Easier for who? You?

[*Beat.*]

You and your God. Disguisin' corruption as charity.

MARSHALL Corruption's the Devil's work, Miss Norma.

NORMA Talkin' 'bout reachin' out and all that. Only thing I see is a way for you to reach in. Put those holy hands on folks don't need 'em. Don't want 'em. Spread your God's will by any means necessary.

MARSHALL [*Lowering his hand.*] I don't follow.

NORMA It ain't the house you want, Pastor. It's who's inside you after.

MARSHALL This has nothing to do with . . . it's a sheer coincidence.

NORMA You call it that. I call it a, what you say before? Reaffirmin'?

[NORMA *starts to stand.* PASTOR MARSHALL *moves to help her, but she waves him off.*]

I ain't sellin' this place. Even if, I ain't never gonna let you dirty it up with close-mindedness.

MARSHALL I assure you, my mind has never been more open.

NORMA Then think of someplace else to sink your blood money into. I don't want one red dime from you or your church.

MARSHALL Certain point comes along, Miss Norma, when you gotta face facts.

NORMA What facts we talkin' 'bout?

MARSHALL Good people of Mineola find themselves rather frightened of the folks you welcome in these walls. Growin' somethin' of a discomfort.

NORMA What I gotta worry about them for, huh? They in the square flappin' their gums talkin' 'bout marchin' down here with pitchforks and fire?

[*Beat.*]

Ain't no monsters live in this house for them to fear.

MARSHALL Your cancer, then.

[*Beat.*]

Apologies for my directness on that matter, but we all know the hands that got a hold of you, wantin' to rip you away from this world all too soon.

NORMA Don't flatter me, now.

MARSHALL What's gonna happen to the place then? Unless you got someone to take it over, it'll belong to the state. They ain't gonna let a bunch of addicts and felons run a place of their own. They'll be turned out. Abandoned. A wayward flock. What kind of shepherd would you be then?

NORMA   You ain't got any idea . . .

MARSHALL   Eighty thousand dollars.

NORMA   What?

MARSHALL   That's what I'm bringin' to the table. Eighty thousand dollars for the house and property it sits on. You all can stay and keep doin' what you're doin' here, only it'll be under the eyes of God. *My* God.

[*He extends his hand one more time.* NORMA *looks at it.* TILLY *re-enters, carrying the chain saw and wearing goggles.* NORMA *and* PASTOR MARSHALL *turn to him.* NORMA *looks back at* PASTOR MARSHALL.]

NORMA   Think you best leave, Pastor.

MARSHALL   [*Lowering his hand.*] Fine.

[*He starts to exit the way he came. He stops and turns back to* NORMA.]

MARSHALL   You'll think about it at least?

[NORMA *looks at him. He flashes a smile.*]

I'll be back shortly.

NORMA   I'm sure you will.

[PASTOR MARSHALL *starts off.*]

Bring something better than a fruit basket next time.

[PASTOR MARSHALL *exits.* TENNESSEE *enters from inside, carrying the plate of pancakes.* NORMA *turns to her, then to* TILLY.]

You eat yet?

[TILLY *shakes his head.*]

Go on an' get you somethin'. Tree ain't goin' no place.

[TILLY *sets the chain saw down and flips the goggles up on his head. He exits inside as* NORMA *moves up to the porch.* TENNESSEE *hands her plate and goes to the porch chairs. She sets them upright as* NORMA *moves to them and sits.*]

Thank you.

TENNESSEE What he want?

NORMA Nothin'. Gave us a fruit basket.

TENNESSEE Fruit basket?

NORMA For the tree.

TENNESSEE What's he think a fruit basket is gonna do?

NORMA Make us forget about the tree, I guess.

[*Beat.*]

Never really understood them fruit baskets.

TENNESSEE Nothing else?

NORMA Huh?

TENNESSEE He didn't say nothin' else?

NORMA Said a lotta things. Wasn't really listenin' but couldn't help but hear. Nothin' of any real consequence.

TENNESSEE Really?

NORMA Really.

TENNESSEE Bastard.

NORMA He gone, Ten. Let it lie.

[*Takes a bite of pancake.*]

I say, girl. One day you gonna have to tell me your secret with these things.

TENNESSEE I ain't tellin' no one my secrets.

NORMA Shae get somethin' to eat?

TENNESSEE Grabbed a biscuit, I think and went up to her room.

NORMA Got biscuits in there?

[TENNESSEE *nods.* NORMA *holds out her plate.* TENNESSEE *takes it and stands, heading back into the house.*]

Gravy?

TENNESSEE Jelly.

[NORMA *shakes her head and holds out her hand.* TENNESSEE *moves back and gives her the plate.* NORMA *continues eating.*]

NORMA You seen Ferret's lil' ass try to sneak up in here?

TENNESSEE I saw Ferret.

NORMA You tell her somethin'? Show her how to cow ate the cabbage?

TENNESSEE Norma, half the time I don't understand a single word that comes out of your mouth.

NORMA She ain't clear it with you last night.

[*Beat.*]

And why is that, anyhow? Ain't you always in the family room 'round then?

TENNESSEE I am.

NORMA Her window still locked, right?

TENNESSEE Last I checked.

[*Beat.*]

Musta been in the bathroom or somethin'.

NORMA Or somethin'.

[*Beat.*]

Ferret's met a new man. Name Avery. We need to have a lunch. Next week. She can invite him on down so I can get a read on him.

TENNESSEE Next week?

NORMA Don't start with me on that now, girl. I say next week, I mean next week.

[*Beat.*]

If my grandmomma can climb mountains, I can live 'til next week.

[TILLY *enters from inside, dabbing the sides of his mouth with a napkin. The ladies turn to him.*]

TENNESSEE Hi, Tilly.

[TILLY *nods.*]

NORMA   Get enough to eat?

[TILLY *nods again. He goes over to* TENNESSEE *and places a hand on her shoulder. She takes his hand in hers.*]

TENNESSEE   You're welcome, sugar.

[TENNESSEE *pats his hands and they release.* TILLY *goes back for the chain saw. He picks it up and heads for the tree. He flips the goggles down and pulls the choke. Nothing. He pulls again. Nothing. He flips a switch. Pulls again. Nothing.*]

NORMA   You check the gas?

[TILLY *flips open the gas cap, peers inside, then looks back at* NORMA *as he sets the chain saw down. Laughing.*]

Boy, what's wrong with you?

[TILLY *shrugs.* NORMA *turns to* TENNESSEE.]

We still got them gas cans out by the greenhouse?

TENNESSEE   You know damn well I don't mess with no greenhouse. Don't mess with gas cans, neither.

NORMA   [*To* TILLY.] Run on back there, see if you can find 'em.

[TILLY *nods and exits around the side of the house.*]

TENNESSEE   We ever gonna get that tree peeled off?

NORMA   Day still young, Tennessee. Day still young.

[*Holds out her plate.*]

I'm finished.

TENNESSEE   Get enough?

NORMA   Sure did.

TENNESSEE   You like it?

NORMA   Always do, child.

[TENNESSEE *smiles as she takes* NORMA'*s plate.*]

TENNESSEE   Ferret say anything to you?

NORMA   Just stories about her made-up friends and made-up movies. Why? Somethin' I should know?

TENNESSEE . . . I'm gonna' get the kitchen cleaned up.

[TENNESSEE *exits inside.* NORMA *waits a bit before standing and making her way off the porch.* SHAE *enters from inside, fully dressed now and carrying her purse.*]

SHAE Momma, I got it! I got an interview!

[SHAE *holds out her hand.* NORMA *looks at* SHAE's *open palm, then "gives her five."*]

NORMA Alright!

SHAE [*Keeping her hand out.*] I need the car.

NORMA My car?

SHAE Yeah.

NORMA Yours ain't here?

SHAE Still in the shop, Momma. Mechanic's slower than hell.

NORMA Hey, Pete Smalls ain't slow. Just passionate 'bout what he does. Takes his time.

SHAE I still need the car.

NORMA An interview, huh?

SHAE Yes.

NORMA On a Saturday?

SHAE Just got the call.

NORMA I don't know, baby.

SHAE What don't you know?

NORMA The *Monitor*'s great and all, but—

SHAE But what?

NORMA Ain't you a, whatchu call it, a creative writer? Ain't nothin' like that in that paper. Just obituaries and local news. Who bakes the best pies and all that.

SHAE It's a job, Momma.

NORMA Plenty a' folks got jobs. Not all of 'em got talent like you, girl.

SHAE I don't have time for this right now.

NORMA You need to go back to school.

SHAE Wasn't for me.

NORMA Whatchu mean wasn't for you? You loved it over there.

SHAE Not anymore. I don't want to be in school, I want to be here.

NORMA No, you just tell yourself that. Deep down you just think you need to be. Think that if you go off again, I'm gonna wilt and die.

SHAE Momma.

NORMA I was so proud of you, baby. My girl. Up at Yale University. Still got my sweater and everything.

[TILLY *enters.* NORMA *turns to him.* SHAE *grows uncomfortable.*]

Nothin'?

[TILLY *shakes his head.*]

Damn.

[*Turning to* SHAE.]

Tilly gonna have to go to town and get some gas cans for the chain saw.

SHAE What's that got to do with me?

NORMA Think ya'll can ride together? How long the interview?

SHAE I'm not riding in that car with him.

NORMA Please, baby. Just give him a chance. For me.

[SHAE *stares at* TILLY, *then back to* NORMA.]

SHAE I'll reschedule.

[SHAE *heads up the porch and exits inside.*]

NORMA Don't pay her no mind, Tilly. She's somethin' else.

[NORMA *reaches into her pocket as she turns to* TILLY.]

Here.

[NORMA *pulls out her car keys.* TILLY *walks up and takes them.*]

Go on and get that gas. Wonder where them cans went.

[TILLY *shrugs.*]

Let me get you some money.

[NORMA *starts for the porch.* TILLY *takes her arm, stopping her. He shakes his head.*]

You pay for enough 'round here, you don't need to be buyin' . . .

[TILLY *shakes his head again, releasing* NORMA.]

Alright, then. Don't think for a second I ain't gonna get you back.

[TILLY *walks across the lawn and exits.* NORMA *watches him go before heading back to the garden.* TENNESSEE *and* FERRET *enter from inside.* FERRET *holds a large envelope.*]

TENNESSEE Norma?

NORMA I ain't never gonna finish this garden with ya'll botherin' me like this.

FERRET Sorry.

NORMA S'fine, child. What's it now?

[FERRET *looks at* TENNESSEE.]

TENNESSEE Go on, then.

NORMA Whatchu got there, Ferret?

[FERRET *looks down at the envelope, then back to* NORMA *She walks over to her and hands her the envelope.* NORMA *opens it and looks inside.*]

Where'd you get this?

FERRET That's eight hundred dollars.

NORMA Ain't ask you how much it was. Asked you how you got it. Don't lie to me, now.

FERRET That's Avery.

NORMA This Avery? All these little green pieces a' paper called Avery? Best cancel that lunch next week, Tennessee. Got all I need to know 'bout Avery.

FERRET Avery got that money.

NORMA How?

[FERRET *looks to* TENNESSEE.]

TENNESSEE S'okay, baby. You just go ahead with it.

FERRET Knocked off from Merle's Liquor Store, but it wasn't me.

NORMA Knocked off? Thought you told me you wasn't up to nothin' stupid?

FERRET I'm not, I swear.

NORMA Then why come I got an envelope full a' stolen money?

FERRET Avery did it. I stayed in the car.

NORMA Getaway driver?

FERRET No. Told me we were going to the movies. I didn't know he . . .
[*Beat.*]
I didn't know.

NORMA Why he give this to you?
[*Silence.*]
Speak up, now. 'Fore I kick your lil' butt out this place.

TENNESSEE Norma . . .

FERRET We did it for you.

NORMA Chu'mean, we?
[*Turning to* TENNESSEE.]
You knew about this?

FERRET I want to give you all of it. Every penny. For treatment.

NORMA Treatment, huh?

FERRET Yeah.

NORMA Bein' treated already.
[*Beat.*]
You gonna give this back.

FERRET Norma—

NORMA Don't argue with me. I don't need no eight hundred dollars for treatment. I'm bein' treated just fine without it.

TENNESSEE You sure about that?

NORMA What?

TENNESSEE Maybe with a little boost, you get some more treatment. Better treatment. New liver, maybe.

NORMA Whatchu doin', Tennessee?

TENNESSEE Just facin' facts.

NORMA What facts? Ain't no new nothin' for me. I gotta work with what I got.

[*Holding the envelope out for* FERRET.]

And what I got don't need this money.

[FERRET *takes the envelope.*]

Matter of fact, why don't you give that money to Tennessee. Let her handle it for you. Don't want you showin' your face 'round Merle after what you done.

FERRET I didn't do anything. Avery went in.

NORMA You ain't try and stop him.

[FERRET *looks at* NORMA, *then to* TENNESSEE. NORMA *gives* TENNESSEE *the envelope.*]

Tell Avery you won't be seein' him no more.

FERRET I love him.

NORMA Don't matter. Spent too much time on you to be runnin' 'round with the same fools done got you here in the first place. This for your own good. Handle it, Tennessee.

TENNESSEE Okay.

[FERRET *exits inside.*]

She cares a great deal about you, Norma.

NORMA I know. And I care too much about her.

[*Beat.*]

She shouldn't a' done it. And you shouldn't be over here encouragin' her like that.

TENNESSEE I know. I'm sorry. It got a hold of me, is all.

NORMA What?

TENNESSEE Hope. Big ol' glass of it. With a slice a' delusion.

[*Beat.*]

We're tryin' to help you the only way we know how.

NORMA By doin' the stupid stuff done landed you here in the first place?

TENNESSEE Can't rightly make this kind a' money cleanin' bingo halls.

NORMA We don't need that kind a' money. So handle it.

[NORMA *goes back to the garden.*]

TENNESSEE You ever think, I don't know, that maybe I got somethin' to do with it?

NORMA Do with what?

TENNESSEE You still havin' cancer and all. I read all the time about folks beat cancer with the right kind of treatment.

NORMA Got the best cancer doctor in Mineola in my corner.

TENNESSEE Only cancer doctor in Mineola. Cancer doctor who knows about me. Knows that I live with you.

[NORMA *stops.*]

NORMA Whatchu gettin' at, girl?

TENNESSEE I see the faces when I go in to town. Hear the whispers behind my back and feel the fear 'round every corner. I'm a monster in this town. And I think you be best gettin' a new doctor. In a new town. Someplace where they don't know.

[NORMA *stands and moves to* TENNESSEE.]

NORMA This is our home.

TENNESSEE Every mornin' I come out my room expectin' you to not be here anymore.

[*Beat.*]

What's gonna happen to me when you go?

NORMA Hey, now.

[*Taking* TENNESSEE'*s hands in hers.*]

Look at me. Look at me, child. I'm still standin' right here.

TENNESSEE For how long?

NORMA Don't matter. 'Cause even after I done left, you'll always have your home.

[TENNESSEE *looks at the tree.*]

TENNESSEE Place ain't gonna stand much longer after you.

NORMA Tilly gonna peel that tree off. Repair the sidin' and all that. You know how good he is.

TENNESSEE I know what happens to the places when the state gets the keys.

NORMA Ain't no state gonna be gettin' no keys.

[*Releasing* TENNESSEE.]

You ain't goin' no place, child.

TENNESSEE Okay.

NORMA Can I get back to my flowers now?

TENNESSEE What flowers?

NORMA The ones that woulda' been planted by now if it wasn't for you and your naggin'.

[*A smile.* TENNESSEE *kisses* NORMA *on the cheek and makes her way up the porch. She exits inside.*]

The hell am I gonna do?

[*Looking to the sky.*]

What should I do, huh? What do I do with what I got left?

[NORMA *waits a bit before walking back to the garden. She stops, wincing in pain and clutching her side. She starts to keel over.*]

Tilly!

[*She goes to the ground.*]

Tilly—

[FERRET *enters from inside. She sees* NORMA.]

FERRET Norma!

[*She rushes to* NORMA's *side.*]

NORMA Get Tilly.

FERRET He's gone.

NORMA Think you can get me over to that porch, child?

FERRET Holy shit.

NORMA Language.

FERRET Help! Tennessee! Shae!

[TENNESSEE *enters from inside and sees* NORMA *and* FERRET. *She runs to them.*]

TENNESSEE What happened?!

FERRET I dunno, came out here and she was like this!

TENNESSEE Norma, we gonna take you inside now.

[SHAE *enters from inside and sees the others.*]

SHAE Momma!

[*She rushes to them as* TENNESSEE *lifts* NORMA *up and carries her to the porch.*]

NORMA I'm fine, baby. Just need to . . . lie down a spell.

[TENNESSEE *exits inside with* NORMA. SHAE *and* FERRET *watch them go.*]

SHAE She gonna be okay?!

FERRET Dunno. This happened once before, I think.

SHAE And no one called me?!

FERRET Norma didn't want to bother you with it. Take you away from college.

[TENNESSEE *re-enters.*]

TENNESSEE She's alright, girls. Just overworked. She's lyin' down now. Talkin' to me just fine.

SHAE Good./

FERRET /Okay./

TENNESSEE I'm gonna stay with her a bit.

[TENNESSEE *exits inside.*]

SHAE It's bad, huh?

[FERRET *nods.*]

Goddamnit. This whole time I . . . I didn't know . . .

FERRET Do now.

SHAE Didn't want to bother me?

FERRET Said that if her grandmomma could climb mountains at eighty-seven . . .

SHAE Momma and her logic. Never was able to make sense of it.

[*Beat.*]

You like it here?

FERRET It's home, so, yeah, I guess.

SHAE If you could change anything about it, what would it be?

FERRET I dunno. Get that tree off the house. Why?

SHAE Just making a list for when I get the keys.

FERRET Get the keys?

SHAE When my mom . . . passes. I'm taking the place over. She didn't tell you?

FERRET Norma's not gonna die.

SHAE I pray for that, too.

FERRET I don't need to pray. Norma's not gonna die.

SHAE I was young like you once.

FERRET I'm not young, I'm eighteen.

SHAE I know it's hard. This being your home and all. Your family.

FERRET She's not gonna die. We don't let her.

[SHAE *reaches to place a hand on* FERRET'*s back, who pulls away.*]

And you're not taking this place. I don't like you.

[FERRET *rushes up the porch and exits.* SHAE *watches her go, before looking around the lawn. She walks over to the birdbath and tries to lift it up. It won't budge. After a few more tries, she gives up and heads up the porch. She exits inside.* PASTOR MARSHALL *enters from across the lawn. He sees his fruit basket and shakes his head. He walks up to the porch to knock on the front door.* TENNESSEE *enters from inside. The two lock eyes.*]

TENNESSEE What're you doing here? We got your fruit already.

MARSHALL Miss Norma inside?

TENNESSEE She's lyin' down.

MARSHALL She okay?

TENNESSEE Fine. What do you want?

MARSHALL How are you, Samuel?

TENNESSEE It's Tennessee now.

MARSHALL Right. Beautiful state. Been there?

TENNESSEE No.

MARSHALL Norma tell you about my offer?

TENNESSEE What offer?

MARSHALL Want to buy this place.

TENNESSEE She didn't say nothin' to me about it.

MARSHALL Not surprised. Norma and I don't exactly see things the same way.

TENNESSEE   And what way do you see things here?

MARSHALL   To be honest, son, I see this house. That tree. And I can't think of nothing but smite.

TENNESSEE   Smite?

MARSHALL   The Good Lord saw fit to act on this place last night. Show you all the path to damnation you're walking.
[*Beat.*]
Ya'll need God in your lives.

TENNESSEE   Us? Or me?
[*Beat.*]
How much you offerin'?

MARSHALL   Enough to keep this place what it is after Norma's . . . not with us anymore. Enough to keep you within four walls and a roof.

TENNESSEE   'Cause God won't let me stay at your house, huh?

MARSHALL   I'm tryin' to make sense of all this, Samuel.

TENNESSEE   Tennessee.

MARSHALL   When your mother was taken from us, I tried. Tried to help you.

TENNESSEE   The only way you knew how.

MARSHALL   Yes.

TENNESSEE   Well, we don't need your help. And don't want it.

MARSHALL   You're lost, son. Wayward. Now I know how much this place means to you and I want to do everything I can to ensure it stays like it is.

TENNESSEE   Out of love?

MARSHALL   God's love, yes. I want to fill this place with God's love.

TENNESSEE   I don't care about God's love, Daddy. All I ever wanted was yours.

MARSHALL If your mother was alive to see you like this . . .

TENNESSEE [*Pointing inside the house.*] My mother sees me every day. And she loves me every day.

MARSHALL You need God.

TENNESSEE I needed you. I tried God once already and he wasn't enough.

MARSHALL Didn't try hard enough, then.

TENNESSEE Kinda hard to give it my all with a needle in my arm and a pill down my throat. Or are you talkin' about something else?

[*Beat.*]

This is who I am. Who I've always been. Long before the drugs. Those came later, after I was kicked out of my own home. My own family. Because they didn't love me enough to stand to look at me.

MARSHALL That's not true, now.

TENNESSEE Then say it. Say you love me.

[*Pause.*]

Say you love me.

MARSHALL I want to, son. With all my heart and soul.

TENNESSEE Go away.

MARSHALL Every day I ask God for the strength to love you.

TENNESSEE Go away!

MARSHALL Son, please.

TENNESSEE Go away, I said! Go away!

MARSHALL No!

[NORMA *enters from inside.*]

NORMA What's all this hollerin', now?

[*To* PASTOR MARSHALL.]

Whatchu doin back here? No fruit this time?

MARSHALL [*Collecting himself.*] Have you reconsidered my offer?

NORMA I . . . I need more time.

MARSHALL Time's a fleeting luxury nowadays, Miss Norma. One you don't have. That tree is just the beginning. If this house doesn't find God and choose to obey His will, then—

TENNESSEE The house? Or me?

MARSHALL Both. I'm your father, Samuel. I just want what's best for you.

TENNESSEE That why you kicked me out?

[TENNESSEE *approaches her father.*]

See, that's the problem with you and your God. Only see folks for what they are, not who they can become. To you, I'll always be Samuel. Always be Samuel and always have a needle stickin' out my arm. But here, and in Norma's eyes, I'm somethin' else. Somethin' greater than your God intended.

[*Beat.*]

We all make choices, Daddy. That's really all we have in this world. I made mine. I chose to do the things that got me here and I choose to make my life better for it. You can choose, too. You can choose to love me for who I am, rather than condemn me for what I am. Or you can leave, and we can go back to pretending we don't share the same sky or breathe the same air.

[*Beat.*]

The place ain't for sale.

MARSHALL You know what's gonna happen to you after Miss Norma . . .

NORMA I ain't goin' no place.

MARSHALL [*To* NORMA.] Every day I pray for a miracle. Pray that God sends his love and compassion down on this house and blesses you with more life.

NORMA [*Looking to the tree.*] Looks like he misunderstood you.

MARSHALL   But facts are facts. Cancer's cancer. After you're gone, this house—

TENNESSEE   Is gonna be looked after by Shae. Her daughter.

[*Pause.*]

MARSHALL   Eighty thousand dollars.

NORMA   I remember. No sale.

MARSHALL   Miss Norma, it's in your best interest to—

NORMA   No sale.

MARSHALL   I know you and I aren't exactly the best of—

NORMA   No. Sale.

MARSHALL   I'd like to share with you some passages, Miss Norma.

[*He reaches into his coat and removes a pocket Bible. Colored tabs stick out of the pages. He flips to a tab.*]

NORMA   Don't need to share nothin' 'round here.

MARSHALL   Psalm One-nineteen.

[*Reading.*]

Blessed are those whose way is blameless, who walk in the law of the Lord. Blessed are those who keep his testimonies, who seek him with their whole heart.

NORMA   That's enough, Pastor.

[PASTOR MARSHALL *raises his hand.*]

MARSHALL   [*Reading.*] Who also do no wrong, but walk in his ways. You have commanded your precepts to be kept diligently. Oh, that my ways may be steadfast in keeping your statutes.

[*He flips to another page.*]

TENNESSEE   Please stop.

MARSHALL   James. One-twenty-two.

[*Reading.*]

But be doers of the word, and not hearers only, deceiving yourselves. For if anyone is a hearer of the word and not a doer, he is like a man who looks intently at his face in a mirror. For he looks at himself and goes away at once.

[*To* TENNESSEE.]

Forgets what *he* was like.

[*A car is heard pulling up. Reading.*]

But the one who looks into the perfect law, the law of liberty, and perseveres, being no hearer who forgets but a doer who acts—

[TILLY *enters, carrying two gas cans. He observes* PASTOR MARSHALL.]

He will be blessed in his doing.

[*Sees* TILLY.]

How you doing, young man?

TILLY   The good person out of his good treasure brings forth good, and the evil person out of his evil treasure brings forth evil. Matthew seven-thirteen. Verse fourteen.

MARSHALL   You know the word of God?

TILLY   Do you?

[*Beat.*]

Isaiah sixty-four. We have all become like one who is unclean, and all our righteous deeds are like a polluted garment.

[*He opens his shirt, revealing a swastika tattoo on his chest, surrounded by various other indiscernible, yet equally evil, tattoos.*]

We all fade like a leaf, and our iniquities, like the wind, take us away. I know the Bible, Pastor. Bein' locked up'll make a man wanna read just about anything. You know who I am, Pastor? Know what I done?

MARSHALL   I've heard, yes.

TILLY   Heard I was the monster damn near killed two boys in an alley one night. Got me six years. I didn't have this ink then. Learned real quick when them bars shut behind me. Learned that if I didn't pick a side. Pick a color. Those six years, locked up with all that evil, woulda been a lot shorter for me. So I made my choice. Got the ink. Got out in three years. Started runnin' 'round with other folks had the same skin I did. Only folks I knew to run around with. The world don't take kindly to folks been locked up like I was. I live with my regrets. Live with my choices.

MARSHALL I can pray for you, son. For your salvation.

TILLY I don't deserve it. Don't want it from you anyway. Far as I see it, you got more ink than me.

[*Beat.*]

Only one thing I pray for, Pastor. I pray for a new skin.

MARSHALL You should pray for God's mercy. For God's love.

TILLY [*Looking at* NORMA.]

I got hers. And I got this place. That's plenty of love for now.

[*To* PASTOR MARSHALL.]

I suggest you start walkin'. I really don't feel like goin' back to prison today.

MARSHALL That a threat?

TILLY You tell me.

[PASTOR MARSHALL *stares at him, then looks to* TENNESSEE, *who comes up behind* NORMA *and places a hand on her shoulder.*]

MARSHALL Fine.

[*He pockets the Bible and walks to the fruit basket. He picks it up.*]

May God bless and keep you, Miss Norma.

NORMA Already has.

[PASTOR MARSHALL *exits.*]

NORMA Thank you, Tilly.

[TILLY *nods. He buttons his shirt and goes back for the gas cans. He walks around the house and exits.* TENNESSEE *releases* NORMA *and lets out a large breath, tears welling up.*]

Hey, come on now. It's handled. Dry them eyes, girl.

[TENNESSEE *nods and wipes her face.* SHAE *enters from inside.*]

SHAE Everything alright, Momma?

NORMA We're fine.

[*Beat.*]

I wanna talk to you a minute, girl.

SHAE Okay.

[TENNESSEE *turns and exits inside.*]

NORMA I'm kickin' you out, Shae.

SHAE What?

NORMA This ain't no place for you.

SHAE It's where I need to be.

NORMA I know you want that to be true. But you a city girl. With a city life. Can't even wake up 'fore ten.

SHAE I can start. I'll try, I swear.

NORMA I don't want you to try. And you don't run a sober house because you want to. You do it because you have to. 'Cause there ain't many people who will. You learn to love it, sure, but . . . when I was your age I wanted to see the world. Me and your daddy traveled all over the place. Been up and down the lower forty-eight. Mexico. Canada. Even on down South America. We was only beginning. Then I had you. And what I wanted to do didn't fit with what I had to do. And, boy, did I learn to love it. It's the same thing here. You don't have to do these things yet. You only just beginning.

[*Taking* SHAE's *hand.*]

You need to live your life. Finish what you started up at that college. Don't be worryin' about me.

SHAE What if you're not here when I get back? I don't want to leave you to . . . leave you to die.

NORMA Hey, now. If your grandmomma could climb mountains at eighty-seven I can live long enough to wait for you.

[*Beat.*]

I want you out of here by middle a' next week. Give you some time to arrange things with Yale. Make some calls and all that.

SHAE And if they don't take me back?

NORMA Good a writer as you are? Be stupid not to.

SHAE What if?

NORMA Then you figure out someplace else. Either way, you leavin'. I won't hear another word of it.

[*Pause. SHAE nods.*]

I love you, girl.

SHAE Love you, too.

[SHAE *begins to cry as she walks away from her mother and up the porch.*]

NORMA And, Shae?

[SHAE *stops.*]

Find yourself a man. Want me a couple grandbabies 'fore I go.

[SHAE *laughs a bit, then starts crying again. She exits inside. NORMA watches her go before walking to the porch and sitting at the edge. TENNESSEE enters from inside.*]

What am I gonna do, Tennessee?

TENNESSEE Don't know.

[TENNESSEE *moves next to NORMA and sits.*]

NORMA I'm not ready. Not ready to leave this place just yet.

TENNESSEE I know.

NORMA If I . . . if I go soon—

TENNESSEE Norma, don't.

NORMA If I do, I want you to look after the house awhile.

TENNESSEE What?

NORMA You heard me.

TENNESSEE I don't think that's a good idea.

NORMA Why not? Practically do already. You come a long way, girl. Time to help some other folks do the same. 'Sides, you'll have Tilly around to help you with all the heavy stuff.

TENNESSEE I . . .

NORMA And keep a close eye on Ferret, now. That girl's a lotta trouble but she's worth it.

TENNESSEE The state ain't gonna go for this.

[*Pause.*]

NORMA Such pretty hair.

[NORMA *runs her fingers through* TENNESSEE's *wig.*]

TENNESSEE What, you want it?

NORMA Nah.
  [*Placing her hand on her hair.*]
  Mine's holdin' up just fine.

TENNESSEE Can't even tell.

NORMA Get my wigs custom.
  [*Beat.*]
  'Sides, I want that pink one you got.

TENNESSEE Over my dead body.

[*Pause.* NORMA *stands.*]

NORMA I'm tired. All this jaw-flappin' done wore me out. I need a rest.

TENNESSEE Okay.

[NORMA *starts for the door.*]

NORMA You know the damndest thing about climbin' a mountain?

TENNESSEE What?

NORMA You look back and see how far you come, only to look ahead and see how much further you got to go.

[*She opens the door.*]

TENNESSEE What about the garden?

NORMA What about it?

TENNESSEE Ain't you gonna finish?

NORMA When I feel like it.

TENNESSEE Crotchety old coot.

NORMA Uppity lil' nag.

[NORMA *exits inside.* TENNESSEE *looks around a bit, settling her eyes on the hanging sign. She walks over to a chair on the ground and picks it up, setting it upright under the sign. She stands on the chair and reaches up to the sign, hanging the loose side back up. She steps off the chair and places it back on the porch. She turns to the garden and walks toward it.* TILLY *enters and sees* TENNESSEE. *He nods as he moves to the chain saw and begins filling it with gas.* FERRET *enters from inside, looking as if she's been crying. She looks to* TENNESSEE, *who looks back, then begins picking up the garbage and debris around the house.* TENNESSEE *watches her a bit before kneeling down in the garden. She picks up the spade and continues the work that* NORMA *started. Blackout.*]

• • •

The Hour

Susan Goodell

Susan Goodell

Susan Goodell is the author of the full-length plays *Hope Throws Her Heart Away* (premiere Chicago's Genesis Theatrical Productions) and *Heels Over Head* (first produced by Tri-State Actors Theatre; Rova Dramawerk's Seconds Award). These scripts were developed at theaters including Virginia Company, the Barrow Group, and Atlantic Stage in Myrtle Beach. Her short plays have been seen at the Abingdon, the Boston Theatre Marathon, NYC's Fresh Produce'd, Source Festival, Philly's Primary Stages, the Strawberry Festival (finalist), and the Turnip Festival. Other recognition: Steppenwolf Theatre Company commission, Djerassi Resident Artist, Denver Drama Critic's Circle nomination, and the *Denver Post's* 10-Best List. A former small-town newspaper editor and Madison Avenue public relations executive, she lives in New England.

···production history···

The Hour received its world premiere on January 3, 2014, as part of Chicago's Landmark Festival, produced by Prologue Theatre Company. The production was directed by Damon Krometis and featured the following cast:

DEXTER   Chad Eschman

DARRYL/MAN WITH HAT   Logan Hulick

AMBER/JADE/CRYSTAL   Allie Fleschner

It was performed again in Hollywood on August 28–September 20, 2015, as part of Punk Monkey Production's PL.A.Y Noir, directed by Rich Cassone with the following cast:

DEXTER   Gordon Martin Meacham

DARRYL/MAN WITH HAT   Jim Shipley

AMBER/JADE/CRYSTAL   Angela Bray

characters

DEXTER   20s to 40s, sincere to geeky

DARRYL/MAN WITH HAT   30s to 40s, tough cop/smarmy dealer

AMBER/JADE/CRYSTAL   20s to 40s, femme-fatale buyer/crisp lawyer

setting

Police department interview room.

props

A black wig (can be weird/Halloween) for AMBER, two drinking glasses, quirky hat for DARRYL, and another accessory for AMBER as CRYSTAL.

[DEXTER *sits uncomfortably in chair. Impatient* DARRYL *paces above him, determined to get information he seeks. Both men push exhaustion.*]

DEXTER   I see why you don't believe me.

DARRYL   Because you're guilty.

DEXTER   Guilty of what? I know the story sounds weird.

DARRYL Because you're lying.

DEXTER I don't believe it myself, but it's the only story I have.

DARRYL So I need to hear it again. . . .

DEXTER I'll tell you again, but nothing will change.

DARRYL Humor me.

DEXTER You have a sense of humor?

[DARRYL *reacts.* DEXTER *regroups.*]

Okay, here we go. Just like I told you before. I enter Tiki's Bar, Grill and Vittles.

[*Rises.*]

DARRYL March 13, some time after noon on the first day of daylight savings time. Subject enters Tiki's Bar Grill and Vittles.

DEXTER I look for a raven-haired lady in a red dress sitting alone at a table.

DARRYL That alone is a clue you're headed for trouble. Okay, so this woman is named—

DEXTER Her name is Amber. Or I thought it was Amber.

[AMBER *enters, sits in chair.* DEXTER *spots her and happily extends hand to her.*]

Hello. I'm . . .

AMBER I know.

DEXTER And you must be . . .

AMBER Let's do without the pleasantries. We both know what we came here for.

[DARRYL *sits down beside* DEXTER *to hear his story.*]

DARRYL You didn't think that strange? Red dress and now just business?

DEXTER I did. And I'm already on edge.

DARRYL [*Makes note.*] Goes over edge easily.

DEXTER [*Offended.*] Not usually.

DARRYL You've been on edge since I met you. So you and raven-haired Amber skip the pleasantries.

DEXTER [*Turning to* AMBER.] Look, Amber.

AMBER Jade.

DEXTER When we talked over the telephone your name was Amber.

AMBER We didn't talk on the phone. Your friend said you'd be here, ready to deal.

DEXTER You were so pleasant on the phone. Now you're just fussy.

DARRYL Not exactly charming, are you?

DEXTER I can be charming. Sometimes.

DARRYL I doubt that. So what happens next?

DEXTER [*Looks at* DARRYL, *who's already heard the story, but seeing his insistence, continues.*] Okay, Jade or Amber, whoever you are today.

AMBER Not exactly charming, are you?

DEXTER I am charming! You told me to skip the pleasantries. What do you want? Let's just get this over with and do the deal.

AMBER Whoa. Such a big hurry to deal. We'll deal, all right? Buy me a drink first.

[DARRYL *sets two empty glasses on table; they pretend to drink.*]

DEXTER You want a drink first? Okay.

[*Chit-chatting.*]

You came highly recommended by my friend Randolph.

AMBER I thought it was Rudy.

DEXTER Randolph.

AMBER How could you hear Randolph? Rudy enunciates too clearly.

DEXTER I've known him since college.

AMBER What if he changed names and didn't tell you?

DEXTER He tells me everything.

AMBER Give me another drink. There's nothing in this glass.

[DARRYL *takes her glass and returns it to her.*]

This drink is even worse.

DEXTER They're very busy here.

AMBER [*Daring.*] You're not going to . . . back out are you?

DEXTER You're the one who wanted a drink. . . . Okay. Look, just show me the Jack and the Bazooka, and if they're what you describe, we transact business, and I get out of your raven hair.

AMBER Uh-uh. First you show me cash; then you see the merchandise.

DEXTER You agreed on a check . . . over the phone call . . . you say we didn't have.

AMBER Look, if you're doing this, let's go. Show me your . . . check? How can anyone pay by check?

[DARRYL *hands* AMBER *check. She rises to leave.*]

DEXTER Aren't you forgetting something? Where are my Bazooka and Jack?

AMBER [*Tucks check.*] Are you kidding? You actually expect to leave here with a Bazooka? You lowlife creep. The more guys like you we get off the streets, the safer we'll all be.

[*She exits.*]

DEXTER Wait. Where're you going? I trusted you to be honest.

[*To* DARRYL.]

She's gone. Probably never even brought the merchandise.

DARRYL You complain she's dishonest?

[*Snorts a laugh.*]

In your business?

DEXTER Every one of my trades has been straightforward. Then this. But things don't end there. 'Cause it seems like Amber or Jade sent this man over to see me.

DARRYL Later March 13, about what time?

DEXTER Think it was 12:40. Might have checked my watch. Why do you act like you haven't heard this story?

DARRYL To trip you up, but so far you've outsmarted me. Okay. Approximately 12:40 p.m. daylight savings time. A male approaches. What's the male's appearance again?

DEXTER You know this. About [DARRYL*'s height.*] with [DARRYL*'s eye color.*] but with a weird hat.

[DARRYL *puts on weird hat.*]

That's him.

DARRYL And he . . .

DEXTER Starts talking about . . .

DARRYL [*Turns into smarmy drug dealer type.*] Hello. Can I join you?

DEXTER Bad idea.

[DARRYL *sits anyway.*]

I'm rotten company. A long story, but just met this crazy woman, who promises a great deal on a Bazooka and a Jack, takes my check, and bolts like I gave her crime evidence.

DARRYL Wouldn't that happen all the time to you creeps?

DEXTER Huh? I always thought people who like this sort of thing don't do this sort of thing.

DARRYL Idealistic for your business, huh? Never mind. Say, dude, I might be able to make this up to you.

DEXTER Look, I don't know you, don't want to talk, just want to go home, be miserable.

DARRYL What if I offer you an assortment at a very good price?

DEXTER Oh . . . No. I never want to trade again.

[*But too tempted.*]

You have an assortment? Like what stuff? What price?

DARRYL [*Removes hat and plays cop again.*] That doesn't faze you? A stranger who just happens to have an easy offer like that?

DEXTER I thought he might have overheard me talking to Amber or Jade or Topaz.

DARRYL You're not a careful man, Dexter. I don't know how you slipped away until now.

DEXTER I have no idea what you're saying, but do I need a lawyer?

DARRYL You want a lawyer?

DEXTER Can I ask for one?

DARRYL Don't you watch television? Of course.

[AMBER *enters with different accessories. She's a crisp lawyer, maybe with different speech to contrast with other character.*]

DEXTER Oh, no, she looks just like . . . you're Amber, Jade.

AMBER Crystal.

DEXTER You look just like . . .

AMBER Maybe you know my sister, Opal.

DEXTER Maybe you shouldn't be my lawyer. You look too much like the woman who took my . . .

AMBER You are arguing with me?

DEXTER Oh no no no. I won't argue. I'm desperate. I will treat you pleasant, treat you rough, anything. Be my lawyer. Please . . . ask him . . .

[*Pained and desperate.*]

Why he won't stop asking these crazy questions!

DARRYL That's easy. 'Cause you're not easy to break.

DEXTER *Talk to him.* What's going on?

AMBER Look, I'm just a lawyer. I don't undo lives for people who mess them up.

DEXTER   You're a big help.

DARRYL   He's close to a total breakdown. This will be good. Come on . . . I love this part when the guy enters. Dexter. Tell us about your arrest again.

DEXTER   Right, the guy enters. Okay. So I tell the guy who sat at my table, after missing the Bazooka and the Jack, I'll take his assortment and . . . you know this part. . . .

DARRYL   I love the way you tell it.

DEXTER   Then you appear and say, "You're coming with me."

DARRYL   Completely accurate. You're coming with me.

AMBER   You just say out loud you'll buy an assortment? Stupid. See you in fifteen years.

DEXTER   Is that bad? How is it bad?

DARRYL   Look, repeat the story. You're so inept, now even I want to help you.

DEXTER   Inept at what?

[*Gets no answer.*]

Okay. Today is Sunday, March 13, you know this, and as I told you, and I'm about to enter . . .

DARRYL   About to meet Jade, whom you guessed by now was a close associate with the man with the hat. What time again?

DEXTER   I remember now. I did check my wristwatch. It was exactly 12:15 p.m. when I was about to meet Amber.

DARRYL   Jade, and it was 1:15 p.m. daylight savings time.

DEXTER   I have a new watch, and it was 12:15 precisely.

AMBER   Stop. Right there. Officer, did you hear that?

DARRYL   Curious. Dexter? Repeat our chronology. Amber, 12:15?

[*Removes hat.*]

DEXTER   Exactly. For a Bazooka and a Cracker Jack.

AMBER   Cracker Jack? That's what they call illegal weapons these days?

DEXTER   That's what they also call baseball cards. Cracker Jack and Bazooka gum. Amber promised to sell me two rare baseball cards, a Bazoo . . .

DARRYL   No. He is pretending to buy baseball cards, but smuggling weapons, exotic animals, and bootleg mushrooms. This arrest clears half the unsolved cases in Slippery Rock.

DEXTER   I didn't need to pretend to buy baseball cards because I was buying baseball—

AMBER   But he said . . .

DEXTER   But not from Jade. From Amber.

AMBER   First day, daylight savings. Curious. Oh no. What if Dexter has been *caught*?

DARRYL   But so much evidence.

AMBER   Recheck your timeline.

DARRYL   We spot subject. Sunday, first day, daylight savings . . .
[*He understands mistake.*]
Oh no. *Oh no.*
[*Pounds fist.*]
Dammit! He was caught!

DEXTER   Dammit, caught in what?

AMBER   Caught in "the hour."

DARRYL   Oh gawd no, don't tell me.
[*Pounds fist.*]
Dammit, Dexter, you went and blew everything. Had to get caught in "the hour," didn't you?

DEXTER   Tell me, tell me. What is going on!

AMBER   Another chump who forgot to spring . . .

DARRYL   How did we miss this with all the evidence right here. . . .

AMBER I hate it. Failure to spring forward. Destroys months of . . .

DARRYL *An hour late*, 'cause you didn't reset your new watch, you sit down with . . .

DEXTER Jade. But my new watch . . .

DARRYL Amber, whom we presume arrives approximately at 12:15, departing, sometime later, furious, thinking she was stood up. We'll have her on surveillance.

DEXTER So Amber was there? Whatever it is, I didn't do it intentionally.

DARRYL How did he let this happen?

AMBER Some men are . . .

DARRYL They pretend time doesn't march forward.

AMBER They never want to get older and even want time to stand still.

DARRYL You were caught not ready for a new season, weren't you, Dexter?

DEXTER I was ready . . . shiny new watch . . . daylight savings . . . ooohh . . . oops, I always remember, but with the excitement of getting my hands on a Bazooka and Jack . . . I forget to reset my new watch. You can't arrest me for that, can you? Gee, looks like I caused trouble here.

DARRYL You blew apart the precise sting twenty men in the department planned for months.

DEXTER I didn't mean it.
[*Idea.*]
Why don't you just return to the Tiki . . .

DARRYL Too late. As you know, timing is everything.

DEXTER I caused . . . I did? Oh, terrible. Look, I'll go home, reset the clocks, even change the battery in my smoke alarm.

DARRYL No, that's when you fall back. Not as important.

AMBER   No damage done when you arrive an hour early.

DEXTER   You're finally convinced I've done nothing wrong.

AMBER   You were wrong. But not illegal. Completely out of step.

DARRYL   Disorganized, tardy, but within the law.

DEXTER   So, I'm free to go? Yippee.

> [*Rises.*]

> He's been starving me for hours. Talk about caught in the hour.
> Haven't had food since . . .

[*Checks his watch proudly. Shrugs and exits.*]

AMBER   Unlucky bastard.

DARRYL   What a low-life creep. Dammit.

> [*Pounds fist.*]

> He even got to sleep late.

• • •

The Lilac Ticket

C. J. Ehrlich

C. J. Ehrlich

C. J. Ehrlich's award-winning one-acts have enjoyed dozens of productions around the U.S. and internationally on five continents, and are published in several editions of Smith & Kraus's annual *Best Ten-Minute Plays* anthologies (2011–2015) and by Heuer Press. Her full-length comedy collaboration, *The Cupcake Conspiracy: "Terrorism Is Easy. Marriage Is Complicated"* (with Philip J. Kaplan), opened Rover Dramawerks (Plano, Texas) 2015 season and was a finalist for the Charles Getchell Award and the Mountain Playhouse International Comedy Competition. Among its accolades, *The Lilac Ticket* is a Heideman Award finalist. A proud member of the Westchester Collaborative Theatre and the Dramatists Guild, Ehrlich is also a freelance editor and writing consultant and runs workshops in animation, improv, stagecraft, and playwriting. But by far Ehrlich's greatest accomplishment is teaching her sons the fine art of the spit take. Visit www.CJ-Ehrlich.com.

···production history···

West Coast Players, 2015 One-Act Play Festival, Clearwater, Florida. First Place Winner, Audience Choice Award, July 2015. Directed by Judy Landis.

SAM   Richard Michaels Stefanik

BARB   Elyse Van Breemen

The Lilac Ticket toured senior centers, retirement communities, assisted-living facilities, community centers, churches, and synagogues in Atlanta, Georgia, with Atlanta Theatre-to-Go, directed by Lee Buechele, June–September 2014.

The Pakriti Foundation, Short & Sweet Chennai, Chennai, India, July 2013. Directed by Vaishnavi Sundar.

SAM   Vasudev Menon

BARB   Latha Venkatraman

The Boston Theatre Marathon XIV, Boston, Massachusetts, May 2012. Directed by Bridget O'Leary, New Rep Theatre, Watertown, Massachusetts.

SAM   Stephen Benson

BARB   Kippy Goldfarb

Developed in the Jewish Women's Theatre of Los Angeles Salon Series, May 2012: "The Moment You Knew." Directed by Ronda Spinak.

SAM   Steven Macht

BARB   Kate Zentall

A reprised production was undertaken May 2013.

setting

A car, then a doctor's waiting room

time

Recently

characters

SAM   70s

BARB   70s

synopsis

SAM and BARB confront two crises threatening their fifty-year marriage: one happening now in the doctor's office, and the other a long-buried secret.

set

The set is played by two chairs.

director's notes

SAM and BARB are in their seventies, fairly healthy, but with typical decline of vision, some tremors perhaps, slower movement and reaction time, and lots of aches and pains. They lead a simple life, physically and socially, but are mentally "with it." They have been married for fifty years. Note on language: Several curses supporting the story line are refined for family audiences. The "f-word" could be whispered or replaced with "eff" if it seems appropriate.

[SAM *and* BARB *sit next to each other on two chairs facing the audience. They are in a car.* SAM *may have his right arm over the back of* BARB's *chair as he steers. He is trying to back into a parking space at a shopping center.* SAM *is slightly stiff when he turns his head. Their movements coordinate to convey sharp jerks as the car starts, stops, lurches forward, back.*]

BARB Watch it, watch it, Sam! Stop! Stop! The basket man!

SAM What the hell is a—

BARB The man pushing the baskets! Brake! BRAKE!

SAM You mean the shopping wagons! The wagons!

BARB Whatever ya call 'em—You're gonna hit him!

SAM For godsakes! He's half a mile away!

BARB Oy, Sam. He's crossing—like the boy with the Red Sox cap!

SAM I SEE him!

BARB Okay. Go, go—stop! Watch it! Oy, oy, oy!

SAM Barb, I beg you. Calm down and let me PARK!

[*He parks. They both sit, exhausted from the adrenaline rush. After a moment:*]

BARB A hundred shopping carts, you don't even see him!

SAM I SAW HIM! And I saw the Red Sox cap.

[*They sit quietly. Shaking. SAM gets out of the car and goes to BARB's side. He opens the door for her. She gets out.*]

BARB Why we go to this medical group—! It's impossible to park!

SAM What impossible. I JUST PARKED!

[*They walk slowly to the medical office.*]

BARB You telling the doctor, or should I?

SAM Enough with the backseat driving! You hate my driving so much? Don't drive with me!

BARB We're done here, we do the marketing.

SAM You heard?

BARB I hear fine.

SAM Don't drive with me.

[*They enter the medical office.*]

BARB Who else is driving with you.

 [*To the invisible receptionist.*]

 Sam Becker for Doctor Finkelstein, eleven o'clock. No co-pay.

[*They return to the chairs, which now represent the waiting room.*]

SAM You made a list?

BARB Quart of milk, loaf of bread, can of peaches . . .

SAM Coffee.

BARB No coffee!

SAM A cup in the morning. It's all I ask!

BARB Dr. Finkelstein says it's bad for your heart.

SAM Dr. Finkelstein needs to know?

BARB One cup keeps you up all night.

SAM So? You need me to milk cows at dawn?

BARB Fine! We'll get some decaf! Milk, bread, decaf.

SAM You remember . . .

BARB Peaches.

SAM the coffee they served at that hotel?

BARB What hotel?

SAM The hotel with the coffee.

BARB Fifty years together. I'm supposed to know what you mean, "that hotel."

SAM We used to go. When the kids were little. In the Catskills.

BARB . . . Grossingers?

SAM Grossingers.

BARB That was ages ago! A lifetime! Who remembers a hotel?
[*Beat.*]
Coffee was okay. I've had better, plenty of places.

SAM Those buffets. Breakfast. You could have anything.

BARB I remember now. Summers. With the kids. Breakfast as far as the eye could see! Pastries. Herring! Strawberries . . .

SAM Steaming coffee . . . in silver carafes. You felt like a pasha.

BARB First time I ever saw a kiwi fruit.

SAM You remember, the Katzes, the Madoffs . . . the Kamolwitzes . . .

BARB Sure, every morning. One big table. Breakfast. Then tennis . . .

SAM Gossip . . . Then tennis.

BARB I played doubles, with Sylvia, Ruthie Kamolwitz, Lucille Fishbein, oy oy . . .

SAM I played poker. A little basketball maybe.

BARB They're all gone now. Lucille with the kidney disease. Poor Ruthie—the brain cancer . . .

SAM Jerry Madoff's still around. In Arizona maybe.

BARB We were so active then. So . . . attractive!

SAM Hey. I'm still attractive. And every morning I wake up, still breathing, it's a bonus.

[*Beat.*]

They had "to do" there. The kids—made their—wax turtles . . . leather bracelets—And for us. Rumba lessons . . . You wouldn't rumba with me . . .

BARB Who needs that stuff. Too Carmen Miranda!

SAM The nightlife! Bands. Comedians . . . Buddy Hackett . . .

BARB What a mouth on that one! Remember that magician? Made Jerry Madoff disappear.

SAM Jerry's in Arizona now. His nephew, Bernie, what a schmuck.

BARB Sam, shhh. There's people here.

SAM People say anything now. Schmuck's nothing! You know how they talk. Ass is nothing. Fuck is nothing.

BARB SAM!

SAM You can say it all day long. Hello, madam, how the eff are you? May I have some effing milk in my effing decaf?

BARB Watch your language! They'll think you have Tourette's.

SAM Fine. I'll be quiet. I'll say nothing.

[*Beat.*]

And you. Can say nothing.

BARB I have to tell Dr. Finkelstein.

SAM Don't. You tell him, he has to take "action."

BARB Sam, you nearly . . .

SAM I didn't "nearly," by a mile! For the sake of our marriage, Barb . . .

BARB What. After fifty years, I'm gonna leave you?

SAM You want to take away my driving, the one thing I can still do that makes me happy? Where I can't break a hip, I mean.

BARB It was a *miracle* you didn't hit the boy in the Red Sox cap.

SAM How many pleasures I have left? I have you. Such a pleasure. Large-print books, I have. Senior matinees.

BARB The grandchildren!

SAM They visit once, four times a year, tops. Their "Skyppee" computer calls, big deal. We can't travel. So what else. Canned peaches. Decaf coffee?

BARB You have interests. The Rabbi's seminar on Martin Buber . . .

SAM You know what? Hit me with a shovel! Bury me now. I like Sundays, to take a little drive!

BARB The boy . . .

SAM A boy, raised by Neanderthals, runs into the street . . .

BARB He was chasing his ball!

SAM Sixty years behind the wheel. First time a kid decides to jump in front of me—like I'm some kind of bullfighter . . .

BARB You didn't even see him!

SAM I saw him! Could have been an eighteen-year-old driving, would have "almost" hit him.

BARB I'm telling the doctor. You almost killed someone!

SAM I almost nothing! I "almost" effed Ruthie Kamolwitz!

BARB You—? What do you mean, you "almost." You almost WHAT?

SAM [*Beat.*] She had a few other sports she liked to play doubles.

BARB WHAT ARE YOU TELLING ME?

SAM Calm down, Barb. Shh. There's people here!

[*Beat.*]

What are you so excited. She's dead. Fifteen years she's dead.

BARB GOD PUNISHED HER!

SAM What a tush on her. I can almost taste it to this day.

BARB You tasted!

SAM No, no, no!

BARB Sam Becker. What "almost" happened?

SAM Forty years ago, more. You don't want to know.

BARB I want to know!

SAM It's ancient history, like the Babylonians!

BARB You can take a bus home, with the Babylonians!

SAM All right! . . . It was one of those blazing afternoons. You had the kids, at the pool. I won a few bucks at poker, couple of beers in me. I feel great. You know? Content. My job, my family—Grass is green, flowers flowering . . . I order a cup of coffee, on the patio, like a prince . . . And there's Ruthie Kamolwitz. Crossing the lawn. In her white shorts and sandals. Those legs . . . one more perfect thing God created.

BARB Oy, now she has legs!

SAM Oh, sha. You had legs too. She comes over. To me! Asks could she share my umbrella.

BARB That tramp!

SAM I knew they were talking divorce—you and the girls never stopped squawking about it behind her back. I thought maybe she needed legal advice. So why not. She sits. We talk. Next thing I know, her hand is on my knee.

BARB [*She smacks him.*] You! Why were you sitting so close?

SAM I was no rocket scientist in that department, but it didn't take a genius. Her in her two-piece bathing suits. She says, "My husband's gone back to the city for a few days. I'm feeling a little blue."

BARB You remember!

SAM Like it was yesterday. She pushes to me, across the table . . .

BARB Her room key! That's it, Sam. I'm calling a lawyer . . .

SAM No, no—stop. Stop! It was a card.

BARB What card.

SAM A lilac ticket to the evening comedy show. "Turn it over," she whispers. On the back, in pencil, her room number.

[*There is a pause.*]

BARB And you said.

SAM I said nothing.

BARB Nothing.

SAM But I thought . . . Why me? So we rumba-ed once or twice. She knew I was happily married.

BARB She hated me! I always beat her in tennis.

SAM No! She was . . . lonely and confused . . . and . . .

BARB How the hell do you remember "lilac" after forty years?

SAM Because, petal . . .
   [*Pause.*]
   I still have the ticket.

[*He looks at her. Then takes out his wallet. He slowly extracts a faded purple card.*]

BARB Oy, my heart, Sam! Why? Why do you have that?

SAM To remind me. That in fifty years of marriage. This is the closest I came to messing it up. A hand on my knee. And a lilac ticket with three numbers on the back. Because in all that time, you're the only ticket I ever needed. I love you, Barb. And that's God's truth.

BARB [*Beat.*] I don't know if I should beat you . . . or kiss you.

[SAM *puts the ticket away.*]

SAM You hit me, it's elder abuse. They can put you in jail.

BARB You regret it, don't you. Every time you see that thing, you think about what could have been. I mean, look at us, Sam. Look at us!

SAM Exactly, Barb. Look at us . . . I didn't miss a thing.

[*Beat.*]

Look, if you want me to stop driving—I'll stop.

BARB No, Sam . . . When it's time . . . you'll make the right choice.

VOICE [*From offstage.*] Mr. Becker? The doctor will see you now.

BARB I'm waiting here. But I'll show you a tush. Later.

SAM And much cuter than Ruthie Kamolwitz's.

BARB Oh really . . .

SAM She is dead fifteen years.

BARB You're disgusting! I don't know why I put up with you.

SAM . . . And this one is all mine.

[*He pinches her butt. They kiss.*]

• • •

The
Subterraneans

Adam Kraar

Adam Kraar

Adam Kraar's plays include *Alternating Currents* (Working Theatre commission), Wild Terrain (EST Marathon of One-Act Plays), *Empire of the Trees* (NY Innovative Theatre Awards nominee, Outstanding New Script), *New World Rhapsody* (Manhattan Theatre Club commission), *The Spirit House* (premiered at Performance Network), and *Freedom High* (Queens Theatre in the Park). Kraar's work has been produced and/or developed by Primary Stages, NY Stage & Film, Public Theatre, the New Group, and many others. His plays are published by Applause Books, Dramatic Publishing, and Smith & Kraus. Awards include the Bogliasco Fellowship, Sewanee Writers' Conference Fellowship, Reva Shiner Award, Inge Center Residency, and Manhattan Theatre Club Fellowship. He is a member of Ensemble Studio Theatre and an affiliated member of the Playwrights' Center. Kraar grew up in India, Thailand, Singapore, and the US. He earned an MFA at Columbia University, taught playwriting at the University of Rochester and Adelphi University, and lives in Brooklyn with his wife, Karen.

···production history···

The Subterraneans was commissioned and originally produced by the Stella Adler Studio—Tom Oppenheim, artistic director, and Christa Kimlicko Jones, director of teen programs—as part of the Advanced Teen Program, 2015. The cast included Kat McMahan, Kirsten Mossberg, and Zach Palomo, under the direction of Judson Jones.

characters

> **ROBBIE** 16, a loner who often hides his wild imagination and sensitivity behind an intellectual demeanor. Full of intense emotions, but inhibited to express them openly. Though he finds his sister irritating and sometimes disturbing, he loves her more than anyone else.
>
> **PATTI** 15, Robbie's sister. An odd, super-sensitive, kindhearted creature. She is curious, somewhat naive, sometimes confused and awkward, and sometimes outspoken.
>
> **LISA NOVA** 18, a famous pop star (seen through Robbie's fantasy).

place

The suburbs of a mid-sized city somewhere in America

time

The present

[*A teenage boy's bedroom, which also resembles a cave. Interspersed with the realistic domestic elements are stylized stalactites and stalagmites. It is dark: the main sources of light seem to be a computer screen and several prospector's lamps on the floor. The walls have nothing on them. The room is cluttered with clothes and junk, piles of books and magazines, drawing pads, a suitcase, and several cardboard moving boxes. ROBBIE sits at his desk, on the computer with headphones on, raptly watching a music video. There's a knock at the door, but ROBBIE pretends not to hear it.*]

PATTI Robbie?

> [*Knocks.*]
>
> . . . Robbie!

[PATTI *opens the door and pokes her head in.*]

Robbie?

ROBBIE What are you . . . ? How did you . . . ?

PATTI You jiggle the handle—

ROBBIE You're not allowed in here.

[*He quickly puts his computer to sleep and gets up.*]

PATTI You have to help me.

ROBBIE [*"What is it?"*] What?

PATTI Can I come in?

ROBBIE [*About to drive her out.*] No.

PATTI But . . . But . . . I'M FREAKING OUT!

ROBBIE . . . You can come in for one minute. But don't touch anything.

[PATTI *comes in.*]

PATTI Thank you, Robbie. I really appreciate it.

[*Looking around.*]

. . . Aren't you gonna unpack?

[*He replies with an impatient look.*]

I know I get on your nerves, I know you think I'm really uncool.

[*Interrupts herself, and picks up a somewhat wadded tissue from a pile of stuff.*]

Can I use this?

ROBBIE No!

[*He grabs the tissue away from her and stuffs it in his pocket.*]

PATTI Do you have a tissue I could use?

ROBBIE Is that what you . . . ?

PATTI My nose is running, and I'll get that thing, where you'll be annoyed 'cause I'll be talking through the waterfall of phlegm.

[ROBBIE *looks around and unearths a roll of toilet paper, which he tosses to* PATTI.]

How come you have all that toilet paper? You getting allergies too?

ROBBIE Just blow your freakin' nose and tell me what's up.

[PATTI *blows her nose elaborately, seeming to lose herself in the task. Getting impatient.*]

Jesus!

[PATTI *suddenly bursts into tears.*]

. . . I mean . . . How much snot is in there?

PATTI I think my brains are coming out!

ROBBIE *What?*

PATTI I think my brains are coming out. Will you look?

[ROBBIE *stares at her incredulously.* PATTI *shows him the tissue.*]

I can't look.

[ROBBIE *glances at the tissue, then shakes his head derisively.*]

Is it . . . ?

ROBBIE It's snot, you idiot. . . . What the hell is going on?

PATTI You're gonna be mad. Please don't be mad. Ever since we moved here, you act like I'm invisible. You're always . . . locked up in here. What do you do in here?

ROBBIE What I do is none of your business. You shouldn't even think about it.

PATTI And this school is weird, isn't it? Don't you find the people there weird? You can't talk to them; they don't believe in conversation. What do they even care about?

ROBBIE They're rich kids. They care about what they can buy.

PATTI Yeah! Why are so many of 'em from Texas?

ROBBIE 'Cause their parents are all in the energy business.

PATTI [*Somewhat manic.*] All the places we've lived, I never heard kids talk like this. Like they think they're—executives, you know? They have multiple credit cards! Some even have lines of credit. I asked what a credit line was; they all laughed at me, like I was some kinda . . .

ROBBIE   Patti: what's going on?

PATTI   . . . Why do you smoke pot?

ROBBIE   I told you—

[*"What I do is none of your business."*]

PATTI   I smell it, I see it in your eyes, the way you talk to Mom and Dad. Does it help you? 'Cause . . .

[*Pause.* PATTI *takes deep breaths, fighting against panic.*]

ROBBIE   Did you . . . ?

    [PATTI *nods.*]

    You smoked? . . . Why?

PATTI   Because . . .

    [*Suddenly:*]

    It's so weird! I hate it. I hate myself. My voice . . . sounds like . . . a phlegm waterfall!

ROBBIE   [*Sort of comforting her.*] You're tripping.

PATTI   I don't wanna be tripping! How can you stand this? You gotta make it stop.

ROBBIE   What do you want me to . . . ?

PATTI   Make it stop!

ROBBIE   I, I, I don't know what you . . .

PATTI   Take my hand.

ROBBIE   Really?

PATTI   Just take it!

[*He does. Pause.*]

ROBBIE   Now what?

PATTI   I knew you'd help me.

ROBBIE   Where'd you get it?

PATTI   Please don't be mad.

[*Letting go of her hand,* ROBBIE *goes to his desk and opens a drawer, looks around inside.*]

ROBBIE   You took it from . . . ?

PATTI   Just a little bit.

ROBBIE   You just snuck in here and . . . ?

PATTI   You never let me / in.

ROBBIE   /went through my drawers? You little shit.

PATTI   You still have the coral we got in Bali. And the acorns we painted in Virginia?

[*Beat.*]

You don't really hate me . . . but why don't you like me?

ROBBIE   You always gotta stick your pudgy little pig fingers into anything that's mine! You are terminally weird! And you . . .

PATTI   You got all those pictures of Lisa Nova.

ROBBIE   [*She's crossed a line.*] Get outta here.

PATTI   [*Half-curiosity, half-provocative.*] What is she, like your cave woman? You drag her in by that bad hair?

[ROBBIE *grabs a tennis racquet.*]

ROBBIE   Patti: I mean it.

[PATTI *giggles.* ROBBIE *swings the racquet at her, narrowly missing her.*]

PATTI   [*Now serious.*] You . . . ! You coulda hurt me!

ROBBIE   Well, you asked for it. Now, get . . .

PATTI   But . . . !

ROBBIE   Out!

PATTI   [*Upset.*] You . . . You used to protect me!

ROBBIE   Walk around the house ten times. Deep breaths.

PATTI   Will you come with me?

ROBBIE   No!

PATTI You don't give a damn, do you?

ROBBIE Walk it off: You'll be fine. Go!

[PATTI *leaves.* ROBBIE *shuts the door. Then he walks around the room, trying to unwind. Then he goes to his drawer, takes out a photo torn from a magazine, and studies it for a moment.* LISA NOVA *appears from behind a stalagmite.* LISA *is a sophisticated teen pop star, perhaps dressed something like an emo model, in a tank top, torn jeans, and glasses.*]

LISA NOVA They just don't understand, do they?

ROBBIE They don't even know what it is they don't know.

LISA NOVA God, you're intense.

ROBBIE Come here.

[*She doesn't.*]

LISA NOVA How far down are we?

ROBBIE Twenty-two miles beneath the earth's crust.

LISA NOVA Wow . . . What's that sound?

ROBBIE The cascading of subterranean rivers.

LISA NOVA [*Suddenly worried.*] Could we drown?

ROBBIE Well, this vault's made of fortified titanium, but when you're this far down, anything's possible. You could scream your head off and no one would hear.

LISA NOVA Wow. Kinda scary.

ROBBIE Come here.

[*She hesitates. . . .*]

LISA NOVA Are my eyes really like renegade quasars?

ROBBIE Your eyes are different now. Blacker, deeper—underground pools.

LISA NOVA I can't believe I'm finally here with you. Are you really real?

ROBBIE Let me show you.

LISA NOVA Robert: Why do you think it is that no one else knows who you really are?

[*In the distance, faintly, under the next couple of speeches, we hear a strange rumbling sound.*]

ROBBIE I don't know. Maybe they're afraid of the new, and the strange? . . . I don't know!

[*Pause: perhaps for a moment he chews a cuticle. Then:*]

We work in the dark, as best we can, using our secret powers to light our way. Slashing through unseen enemies, moving boulders with sheer force of mind, and eventually . . .

LISA NOVA What's that sound?

ROBBIE [*Listens for a moment; then, covering his fear.*]

. . . The groaning of the earth, from all the lava.

LISA NOVA Don't you ever get scared?

ROBBIE I've got seismic sensors all over the place. As long as we track all the data—

[*Then we hear, from the other side of the door, a couple of weird whimpers.*]

LISA NOVA Is that . . . ? Is that Cerebus?

ROBBIE Cerebus?

LISA NOVA The creature that guards the entrance to the underworld. The hellhound!

[*Two more whimpers are heard. Then* ROBBIE *goes to the door, and* LISA NOVA *disappears.*]

ROBBIE [*Talking through the door.*] Patti? Is that you?

[*More whimpering.*]

. . . Could you please . . . do that somewhere else? I'm trying to work.

PATTI [*Through the door.*] You're so . . . freakin' . . . mean! . . . That time when we were little, in the deep end of the pool? You remember? . . . By mistake we let go of that float . . . we were floundering. Neither of us knew how to swim. And you used me to stay afloat. I coulda drowned! . . . But you don't give a damn.

[*We hear a couple of sobs.*]

ROBBIE Jesus!

[ROBBIE *opens the door.* PATTI *sits in the doorway on the floor.*]

What is your problem?

PATTI I'm high, and I don't like it.

ROBBIE Well, you shouldn'ta . . .

PATTI I know, I know; can I come in, please . . . *please?*

ROBBIE . . . Five minutes, that's it.

PATTI Thanks.

[PATTI *comes into the room.* ROBBIE *goes back to sit at his desk.*]

PATTI . . . I'm sorry I said that about Lisa Nova.

ROBBIE Forget it.

PATTI She's got some good songs. And I like her glasses.

ROBBIE I said, forget it.

PATTI This room is gonna be really cool. You're so lucky you don't have to be on the same floor as Mom and Dad. You can really hear things. Last night . . . she completely melted down. You know that green ceramic vase we got in Thailand? It's in a million pieces now. I think she threw it at him. Screaming she's gonna move back to Boston, start a photography studio, all these crazy plans you know she'll never do. And Dad says nothing. I know he's in there, but I never hear him.

[*Silence.* ROBBIE *looks distant.* LISA NOVA *appears by a stalagmite, looking at* ROBBIE. ROBBIE *looks at* LISA. PATTI *does not see her.*]

PATTI . . . Is it me? Is it something I put out?

ROBBIE What are you . . . ?

["*. . . talking about?*"]

PATTI Ever since I was eleven, you treat me like I'm some kind of cootie nightmare. But we're grown up now. So what's the problem? Just tell me, and I swear I won't bother you anymore.

ROBBIE You know what your problem is? You're too wrapped up in this family.

PATTI . . . What am I s'posed to do? I'm invisible! No one will talk to me. And you just sit in here, drawing stuff, getting high . . . What's gonna happen? What's gonna happen to this family?

[*Slight pause:* LISA NOVA *disappears. Then* ROBBIE *opens a drawer in his desk, takes out a can of Red Bull, and brings it to* PATTI.]

ROBBIE Drink this.

PATTI If I drink that, I'll break out in a substantial rash.

ROBBIE Then make some coffee.

PATTI I can't. . . . Coffee makes me . . .

ROBBIE What? The butt explosion?

PATTI It wasn't a . . . ! It causes problems.

ROBBIE Well, you need something.

PATTI Why?

ROBBIE 'Cause you're talking like . . .

PATTI Like Mom?

ROBBIE Like you need to come down a little.

PATTI Hold my hand?

[ROBBIE *looks away from her. It's too weird.*]

. . . Just for a minute, so I know I'm not invisible!

ROBBIE I don't want you ever coming in here again.

PATTI Unless you invite me, right?

ROBBIE Don't expect that.

PATTI [*Her hand:*] Please?

[*Still looking away from her,* ROBBIE *holds out his hand and she takes it.*]

Remember that monster canine in Phoenix? You used to take my hand when we had to walk by there. How come you're not afraid of anything?

ROBBIE I'm not afraid of my shadow.

PATTI It coulda had rabies. All that slobber, all over the sidewalk. Remember its eyes? But you didn't blink. You took my hand and we walked right past it. How do you . . . ?

ROBBIE Superpowers, of course.

PATTI . . . I'm afraid of my shadow. Late at night, if I get a drink of water, this shadow runs down the hall ahead of me. I'm not even sure it's my own shadow.

ROBBIE What else could it be?

PATTI Something that's . . . not me. Something like Mom; like mercury on a glass slide. You try to pin it down, it darts away. But it's always there; in front of me, or behind me . . .

[*Slight pause.*]

I feel like I've fallen into a hole. Just falling and falling. Bottomless . . . spiraling down, whirling—*whirling!*—no matter what I do, I keep falling. No one sees me. No one ever will. So I might as well just . . . !

ROBBIE [*Getting scared, but hiding it.*] . . . Let go.

PATTI Why?

[ROBBIE *pulls his hand away from hers and goes to a dark corner of the room to center himself. To cover his fear, he picks up a drawing pad and flips through it. PATTI watches him.*]

ROBBIE [*Covering.*] . . . Air-conditioning here sucks.

PATTI You ever feel like you're falling?

ROBBIE You'll get over it.

[*Pause.*]

PATTI Do you think Mom's lost her mind?

ROBBIE She's always been a little nuts . . .

PATTI She's out of control. Look around this house. We've been here a month, and it's like a tornado hit it. A twister. Our mom is like a twister. What if she blows this house away?

ROBBIE   I wouldn't worry about it.

PATTI   Why not? What happens when—?

ROBBIE   Patti: There's nothing we can do about it.

[*Pause.*]

PATTI   I could help you unpack.

ROBBIE   [*Reflexively.*] You're not allowed in here.

PATTI   *Why not?*

ROBBIE   . . . Because I'm trying to accomplish things.

PATTI   I could help you put up shelves . . . for your dinosaur collection.

ROBBIE   No thanks.

PATTI   . . . Probably wish you could run off with Lisa Nova, start a new family.

ROBBIE   [*Sarcastically.*] That's my plan.

PATTI   Or get really high with her . . . get wrecked, right? . . . and have sex with her.

ROBBIE   Do you have any concept of how weird you are?

PATTI   Yes. And now I know why you get high.

ROBBIE   [*Dismissively.*] Oh yeah?

PATTI   'Cause when you're looking out at the world from inside a cave, being weird isn't so horrible.

ROBBIE   . . . I'm not the weird one.

PATTI   Don't you wish you had like one friend?

ROBBIE   [*Lying.*] I've got friends.

[*Pause. For a couple seconds, from deep within the cave, we almost hear the sighing of the earth. It's mysterious and somewhat scary.*]

PATTI   The shadows in here are kinda cool. I bet that's why you keep those lamps on the floor. Makes the shadows so enormous. Like they could swallow us. They could swallow us and there wouldn't be a sound.

[*Silence.*]

ROBBIE Wanna hear a song?

PATTI . . . Sure.

[ROBBIE *goes to his computer, unplugs earphones, and brings up the link to the song. As he does this,* LISA NOVA *appears with a microphone, waiting.*]

ROBBIE Why don't you sit down. But don't touch anything.

[PATTI *sits on a milk crate or something. Then* ROBBIE *starts the song, and* LISA *sings, or recites over music.*]

LISA NOVA [*Singing:*]
Deep in the earth
There's a wild wild beast
You can't keep it down
No, you can't keep it down
'Cause it's cryin'
And it's sighing
For the long lost days
When it lived up above

PATTI I like it.

ROBBIE It's cool, right?

PATTI Yeah.

LISA NOVA [*Singing:*]
Let it sing
Let it howl
Let it go
Let it free!
Let it dream of the days
It can live up above

[ROBBIE *pretends to watch his computer screen.* PATTI *looks at* ROBBIE. *Lights fade.*]

• • •

Feathers

Judd Lear Silverman

Judd Lear Silverman

Judd Lear Silverman is a Brooklyn-based playwright/director/teacher, whose work has been seen across the country as well as in the Vancouver, London, and Edinburgh fringe festivals. Recent plays in addition to *Feathers* (Brooklyn's Gallery Players; Manhattan's Puzzle Theater Festival) include *A Shot at the Big Time* (Gallery Players; Clearwater, Florida's West Coast Players), *Recovery* (Edmonds Driftwood Theater, Washington), and *Form Follows Function* (Michigan's LowellArts!). A grant recipient from the Berrilla Kerr Foundation, he has been published by ArtAge Publications and in anthologies published by Samuel French, the Last Frontier Theatre Conference (through Focus Publications), and previously by Applause Theatre & Cinema Books in *Best American Short Plays 2011–2012*. A member of the Dramatists Guild as well as Charles Maryan's Playwrights/Directors Workshop, he currently teaches playwriting and English at Pace University in New York City.

···production history···

Feathers was developed in Charles Maryan's Playwrights/Directors Workshop in NYC (January 24, 2014), where MARIE was first read by Mollie Collison Wise and DANIEL was read by Jim Ireland. A subsequent public reading was presented by Piney Fork Press Theater (June 7, 2014), with MARIE and DANIEL read by Jane Titus and John Moss, respectively. Its premiere production was presented at Brooklyn's Gallery Players (May 28–30, 2015), directed by Sara Lampert Hoover, featuring Rachel Marcus and David Carlson, which was shortly followed by a public reading as part of the Puzzle Festival at the Marble Collegiate Church in NYC (June 16 and 19, 2015), where it was read by Emily and Derrick Begin under the direction of Justin Bennett.

characters

> MARIE
> DANIEL   her husband

[MARIE *stands, sobbing, looking off into the distance. She waves for a moment, then slowly lowers her hand. Her husband,* DANIEL, *enters, stunned by her demeanor.*]

DANIEL   Honey . . . what is it?

MARIE   She's gone.

DANIEL   What? Who's gone?

MARIE   Becca. She's gone.

DANIEL   What do you mean, she's gone?

MARIE   She flew away.

[*Pause.*]

DANIEL   She flew away?

MARIE   She flew away.

DANIEL   That's not possible.

> [*Pause.*]

> How do you mean, she flew away?

MARIE She spread her wings and . . .

DANIEL Her wings? Sweetie, she doesn't have wings.

MARIE She has wings.

DANIEL She may be our angel, but . . .

MARIE She has wings!

DANIEL Okay. She has wings.

MARIE Don't you remember? That time when she was a baby, that protrusion . . .

DANIEL You mean, when we thought she had an infection . . .

MARIE And we took her to the hospital . . .

DANIEL Awful thing, on her neck, looked like a really bad pimple or something . . .

MARIE And they didn't know what it was, and then . . .

DANIEL That string-like emergence . . .

MARIE And the doctor pulled out . . .

DANIEL A feather! I remember. They thought she must have swallowed it somehow and it was working its way out of her body. Which makes sense . . .

MARIE But what if that wasn't what it was?

DANIEL It was a feather.

MARIE No, I know that. I mean, what if it wasn't just a freak accident, an ingested feather the body rejected. What if it was . . .

DANIEL What?

MARIE Part of her. A part of her.

DANIEL It never happened again.

MARIE That we know of. That we know of, Daniel.

DANIEL We wouldn't know?

MARIE Did you tell your parents everything? She was so shy and private as a teenager. Surly, sometimes.

DANIEL Every teen gets grumpy, impossible.

MARIE She wouldn't let me in the dressing room with her when she tried on clothes.

DANIEL No one wants their mother in the dressing room, do they?

[*Pause.*]

Besides, I would have known.

MARIE What?

DANIEL I would have known. I'm her father.

MARIE What's that supposed to mean?

DANIEL Girls and their dads . . . have a bond.

MARIE She could have told me!

DANIEL Things they can't tell their mothers! You were a daughter.

MARIE My daddy was remote.

DANIEL But weren't there things—

MARIE What?

DANIEL That you wanted to tell your father but that you didn't want to tell your mother.

MARIE I guess.

[*Pause.*]

Still . . .

DANIEL What?

MARIE I think I would have known before if our daughter had wings!

DANIEL Right.

[*Pause.*]

Right. So would I.

MARIE So how come we didn't . . . ?

DANIEL I—wait, I didn't say that she did. You did.

MARIE She just said good-bye and flew off. Out there. Towards the horizon.

[*Pause.*]

She didn't pack enough clothing.

DANIEL She was flying with a suitcase?

MARIE No. She had nothing but her wings.

DANIEL Well, she'd have to travel light, I should think.

[*Pause.*]

Are you sure—

MARIE She was as real and present as you are. She had these beautiful . . . wings, sprouting from her shoulder blades. And the feathers were all sparkly. You would have been so proud. She embraced me, she enshrouded me in her winged embrace, and then she turned towards the sun, feathers glistening, and she spread her arms outward, and then . . .

DANIEL And then?

MARIE She flew away.

DANIEL Did she say anything?

MARIE Well, the usual I love yous and such. At least, I think she did. Not sure if I actually heard it or if she said it or if I just felt it.

DANIEL And what did you say?

MARIE "Will we hear from you?"

DANIEL And she said . . .

MARIE "I will always be in touch."

[*Pause.*]

She was so graceful. Ethereal, sort of. And her skin was so pale, it was almost translucent—like one of those beautiful statues from the renaissance, solid but seemingly lit from within. And yet also soft, not cold to the touch.

DANIEL She let you hold her.

MARIE No. She enveloped me, but I can't say we actually touched. But she was . . . radiant.

DANIEL I'll bet.

[Pause.]

She flew away. And I didn't even get a chance to say good-bye.

MARIE She had to go. She sent you her love.

DANIEL It's not the same.

[*Pause.*]

She flew away without saying good-bye.

MARIE Well, it wasn't any easier being here to watch her fly off, let me tell you.

DANIEL Dammit, Marie, didn't it even occur to you to call out to me? I was only in the next room. . . .

MARIE It happened so quickly, it was a momentary thing, there wasn't time, I had no voice, there was nothing to say, I . . .

DANIEL You left me out!

MARIE Don't blame me. It was her moment to go. I had nothing to do with it. It wasn't my choice.

[*Pause.*]

I doubt she meant to hurt you. At that moment, it seemed like there wasn't really a cruel bone in her body.

DANIEL She could be mean when she wanted to be.

MARIE All kids can be mean sometimes. But in that moment, I think she was the furthest she's ever been from being mean.

DANIEL Still, I would have liked to have been there. To have been a part of that moment.

MARIE Mothers and daughters have their moments, too, Daniel.

DANIEL I won't forgive her.

MARIE You must. You will.

DANIEL We'll see.

[*Pause.*]

She won't, you know.

MARIE What?

DANIEL Always be in touch.

MARIE You think she was lying?

DANIEL No. It's just that—they always think they'll be in touch, but they never are.

[*Pause.*]

MARIE You'd have been so proud of her.

DANIEL I am.

MARIE Are you?

DANIEL I am.

[*Pause.*]

She won't be back.

MARIE You don't think?

DANIEL No. Not really.

MARIE That would be a shame.

DANIEL It's how it works, I guess. Who'd come back to earth when you can fly out there in the clouds?

MARIE She's got to come back sometime, doesn't she?

DANIEL No. Once you have wings—

MARIE It's not fair.

DANIEL Fuck fair. It is. It just is.

[*Pause.*]

Come inside. You've had a shock. I'll make you something.

MARIE No. I mean, I want to. I feel cold somehow. But I feel like I can't move from this spot. The spot from which . . .

DANIEL She flew away.

[*Pause.*]

Do you wish . . .

MARIE What?

DANIEL She had taken you with her?

MARIE I hadn't thought about it. Do you?

DANIEL Maybe. Maybe so. I'm not sure.

MARIE [*Pause.*] I suppose we're too old now.

DANIEL We're not old.

MARIE We're not old. But we are too old to fly away. At least with her.

DANIEL Yes.

[*Pause.*]

But did she get it from us?

MARIE She must have. She had to have gotten it from somewhere.

DANIEL Because that should mean we too can fly. Or could have.

MARIE Perhaps.

DANIEL Isn't that curious? I dreamed about it sometimes. But I never thought I could. Did you?

MARIE No. Not that I recall. Not that I didn't want to leave from time to time.

DANIEL Fly the coop?

MARIE In a manner of speaking. Spread my wings, perhaps.

DANIEL That would have been an amazing moment, wouldn't it? To feel the wind under you, that you could do almost . . .

MARIE Anything!

[*Pause.*]

But the moment has passed. Thank God at least one of us flew.

[*Pause.*]

It's such a big sky.

DANIEL Yes, it is.

MARIE Such a big . . .

DANIEL Unfathomable.

MARIE Yes.

[*Pause.*]

Tea.

DANIEL What?

MARIE You offered to make me something, I believe.

DANIEL Oh.

MARIE I feel like I need something normal. Earthbound. To anchor me.

DANIEL I already feel anchored. Tethered.

MARIE Tied down?

DANIEL No cement overshoes. Just not . . . airborne.

[*Pause.*]

Do you think that feather was a sign? Back then?

MARIE Who knows? I suppose there were signs all along.

DANIEL Probably.

[MARIE *takes a last look over her shoulder, while* DANIEL *looks off into the distance.*]

MARIE Well, if you're not going to make that tea, I'm going to. It's getting cold out here, anyway.

[*Pause.*]

Do you want some?

DANIEL Uh . . . sure.

MARIE Aren't you coming in?

DANIEL   I'll be there in a minute.

MARIE   Don't be long.

[*Pause.*]

And don't go getting any ideas. I still need you down here.

[DANIEL *doesn't respond but looks off into the distance.* MARIE *takes one more look, smiles, goes inside.* DANIEL *stares off into the distance.*]

• • •

The Gulf

Audrey Cefaly

Audrey Cefaly

Audrey Cefaly is a Southern playwright and director whose work often draws inspiration from her home state of Alabama. Her writing is finely tuned to the voices and colorful stories of working-class people and seeks to explore the human condition with a darkly comic style. Her play *Fin & Euba* won the Strawberry One-Act Festival and is published in *Best American Short Plays 2004–2005* (Applause Books). She is currently working on the full-length adaptation of *The Gulf*, which was a finalist for Ensemble Studio Theatre's Marathon of One-Act Plays and winner of the 40th Annual Samuel French Off-Off-Broadway Short Play Festival. Cefaly directed the world premiere of her Southern drama *Maytag Virgin* for Quotidian Theatre Company in the fall of 2015 as part of the inaugural Women's Voices Theater Festival. She is a recipient of the Maryland State Arts Council's Individual Artist Award and a member of the Dramatists Guild.

··· production history ···

The Gulf received its world premiere in 2010 as part of the Silver Spring Stage One-Act Festival:

BETTY   Erika Imhoof

KENDRA   Audrey Cefaly

It received its New York debut in 2015, where it won the 40th Annual Samuel French Off-Off-Broadway Short Play Festival:

BETTY   Effie Johnson

KENDRA   Carolyn Messina

gulf (*noun*)
a portion of an ocean or sea partly enclosed by land;
a deep hollow, chasm, or abyss;
any wide separation, as in position, status, or education;
something that engulfs or swallows up

[*On a quiet summer evening, somewhere down in the Alabama Delta,* KENDRA *and* BETTY *troll the flats looking for red fish.* KENDRA *slowly reels in the line while* BETTY *lays with her feet in* KENDRA'S *lap, reading* What Color Is Your Parachute: A Practical Manual for Job-Hunters and Career Changers. KENDRA *sighs. . . .*]

BETTY   What?

KENDRA   Nothin but rats.

BETTY   Huh?

KENDRA   Man . . . some *scrawny* rat reds tonight . . .

BETTY   Kinda bait are you using?

KENDRA   Baby, if the fish ain't bitin it ain't 'cuz of the bait. It's 'cuz they ain't there.

BETTY   Wan' go somewhere else?

KENDRA   Nope.

BETTY   Rosella was talking about over by Bottle Creek.

KENDRA Bottle Creek?

BETTY I told her we were comin' out here.

[*Beat.*]

She was bein' helpful.

KENDRA Rosella has no idea about fishin' and therefore Rosella is not helpful.

BETTY What's wrong with Bottle Creek? Can't fish in Bottle Creek?

KENDRA Yeah, for boots and dead bodies.

BETTY I thought there was good fishin' there.

KENDRA Well, there was, but not no more.

BETTY How come?

KENDRA B. P. Fuckers

BETTY B.P.?

KENDRA That shit got in . . . choked it.

BETTY Aw, shit . . .

[*Beat.*]

You know . . . you got the whole Gulf of Mexico to fish in, we always end up here.

KENDRA What are you sayin'?

BETTY Right here in the shallows, every time.

KENDRA That's the whole point.

BETTY I don't get it.

KENDRA Exactly.

BETTY What?

KENDRA That's where the—never mind.

BETTY No, tell me. Please.

KENDRA Fish in the shallows, 'cuz that's where the fish are.

[*Beat.*]

Reds like to fight, Betty, they fight . . . deep, shallow, whatever, any water. But in the shallows, they get more traction, see, the fight is bigger . . . more fun . . .

BETTY For you, maybe.

[*Beat.*]

KENDRA When did you talk to Rosella . . .

BETTY Last night . . .

[*Beat.*]

It's warm, idn't it? I might hop in for a swim if I didn't think the gators would get me.

KENDRA Assuming they'd want you.

[BETTY *returns to reading her book.*]

BETTY [*Off* KENDRA's *look.*] What?

KENDRA Nothin'.

BETTY Why can't I do what I want to do? You're doin' your thing.

KENDRA Fishin' boat, not a library.

BETTY I could fish if I wanted to, I ain't in the mood.

[*Beat.*]

I know how to fish. I do!

KENDRA When did you ever fish?

BETTY When I was little. Caught my first fish when I was eight years old. It counts! It does! Stop it, stop laughin'.

KENDRA What'd you catch?

BETTY Sun fish.

KENDRA Sun fish?

BETTY Little ole sun fish. Daddy said to me, Now Betty, the rule is . . . you catch it, you gotta clean it. And then I found out what cleaning was and I thought I don't want to have nothin' to do with that.

KENDRA So what'd you do?

BETTY I just put him in the well, there, under the boat . . . laid there watchin' him. I can't do it. I can't do what you do. You . . . gut those fish wide open like it's nothin'. That catfish last week, his little heart just floppin' all over the boat, why you reckon it does that?

[*Beat.*]

You caught that fish, took out the *insides*, the heart is just layin' there, it's still beatin', Kendra. The fuck . . . why'st do that?

KENDRA [*Playfully.*] 'Cuz it loves me. Even in death it loves me.

[BETTY *swats* KENDRA's *ass with the book.*]

It's what I got, I can't help it.

[*Beat.*]

So what'd you do with him?

BETTY Who?

KENDRA Sun fish.

BETTY Oh . . . umn . . . I just picked him up by his tail and put him back in the water. He didn't move none at first, he just laid there, like he was dead or somethin'. I put my little finger on him and he made a ruckus and swam off. Back to his family.

KENDRA *Back to his family.*

BETTY His family—whatever—you're bein' mean!

KENDRA I ain't bein' mean. You always think I'm bein' mean, I'm just listenin'.

[*Beat.*]

BETTY *Whatever.*

KENDRA Oh, here we go . . . look at this asshole . . .

BETTY Who is it?

KENDRA Oh my god. Will you look at that? What kinda dumbass comes out to fish the flats in a shit-tub like that . . .

KENDRA [*Tries to make out whose boat it is. Calling.*] Duke?! What the fuck are you drivin', man, you just got paid or what? I'm sure the fish love it, they be floatin' up dead at the sight of it.

[*To* BETTY.]

Stupid fuck.

[*To Duke.*]

Man . . . you know what? You can make fun of my coon-ass boat package all you want, but we'll see who's up by the end of the night, won't we? You should try up by Bottle Creek . . .

BETTY [*Overlapping.*] Kendra!

KENDRA [*Continuing.*] Oh, hell yeah. Red fish, gars, trout, whatever, fulla surprises, that Bottle Creek.

[*Beat.*]

Would I lie to you? Move along, Duke, you're spookin' my fish . . .

[*To* BETTY.]

Say good-bye, Betty.

[*They lazily shoot the bird at Duke as his boat rides by.* KENDRA *notices Thelma in the back of the boat. To Thelma.*]

Hey, Thelma!

[KENDRA *turns to see that* BETTY *has pulled out a small picnic basket and is assembling some fancy fixings for a snack.*]

KENDRA What the fuck is all that?

BETTY [*Defensively.*] This is all the same food that you eat every other day of the week, only today it is newly configured into this creative combination for our little fishing excursion.

KENDRA You gon' answer my question?

BETTY Tapenade.

KENDRA *Tapenade.*

BETTY Olive tapenade. Garlic, capers, basil, lemon. All chopped up.

KENDRA Okay, so . . . olives?

[*They glare at each other, as if in a stand-off.* BETTY *holds up another option.* . . .]

BETTY Canapé.

KENDRA That is not a can-a-paint or whatever the fuck word you're sayin', that there is a Ritz cracker with some kind of bullshit green distraction, something like a Vienna [pron: *Vai-yee-ner*] sausage and a snot drop of Cheez Whiz on top.

BETTY Snot drop? That's disgusting.

[*Beat.*]

Are you serious right now? You know what, you remind me of like some kind of Neanderthal cave man except without any of the social skills. Actually, I take that back. You are like a Neanderthal cave man with just enough social skills to kind of blend into your *sewage plant* surroundings, but I would say even that is a little bit of a stretch.

[*Beat.*]

Hello?

[KENDRA *busily digs into the cooler for another beer.*]

I don't even know why I bother . . .

[BETTY *starts packing up the food.*]

. . . try to educate you . . . broaden your horizons, and you are basically a twelve-year-old boy.

[*Beat.*]

What are you doing?

KENDRA [*Busily doing something else.*] I am over here not giving a fuck about anything coming out of your mouth.

[*Beat.*]

BETTY Do you listen to yourself when you talk? Do you hear the things you say or—you know what, forget it.

[BETTY *begins to pack the food back up.*]

For the record, Kendra . . . that there is andouille sausage, or maybe you've heard of it, *arugula* and fucking aged Wisconsin cheddar, which looks nothing like the barbaric mutation that is Cheez Whiz.

Because A, it's not melted, and B, it's just sitting there, not melted. If it was Cheez Whiz—which it NEVER WILL BE—it would look a little different, now wouldn't it? It would look . . .

KENDRA [*Overlapping—deadpan.*] Like a snot blob?

[*Beat.*]

BETTY You see me here holding this piece of cheese, Kendra? This is my kryptonite. I am immune to you and all of your mean-spirited mental terroristics.

[BETTY *pops the piece of cheese into her mouth. She stares at* KENDRA *defiantly as she chews it.*]

KENDRA That's your kryptonite?

BETTY Yep.

KENDRA You're ingesting your own kryptonite?

BETTY Yep.

KENDRA Just checkin'.

BETTY [*Regarding the cheese.*] God-damn that's good.

[BETTY *pulls out her book and resumes reading. Beat.*]

KENDRA [*Under her breath.*] Oh, good. That's good. Let's read a book. Let's all read a book.

BETTY [*Reading aloud from the book.*] *"Theoretically, you could be just as happy as a garbage collector."*

[*To* KENDRA.]

They have the least amount of stress as any job, you know that? I read that someplace. And think about it. What do they have to be stressed about anyway, except maybe, you know, some maggots and dead rats and whatnot?

KENDRA I don't know.

BETTY And you know what . . . I bet after a couple weeks even the maggots would just be routine, whaddya reckon? Alright, now here is a list of possible occupations, however, this is in no way—here it says—"no way intended to be a definitive list, but more a list of suggestions based upon your core competencies and desires."

KENDRA Hand me that push pole, baby.

[BETTY *hands her the push pole. Annoyed.*]

BETTY [*Beat.*] I'll just read the list.

KENDRA [*Seriously annoyed.*] Please.

BETTY [*Reading.*] Prison guard.

[*Beat.*]

KENDRA Prison guard?

BETTY Yep.

KENDRA [*Incredulous.*] You added my whole life up on that worksheet there and that's what came out?

BETTY I may have added a few ideas of my own.

KENDRA Like prison guard . . .

BETTY Yeah, like prison guard, yes, like a lotta things, are you gonna keep an open mind or maybe we'll just quit all this, how bout that? This book *helped me*, K. It's how come I know what I wanna be now, and before I was just driftin' around and whatnot.

KENDRA Good for you.

[*Beat.*]

BETTY Are you jealous of me?

KENDRA [*Increasingly frustrated.*] Could we be more different? I wonder.

BETTY Well, what does that mean?

KENDRA Look, this is *your dream*, not mine, this *social working* whatever, and I want you to go to school. I do. I'm proud of you . . .

BETTY [*Overlapping.*] Why won't you come with me?

KENDRA We have been through this.

BETTY It's junior college, not forever.

KENDRA Exactly.

BETTY Well, I don't like the idea of us bein' apart, do you? Hello?

KENDRA What?

BETTY You gotta see the world sometime. What are you gonna do, fish the rest of your life?

KENDRA Well, I don't know, is it on the list? Why do I need a parachute, anyway? What the fuck is that?

BETTY It's not an *actual* parachute.

KENDRA Just a pretend parachute.

BETTY [*Annoyed.*] It's a metaphor. Do you remember me tellin' you that about twenty minutes ago?

KENDRA Uh . . . I think I'd remember a pretend parachute.

BETTY Well, I guess so, especially when you're stuck somewhere *without* it!
[*Digging in.*]
Welder. Mechanic. Dairy Queen manager. That was a test . . . to see if you were listenin', are you listenin'?

KENDRA [*Overlapping.*] Yes, god, yes!

BETTY Wedding planner.

KENDRA Fuck off!

BETTY Mortician.
[*Beat.*]
What?

KENDRA Mortician?

BETTY You can thank me for that one.

KENDRA Mortician?

BETTY Only because I know how much you like dead people.
[KENDRA *stares at* BETTY *as if she has three heads.*]

That's how come you watch that show all the time, with the "Y" incision.

KENDRA Dr. G is not a mortician, Betty. Dr. G is a medical examiner for the city of Orlando—that's a good one, actually, medical examiner, write that down—and I don't watch that show for the dead people, okay, I told you that.

BETTY [*Flirtatiously.*] Have you got a crush on Dr. G?

KENDRA Just write it down!

[BETTY *freezes for a moment, processing something in her head, as if someone retracing their steps.*]

BETTY [*Trance-like.*] Oh, shoot. I got that kryptonite thing backwards, huh?

KENDRA Yep.

BETTY Shit.

[BETTY *notices* KENDRA's *knife laying nearby. She picks it up and turns it over in her hands, caressing the blade.* KENDRA *is wildly aroused by this. . . .*]

KENDRA You gon' cut me open?

BETTY I was thinkin' about it . . .

KENDRA Let's do it.

BETTY [*Staring at the blade.*] How long does a fish heart keep beatin' after you . . . ya know . . .

KENDRA 3.2 seconds.

BETTY 3.2 seconds?

KENDRA I don't know, Betty! I never counted, Jesus Christ with the fish hearts!

BETTY Don't be mean.

KENDRA I'm not bein' mea—stop trippin'—give me the knife!
[*Beat.*]
I want you to stop thinkin'.

BETTY Why?

KENDRA Because when you think, I'm miserable!

BETTY Why won't you think about it? You been sayin' you need a change, you been sayin' you hate it here.

KENDRA It's just talk.

BETTY No it ain't.

KENDRA It's only one hundred miles away, Betty. What's the big deal anyway?

BETTY Well, it just seems to me you ain't happy and maybe this could be a shot at something different, something good.

KENDRA Could we move on, please, to some topic I give a shit about? I ain't gon' choose my calling offa some list you got from a self-help book.

BETTY This is a career-path *workbook*, Kendra. What color is *your* parachute?

KENDRA Red.

BETTY It is not red. It is not at all red, and if you had been listenin', you would know that. We are on chapter nine, Kendra. *Geography of the Heart.*

KENDRA Is that the last chapter? I sure hope it is.

BETTY [*Overlapping.*] You are being obtuse.

KENDRA Absolutely, I'm being obtuse . . .

BETTY [*Overlapping.*] Do you even know what that means . . .

KENDRA I would *love* to know what that means!

BETTY It means somebody who is smarter than hell, but who is set on pretending to be dumber than shit so maybe nothing is ever expected of 'em and then they don't have to do anything but sit around and fish for all eternity. How's that sound?

KENDRA [*Long pause. Deadpan.*] Is that a trick question?

BETTY Do you have a plan? For your future?

KENDRA Will you stop?

BETTY Do you?

KENDRA I had a plan. Yeah. I had a plan to do a little drum fishing, maybe catch a bull red or two and not have to deal with ridiculous questions and psychotic-analysis, how's that for a plan?!

BETTY [*Overlapping.*] I will never understand you.

KENDRA Thank god for that!

BETTY Open . . . your mind!

KENDRA To what?

BETTY The future.

KENDRA I have a job.

BETTY That's not a job . . .

[KENDRA *turns a steely gaze toward* BETTY.]

You work at a sewage plant.

KENDRA Oh, and your job is saving lives, I guess. Is that it?

BETTY Well, yeah, actually, it is, if you wanna know. I do save a life . . . from time to time. Jenny Pelligrin gave me some of her nitro pills to keep under the bar, just yesterday afternoon, in case she ever goes into cardiac arrest. I keep a box of condoms under there . . . Trojans . . . for Bobby Lee, right next to the margarita mix and the rock salt. Swear to god, it's a damn pharmacy under there. You wouldn't believe the shit I see. These folks, they come in there . . . half of 'em want to get laid, half of 'em want to get drunk, and the other half just need to talk. And it ain't in my job description, but I do it, 'cuz that's what bartenders do . . . they listen. I listen to 'em and you know what I hear?

[KENDRA *stares at* BETTY *in response.*]

Desperation. Quiet desperation. So quiet, only dogs can hear. In the eyes, the shaky voice. Starin' down at the ice cubes in the glass, like readin' tea leaves or some shit. I pour 'em one on the house, I look 'em square in the eye, and I ask 'em the same thing I'm askin' you.

[*Beat.*]

Oh, come on, K, can't you open your mind and think about it. I mean, is it really that hard to imagine? No, seriously. If you could be anything at all in the whole wide world, what would it be?

KENDRA Alone.

BETTY Oh, shut up. You couldn't be alone no more than I could. You can't even sleep with the light off.

KENDRA I'm afraid of the dark now, is that it?

BETTY Afraid of somethin' . . .

KENDRA [*Overlapping.*] Oh my god!

BETTY You sleep with the light on . . . you fish in the shallows . . .

KENDRA And you speak Chinese, the fuck are you talking about? I'm . . . I'm afraid to live or some shit?

BETTY Maybe. Maybe you are.

KENDRA And you don't know how to sit still, how about that? Nothing's ever good enough for you, is it? We came out here to *fish*. But you never fish, Betty.

BETTY Yes, I do.

KENDRA [*Overlapping.*] You don't. And you don't want to learn, either, you just want to sit there with your books and your papers and what not, and rearrange *my life* to make it fit yours in some magical futuristic happy place that exists—where? I don't know, in your mind, maybe? Meanwhile, I'm doin' it. I'm taking part in the miraculousness of life, Betty. REAL LIFE. Where folks catch fish, rip their FUCKING guts out and then eat 'em. And they don't think twice about it and you wanna know why? 'Cuz it's just FISHIN'!

BETTY Do you love me?

KENDRA [*A warning.*] I'm 'on lose it.

BETTY Do you?

[*Inching closer and closer to* KENDRA.]

Sex ed teacher . . . *underwear model* . . . *massage therapist.*

KENDRA Yes. I love you.

BETTY I love you too.

[*They kiss.* KENDRA *pulls open the folds of* BETTY'*s blouse to kiss her neck.*]

KENDRA You smell like roses . . .

BETTY Mmn . . .

KENDRA Wait.

BETTY God, I love you.

KENDRA What is that?

BETTY What?

KENDRA What's that smell?

[*Beat.*]

I fuckin' knew it.

BETTY K . . .

KENDRA You been up to Butler County, hadn't you? You been down there with her? And now you're sittin' here with me, parachute bullshit trying to straighten out my fucking life. That is some fantastic shit.

BETTY I was puttin' an end to it.

KENDRA In person? God. FUCK! I'm such an asshole.

BETTY It's not what you think.

KENDRA [*Mimicking.*] *I've changed, K, I've changed.*

BETTY I have.

KENDRA Oh, please. You are still the same slut I met at Mardi Gras.

BETTY Yeah, well, you took to it pretty quick as I recall.

KENDRA What are you gonna do, Betty?

BETTY About what?

KENDRA About your fucking life! You can't keep that shit locked up for two seconds? Howlin' all over town like some bitch in heat. And you stink too, Betty, by the way. You need some feminine hygiene. All our time together, six years I gave you, took you back, took the BITCH back, WHY? Why the fuck did I . . . junior college? I'm gon' pack up my shit and go with you to junior college?! That is fuckin' hilarious. I'm done. I am beyond done.

[KENDRA *grabs* BETTY's *backpack.* BETTY *reaches to take it from her.*]

LEAVE IT! Leave it.

[*Menacing.*]

Get outta the boat.

BETTY K . . .

KENDRA Get. Out. Of the boat.

[*Beat.*]

What?! What the hell do you want from me? Can't you tell I hate you? Can't you tell I hate your fat ass?!

BETTY No you don't.

KENDRA Oh, I do! I do! You are killing me. I want you to go. I want you to just get your shit and go . . . PLEASE. I can't do this no more. You wanna know the truth? I'm glad you're going to Bay Minette. I'm glad you're leaving. I been wanting you to leave since July! You are bad for me . . . you are bad for my soul, Betty.

[KENDRA *starts throwing* BETTY's *things overboard.*]

BETTY K, please, stop, stop . . .

KENDRA Out . . . get out . . . out, out, out . . . .

BETTY K! I love you!

[KENDRA *looks at* BETTY *a moment and then violently pushes her overboard.*]

KENDRA OUT!

[KENDRA *grabs whatever she can find and begins throwing it all at* BETTY, *who is floundering in the shallows behind the boat.*]

OUT, out, out! And take this psycho-shit with you. Maybe there's a chapter in there about skanks and the morons that love 'em.

[KENDRA *throws the book overboard.*]

Where's that parachute now, BITCH?! That ought to break ya, huh? Egg-suckin' dog.

[KENDRA *collapses, exhausted, into a heap inside the boat.*]

Damn Betty. You wear me out!

[*Long silence. The soaking wet book flies back into the boat.* KENDRA *sees this in her peripheral vision, but pretends not to notice. A hand reaches up and grabs the side of the boat, then another, then a foot, as* BETTY *crawls back in. Silence.*]

BETTY   Kendra . . .

KENDRA   [*A lifeless syllable.*] Hmn.

BETTY   I think maybe you have some pent-up hostility toward me.

KENDRA   How'd you guess that?

BETTY   I'm sorry, K.

KENDRA   [*Barely a whisper.*] Why do you do it?

BETTY   What?

KENDRA   Why do you do it?

BETTY   I wish I knew. I ain't never been any other way. I could never understand it myself 'til that time my cousin told me I had codependence. And then I started to think on it and that's when I realized maybe she was right 'cuz it did seem like I had somethin' wrong with me to where I always needed somebody, you know, like the thought of being by myself was . . . do you hate me?

KENDRA   [*Numb.*] Yeah.

[*Childlike,* BETTY *rather shakily situates herself in the boat and leans back to look up at the night sky.*]

BETTY   One fish, two fish, red fish, blue fish. This one has a little star, this one has a little car, say, what a lot of fish there are.

[*Beat.*]

You ever set and think about your life in reverse . . . like back to that second when it was all just exactly the way you dreamt it could be?

KENDRA   No.

BETTY   You walked into the Judge Roy Bean's on Fat Tuesday. 'Member that? I was sittin' there at the bar and I looked up and saw you . . . holy shit. Leather jacket . . . snake-skin boots. Thirty pounds of Mardi Gras beads hanging off that rack of yours. How'd you get all them beads anyway?

KENDRA   Offa some Baylor boys . . .

BETTY   Baylor?

KENDRA   I just went up to a group of Baylor boys and I asked real nice.

BETTY   What you say?

KENDRA   Hand 'em over.

BETTY   And they just gave 'em up, huh. Just like that.

KENDRA   Yep.

BETTY   Out of the kindness of their hearts.

KENDRA   [*Overlapping.*] Yep.

BETTY   You had your tits out, didn't ya?

KENDRA   All the way out.

BETTY   You flashed 'em good, didn't ya? I'm surprised they didn't go blind.

KENDRA   Few of 'em did.

BETTY   That was it for me. That night. I knew I'd never love nobody like you. And I hadn't. All these years.

KENDRA   I just wish I was enough.

BETTY You are.

KENDRA You are so ridiculous.

BETTY What?

KENDRA That's the difference between us. You ain't never gon' be happy with me.

BETTY I—

KENDRA No. Face it.

[*Beat.*]

We gotta go . . .

BETTY Go where?

[BETTY *touches* KENDRA'*s hand.* . . .]

You've always had the prettiest hands. . . .

[*Beat.*]

I feel like we're disappearin' . . .

KENDRA Shhhhhh. Let's just set here for a while. Tide starts movin' . . . we'll catch a few.

[*Beat.*]

I'm sorry about what I said . . .

BETTY About what?

KENDRA Feminine hygiene.

BETTY Oh.

KENDRA You smell good to me.

[*Beat.*]

BETTY 3.2 seconds . . .

KENDRA I just made that up.

BETTY I know you did. But . . . how long, though. if you had to guess . . . how long before it stops.

KENDRA Maybe a minute. . . .

BETTY A whole minute? Wow. Does it just stop or does it slow down and then stop.

KENDRA Slows down a bit.

BETTY Why does it do that . . .

KENDRA What's that?

BETTY Why does it keep beating like that . . .

[*Beat.*]

KENDRA Habit.

[*Silence.* KENDRA *drinks down the last drop of her beer and tosses her can into the corner of the boat.* KENDRA *casts her line once more into the shallows.* BETTY *opens her book and reads aloud.*]

BETTY Pet psychic. Meter maid. Dental hygienist.

• • •

Winning

Mercilee Jenkins

For Bala

Mercilee Jenkins

Mercilee Jenkins is an award-winning playwright, poet, and fiction writer. Her one-act play *50 Love Letters* premiered in New York in 2015. Her full-length play *Spirit of Detroit* was produced in Detroit in 2014 and premiered at the University of Michigan the previous year. Earlier productions include *Dangerous Beauty: Love in the Age of Earthquakes and AIDS, A Credit to Her Country, The Two-Bit Tango, Menopause and Desire or 452 Positions on Love,* and *She Rises Like a Building to the Sky.* Jenkins is a winner of Poets 11, the San Francisco citywide poetry contest. Her short story "The Day Mel Tormé Died" was published in the anthology *Sisters Born, Sisters Found.* She has received playwriting grants from the Horizons Foundation, the Zellerbach Family Foundation, the San Francisco Arts Commission, and the California Institute for Contemporary Art. She is Professor Emerita in Communication and Performance Studies at San Francisco State University.

···production history···

Winning was a winner of the Redwood Writers Annual Play Contest and Festival, which was produced at 6th Street Playhouse in Santa Rosa, California, May 15–25, 2014: Festival Director, Lennie Dean. The play was directed by Maureen Studer. The cast, in order of appearance, was as follows:

JUNE   Elizabeth Henry

LESLIE   Dana Nelson-Isaacs

Winning was also a winner of the 20th Annual Actors Theatre 10-Minute Play Contest and produced at Center Street Theater, Santa Cruz, at the 8 Tens @ 8 Festival, January 9–February 8, 2015: Artistic Director, Wilma Marcus Chandler; Producer, Bonnie Ronzio. The play was directed by Ian McRae, festival set design by Skip Epperson, lighting design by Sully Taylor, and sound design by Davis Banta.

JUNE   Ruth Elliot

LESLIE   Deborah Bryant

characters

JUNE   a female, 40s, has had recurring bouts of cancer since she was in her early 20s, so she handles it as almost routine and wants no sympathy or pity.

LESLIE   a female, 40s, close friend of June's.

[JUNE *and Andy's home, where their friends have gathered for their annual Academy Awards viewing party.* JUNE *is alone in her bedroom, onstage, sitting on the bed watching TV surrounded by fluffy pillows, a soft down comforter. She is smoking and using the remote control to mute commercials and comment on the action. Sounds of the party going on in the living room and kitchen can be heard intermittently throughout the scene.* LESLIE *knocks at the door.*]

JUNE   Come in at your own risk

[LESLIE *enters with glass of red wine.*]

LESLIE   What ya doing in here?

JUNE   Watching the Academy Awards and smoking.

LESLIE I can see that, but all your lovely guests are in the other room watching on the big screen.

JUNE Most people don't like to see people with cancer smoke cigarettes.

LESLIE Good point. May I join you?

JUNE Sure.

LESLIE I don't think Meryl Streep is going to win this time.

JUNE Why? Because she won last year for playing that bitch prime minister.

LESLIE Yeah, and she's been nominated umpteen times.

JUNE [*Pointing at the TV screen.*] Oooh. See-through dresses are really in this year. I don't think that's the look for me.

LESLIE Me either. June, I'm sorry I brought . . .

JUNE Sorry, I don't need. Sit down here with me. Did you get red wine on your blouse already?

LESLIE [*Sits.*] Oh,
[*Looks down.*]
I guess so. Can I ask how you're feeling?

JUNE No. Put some soda water on it next commercial. Don't let it//set.

LESLIE //set. I know. I like the turban. You can wear that look. Me, I'd look like a gypsy fortune-teller.

JUNE Don't even talk to me with that gorgeous thick hair. Mine was thinning all on its own even before I got help from modern medicine. Besides it makes me look sick.

LESLIE You could wear the Marilyn wig. You looked great in that last Oscars.

JUNE I know but that is so last year.

LESLIE Oh, look—the guy from—what's that show?
[*Spell out.*]
CSI: SUV, CRAP, something with cops and killers.

JUNE *Breaking Bad*, AMC. That's over but it won a Golden Globe this year.

LESLIE That's it. I love that show. Teacher gone bad.

[*Pause watching show for a moment.*]

JUNE I know I'm making Andy be host. Who else is out there?

LESLIE A few neighbors in the living room. The regulars are in the kitchen. Pizza's almost done.

JUNE I have to come out for that.

LESLIE Well, it's a little crazy in the kitchen right now—too many cooks but your hubby is so sweet.

JUNE Don't let him hear you say that. I've been begging him to be abusive and uncaring, so I don't have to feel guilty putting him through all this again.

LESLIE I wish I had one like that.

JUNE So go to rehab and get one. Your problem is you don't need rehab.

LESLIE Yeah, that's what you think. I just need more than twelve steps for what ails me. It seems like rehab is where you meet all the fun people. Are they still as much fun without their drug of choice?

JUNE Well, twelve-steppers know how to network, but you can't beat really sick people for funny.

LESLIE Still going to that group?

JUNE Once was enough. I figured I knew more than anyone else and my doctor was right and theirs were wrong and we're all going to die anyway, so what the hell is there to talk about?

LESLIE Well, since you put it that way.

[*Looking at TV.*]

Oh, look at that cleavage. Real or . . .

JUNE Fake.

LESLIE Real.

JUNE   Look how they mound. Real ones don't do that.

LESLIE   Huh? Not even if you put those chicken cutlet things in your bra

[*Pushes up her boobs.*]

to beef'm up?

JUNE   Ewww. Try not to mix your meat metaphors. Okay, I can't stand it anymore. Is she still out there?

LESLIE   I've been trying to tell you how sorry I am. I should never have brought Missy.

JUNE   This is a party, Goddamn it.

LESLIE   I didn't know she didn't know how to behave.

JUNE   I do not want to be asked by someone I've just met while they touch me on the arm:

[*In slowly exaggerated tone people use with sick people.*]

"How are you?" I'm dying, thank you, but before I do I'd like to win the Academy Award pool at my own party one time.

LESLIE   Say what?

JUNE   We all are, eventually. I'm just going to be first, most likely, but I don't think there's a prize for that.

LESLIE   Hah, you're forgetting how I drive?

JUNE   No, that's why I don't ask you to drive me to appointments anymore. Last time my blood pressure was over the top and I had to convince them not to put me in the hospital.

LESLIE   Oh, oh, this is the documentary category.

JUNE   I need to win this.

LESLIE   Well, you know what we always say. Vote for the Holocaust.

JUNE   I did, I did.

[*Sees she has won.*]

Yes. I won. That's what I'm talking about!

[JUNE *and* LESLIE *high-five. Cheers from other room.*]

LESLIE   You know, we've had other guests who didn't really fit in, like Sophie's husband who knew nothing about movies or the Academy Awards or show business and kept making inappropriate remarks or asking dumb questions, like, "Why do you care what they're wearing?"

JUNE   Yeah, but that was entertaining, if annoying. Missy is just, well . . .

LESLIE   Boring?

JUNE   I don't have time to be bored.

LESLIE   Alright I'll take her home.

[*Starts to get up to leave.*]

JUNE   No, I don't want you to leave. This is the Academy Awards. We do this together.

LESLIE   You mean laughing at what the women are wearing and the stupid things actors say when they don't have a script?

JUNE   Exactly. I do not wish to hear a treatise on the significance of *Inside Llewyn Davis* or whatever the fuck arty Coen brothers movie everyone is loving this year. I mean I like some of their work, *Fargo* but . . .

LESLIE   I want you to know that I have not seen *Inside Whomever* in solidarity with you and I work with that woman every day asking me "Have you seen it? Have you seen it? You really need to see it."

JUNE   Thank you, I'm deeply moved.

[*Pause.*]

Can't you just get her really stoned or something, so she doesn't look at me like that?

LESLIE   Like what?

JUNE   Like I'm dying?

LESLIE   [*Pause.*] How bad is it this time?

JUNE   It's never good. I'm still here. Let's leave it at that.

LESLIE   This sounds different.

JUNE I don't know, maybe I always sound like this at some point. I forget. How many times can you come back from the dead?

LESLIE Depends on the movie.

JUNE True. *The Night of the Living Dead*—those zombies were really hard to kill.

LESLIE They were slow but they kept coming.

JUNE Have you noticed zombies have gotten a lot faster in recent movies? No more of this foot dragging.

LESLIE Yes, I have. Now let's not change the subject.

JUNE [*Pause.*] The doctor says three or four months at the most.

LESLIE I don't believe it.

JUNE I know.

LESLIE [*Pause.*] What can I do?

JUNE I knew you'd ask. When I die I want you to channel celebrity gossip from me during the show, so pay attention now to how I do it, so you can really sound like me.

LESLIE Goddamn it, June, that doesn't take the sting out of the thought of you not being here in the flesh.

JUNE Flesh is overrated

[*Pointing at TV.*]

as you can see.

LESLIE Shit, June. I haven't really been paying attention. You look like hell.

JUNE I feel like it too. And there are all these people out there.

[*Cheers from other room as another winner announced.*]

LESLIE Just friends and they'll understand if you never come out, but they'll probably all end up in here. And blame me for ruining the party by bringing Missy.

JUNE That's good. They'll think that's why I'm in here rather than because I feel like crap.

LESLIE You mean to tell me it's not because of Missy?

JUNE Partly. I guess she was a good excuse.

LESLIE But you were going to let me think that?

JUNE Only temporarily.

LESLIE So it's not just that I'm oblivious to the obvious?

JUNE Well, you are, but hey, you're the one who always makes me feel like I have a future, just in case I need one.

LESLIE Oh, yeah?

JUNE Yeah.

[*Shifts to TV.*]

Look at that dress. Looks like it's made out of shredded plastic.

LESLIE Could be recycled—an eco-dress . . .

JUNE . . . from hell. It's red.

LESLIE [*Looking at another dress.*] Oh, Oh, I like that one.

JUNE Oh, please, she'd look good in a rag.

[*Both laughing.*]

LESLIE Yeah, I'll take the jewelry that goes with that rag.

[*Pause.*]

You know, June, I am serious about us writing the stain book. I mean, if you feel up to it. You know how to get out every stain in the world and I can write about that in a witty and entertaining fashion. That's a bestseller right there and then we can afford to buy you any miracle cure you want.

JUNE If you do all the work, I might be interested.

[*Looks at stain on her blouse.*]

But first, let's get some water on this.

[JUNE *gets off the bed with some difficulty.* LESLIE *comes over to* JUNE *to help her but pretends not to have noticed.*]

LESLIE   I knew you couldn't resist. Let's go into the kitchen. Just one thing, if all else fails, could you will me your husband or something? I just love him.

JUNE   Honey, he can't solve your relationship problems, but he might like to fool around.

LESLIE   Excellent.

[JUNE *is up and walking toward the door but stops, unsure of what to say or do for her entrance, so turns to* LESLIE. *Making a suggestion.*]

Sally Field's acceptance speech 1985.

[JUNE *nods approval.*]

Please let me.

[*Flings door open and announces*]

Step aside, please. Celebrity coming through.

JUNE   [*As Sally Field.*] You like me. You really like me.

[LESLIE *leads applause.*]

• • •

The Grass Is Greenest at the Houston Astrodome

Michael Ross Albert

Michael Ross Albert

Michael Ross Albert is the author of several plays, including *The Big Sandy River Plays* (Jenny Wiley Theatre), *For a Good Time, Call Kathy Blanchard* (Next Stage Theatre Festival, FringeNYC, published by Indie Theatre Now), *Karenin's Anna* (Toronto Fringe Festival: winner, "Outstanding New Play," *NOW Magazine*), and *Starfishes*, which is included in the 2010–2011 edition of *Best American Short Plays*. Albert received an MFA in playwriting from the Actors Studio Drama School in New York City. He is an associate member of the Dramatists Guild of America.

···production history···

The Grass Is Greenest at the Houston Astrodome was originally produced by Outside Inside at 64E4 Mainstage as part of the 18th Annual New York International Fringe Festival in August 2014. The production featured the following cast and creative team:

AMY Kaitlyn Samuel

MARSHALL Greg Carere

CAROLINE Kathleen O'Neal

PABLO David Gazzo

JOHN Jimmy Dailey

Directed by Brandon Stock

Stage Manager: Kristi Hess

Lighting Design: Sophie Talmadge Silleck

Sound Design: Mekeva McNeil

Costume Design: Alexandria Hoffman

Associate Producer: Cihangir "G" Duman

characters

AMY the gallery director

MARHSALL an artist

CAROLINE an artist

PABLO the gallery intern

JOHN Caroline's fiancé

[*A storefront art gallery. The art hangs askew on the walls. Some pieces have been torn off the walls and tossed aside. Sculptures are overturned. Broken glass on the floors. Bottles of wine are scattered here and there, half-empty (or half-full, if you so please). AMY sweeps the floor. MARSHALL is in a corner, hands in his pockets. PABLO drinks wine. CAROLINE is still in her winter coat.*]

AMY Look. Everyone's had a rough night.

PABLO That's putting it mildly.

CAROLINE You don't have to patronize me, Amy. I'm not violent. I'm not unhinged.

PABLO Clearly.

CAROLINE How come you get to drink while your boss is the one sweeping the floor? Aren't you her intern?

AMY Pablo's had enough to deal with tonight as it is, he shouldn't have to clean up your mess.

CAROLINE Ugh, you are still such an art mom.

AMY Okay, Caroline. It's time to go home. You've had a little bit to drink. . . .

CAROLINE That's right. A little bit. I could walk a straight line. I could touch my fingers to my nose. I'm not drunk, Amy. I'm not in the drunk tank. I wasn't even arrested!

PABLO God only knows why not.

MARSHALL Hey, she's upset, you can see that.

CAROLINE Don't speak for me, Marshall. Could you do that? Could you not speak for me, Marshall?

AMY What I was trying to say . . .

CAROLINE What kind of name is Marshall anyway? Who are you? Laser Tag?

AMY Caroline.

MARSHALL What do you mean, Laser Tag?

CAROLINE Oh my God.

AMY Everyone.

PABLO She does this all the time. Even in school.

CAROLINE You didn't even know me in school.

PABLO She makes these statements nobody understands . . .

AMY You guys!

PABLO . . . and when anyone questions her, or criticizes her, she rolls her eyes and says, "Oh my God."

CAROLINE I do not do that.

PABLO Or else she throws a temper tantrum.

CAROLINE I played Laser Tag when I was a child, you asshole, like everyone played Laser Tag and if you needed help, in Laser Tag, you'd yell, "Marshall Upstairs!" if you were upstairs.

PABLO Would someone named Marshall come rescue you?

CAROLINE If you needed rescuing.

PABLO Maybe *you* need rescuing and Marshall's your Marshall Upstairs.

MARSHALL We're on the ground floor, I'm her Marshall Downstairs.

CAROLINE You're not my Marshall anything, what the fuck are we even talking about!?

AMY Everybody calm down!
   [*Her cell phone dings. She looks at it. She sends a text message.*]
   Sorry, sorry one second.
   [*She puts her phone back.*]

MARSHALL Who was it?

AMY Um. Guys, let's . . . let's try to be grown-ups about this. Can we? Can we just breathe and talk and not break any more priceless works of art?

CAROLINE Priceless? Sounds a lot like "worthless," if you want my opinion.

PABLO Nobody does.

CAROLINE Priceless. What a bullshit word. You're telling me the art in this gallery is priceless? You're telling me that, that green monstrosity this jerk sold tonight is priceless?

AMY Okay, what did I just say?

MARSHALL My work wasn't intended to enrage you.

CAROLINE First off, your *work*!? Second of all, fuck you. I'm not enraged.

MARSHALL Then what are you?

CAROLINE Not drunk, that's for sure.

[CAROLINE *gets a bottle of wine, pours a glass.*]

PABLO Please. Drink more. Good idea.

[CAROLINE *starts taking off her coat.*]

CAROLINE God, how is it so hot in here? It's colder than Mars outside and in here, ugh, I'm covered in sweat that's gonna freeze as soon as I hit the curb.

[CAROLINE *takes off her coat.*]

PABLO And when exactly will that be?

CAROLINE What?

PABLO When can we look forward to your sweat-soaked *tucchus* hitting the curb?

CAROLINE Oh boy, would you listen to Harold?

PABLO You did not just call me that.

CAROLINE Why not? That is your name.

PABLO It's Pablo. Okay?

AMY Call him Pablo. He likes to be called Pablo. I guess anything's better than Harold Goldfarb.

PABLO I had it legally changed!

MARSHALL He had it legally changed, Caroline.

CAROLINE Well, bully for Pablo! Unpaid employee of the month.

[*She drinks her wine.*]

PABLO You destroyed a sculpture of mine that took nine months in total to create. That is the period of time it takes to give birth to a human being.

CAROLINE Thanks, Pablo, I was unaware.

PABLO Your rage might have been endearing when you were an art student in Syracuse . . .

CAROLINE Listen to him go.

PABLO . . . but right now it is beyond reprehensible. You've committed a crime. Not just against my work and the work of all the artists represented in this gallery tonight, but, like, an actual crime. Like a legitimate crime.

CAROLINE Then how come I'm not in jail?

PABLO Amy still had to call the police.

[CAROLINE *turns on* AMY.]

CAROLINE That was you!?

AMY I'm the director of the gallery and you were tearing artwork off the walls.

CAROLINE [*Overlapping.*] God, and they said some things would never change, some things would always be the same, and those things were friendship and loyalty and decency, and you had the gall to phone the fuzz over a little demonstration?

AMY [*Overlapping.*] You grabbed glasses of wine out of people's hands and smashed them on the ground. People have lacerations, Caroline. People were afraid, and it's because you were acting like the woman who shot Andy Warhol and this WAS SUPPOSED TO BE A SPECIAL NIGHT!

MARSHALL Okay, okay, enough. Enough.

CAROLINE No! You don't get to say, "Enough!"

MARSHALL Why not?

CAROLINE Because you're irrelevant!

MARSHALL I'm the reason behind this ruckus. Something I made . . .

CAROLINE *Made.* Something he *made.*

MARSHALL . . . pushed you over the edge. Or at least that's how I understand the situation.

CAROLINE You understand it wrong.

PABLO Why can't Marshall say "Enough's enough?"

CAROLINE He can say whatever he wants. It doesn't mean I have to listen.

PABLO You are infuriating, you know that!?

[AMY *gets a text message. She looks at her phone.*]

CAROLINE If I were a man, would you punch me in the face?

PABLO If you were a man, someone would have punched you in the face a long time ago.

MARSHALL [*To* AMY.] Who keeps texting you?

AMY It's nothing. I'm putting out fires left and right.

MARSHALL Is it your boss?

AMY Uh . . . Mmmhmm. Yes. It's my boss.

MARSHALL Did you tell her what happened? Is she okay?

AMY Do you mind if . . . Do you mind if everyone just left? Would that be something you could all do right now? The art gallery that I manage is in disarray. Each of you is my friend, though sometimes I have no idea why or if that's even true, but the fact remains that your work would not have been represented on these walls tonight, or in any group show we've ever hosted, had it not been for my involvement in the curation process. And instead of saying, "Thank you, Amy, how nice that was of you." Or, "Gee, Amy, this sure was a swell opening, sorry the gallery's closing, thanks for the free wine and the hors d'oeuvres, and the exposure in this whatever storefront art gallery, I'm really happy to have been a part of it." Instead of showing even a hint of gratitude, even the slightest bit of thanks for the effort I put into tonight's event, this one is so petty that she literally tears other artists' paintings off the walls . . .

CAROLINE   They're pieces of garbage!

AMY   . . . and all because someone bought Marshall's green thing and not your vaginal thing, whatever the hell it is.

MARSHALL   My green thing?

AMY   I am having a nightmare of an evening, if you haven't noticed. If it hadn't occurred to you yet. I had to convince the police to keep from sending you to a mental hospital, Caroline. Do you understand me? A mental hospital. With padded walls and straitjackets.

PABLO   Maybe it's exactly what the doctor ordered.

AMY   And maybe I don't want to hear your snide remarks either, Pablo. Maybe I'm a little tired. And a little frustrated. And maybe I need to sweep some fucking glass off the fucking floor. So maybe you should all just get the fuck out of my gallery before I take this broom and shove it up each of your assholes. Okay?

[*Pause.*]

CAROLINE   The warrior spirit.

[CAROLINE *goes to hug* AMY.]

AMY   What are you doing?

CAROLINE   You brave, injured soldier.

[*She hugs her tight.*]

AMY   What the hell is she doing to me?

CAROLINE   You've taken such care of us and we've all betrayed you.

PABLO   Who's we, white girl?

CAROLINE   I came back in here to apologize. I didn't want to make another scene. I didn't want to cause another fuss. After the police let me go, I was going to come in here and tell you how ashamed of myself I was and how grateful I am to you for everything you've done. I can't even imagine what this must be like for you, taking care of everyone, of everything.

MARSHALL   Caroline dear, maybe next time you should consider performance art because this is fucking fantastic.

CAROLINE   Marshall thinks I don't mean what I'm saying, and I don't blame him for that. After all he's been through . . . it wouldn't be fair to begrudge him some cynical thoughts.

MARSHALL   Do you mean, what I've been through tonight? (When you had a psychotic meltdown because I sold a piece of my artwork?) Or do you mean . . . what I've been through, with my dad? Because if that's what you're suggesting, if that's what you're bringing up right now . . . in all fairness, that'd make you . . .

PABLO   A bitch.

MARSHALL   It'd make you the definition of a bitch, Caroline.

AMY   What's that sound?

CAROLINE   What sound?

AMY   Do you hear it? It's the sound of all of you not leaving.

[CAROLINE *releases* AMY *from the hug.*]

CAROLINE   We're not going anywhere.

AMY   I was afraid you were going to say that.

CAROLINE   We're going to stay and help you clean up.

PABLO   You're such a Gemini.

CAROLINE   No, I'm not.

PABLO   An hour ago, you vandalized the building and smashed wineglasses on the floor. Now you're crying crocodile tears and guilting us into cleaning up your mess. Gemini.

CAROLINE   I didn't make you feel guilty, Harold. Your liberal Jewish upbringing did that.

PABLO   Amy, give me the broom. I'll sweep up the glass.

CAROLINE   No, let me.

PABLO I am the intern, after all. Cleaning up after other people is part of my job.

CAROLINE The job you don't get paid for, right?

AMY Could you all do this for me: Could you leave? Could you be nice to me and leave? With a cherry on top. Please.

[*Beat.*]

CAROLINE Do you mind if I stay? It's just, John's on his way over. He said he was going to be late and the show is still supposed to be going on, after all, and it's freezing outside. Like, it's so cold. Nothing's open around here, I can't even wait for him in a coffee shop. . . .

PABLO This was the last opening the gallery is ever going to have. It was Amy's big night, and you destroyed it because you're jealous and self-absorbed, and now you're so selfish you can't even leave after she practically begged you to?

[*Beat.*]

CAROLINE It's like minus forty degrees outside.

[AMY'*s phone dings. She looks at it. Beat.*]

AMY Do whatever you want.

[*She hands the broom to* PABLO *and moves towards the back room.*]

CAROLINE I tried to call to tell him not to bother coming. After the police drove off. But his phone's going right to voicemail, he's probably on the subway. He should be here any second.

AMY Great.

CAROLINE You'll finally get to meet him. Amy, can you believe he and I have been together this long and you've never even met?

AMY You never brought him around.

CAROLINE Well . . . John doesn't really like art. He's a normal person. Sort of like you.

AMY I don't know if you mean that as a compliment or an insult.

CAROLINE You know. You're a really, like, adventurous photographer but . . . Since you took this job, you're more of an . . . administrator. You sit on the other side of the desk. That's all I meant.

AMY Of course. I see.

[AMY *exits into the back room.*]

CAROLINE [*Calling after her.*] It's not a bad thing! Sometimes I wish I was on your side of the desk. Everything wouldn't be so depressing!

[*Beat. She looks at the others.*]

What?

MARSHALL Nicely done.

[*He goes to get his coat. Pause.*]

CAROLINE Your work didn't enrage me, by the way.

MARSHALL That's a relief.

CAROLINE It's the fact that someone actually spent three hundred and fifty dollars on three square feet of AstroTurf.

MARSHALL It's how much it cost.

CAROLINE Three hundred and fifty dollars? For what? Fake grass?

[*Pause.*]

MARSHALL Have a nice night, Caroline.

[*He puts on his coat.*]

CAROLINE Where are you going?

MARSHALL Amy asked us to leave. And I don't like discussing my work.

CAROLINE Mr. Big Shot.

MARSHALL I'd prefer not to defend myself to someone who can't even show other people in the community—

CAROLINE The independent visual arts community?

MARSHALL Someone who can't even show her *friends* the smallest bit of respect.

PABLO He's right.

CAROLINE Nobody asked you.

MARSHALL I know tonight was upsetting for you. I get it. No one bought your painting. I see you're hurt, and I sympathize with that. We've all been in shows, we've all been to openings where no one has even looked at our pieces, let alone spent money on them.

PABLO I haven't. This was my first show.

CAROLINE Well, now you know how shitty it feels.

PABLO Someone might have bought my sculpture. Had it not been destroyed.

CAROLINE I doubt that.

PABLO I don't even know what to say to her anymore.

MARSHALL You're mean, Caroline. You let your emotions get the best of you, and you don't care who you hurt. It's unfair. And it's obnoxious. And it makes me not want to be your friend.

CAROLINE It's taking you, like, a million years to leave the room.

MARSHALL See ya, Caroline. Pablo.

PABLO Hold on one second.

[*He picks up a glass of wine. He throws it in* CAROLINE'*s face.*]

CAROLINE WHAT THE FUCK!?

PABLO That didn't feel as good as I thought it would.

[CAROLINE *stomps on his foot. He screams.*]

CAROLINE Why would you DO THAT TO ME!?

[*She stomps on his foot again. He screams.* AMY *enters.*]

AMY Out. Out. Everyone out. Now.

CAROLINE He threw a glass of wine in my face!

PABLO She stomped on my foot. Twice!

MARSHALL I was just about to leave . . .

[CAROLINE *goes to the back room.*]

AMY Where are you going?

CAROLINE I'm covered in wine. I need to clean myself up!

PABLO I think my toe's broken. I legitimately think my toe's broken.

CAROLINE God, everyone I know is so sensitive.

PABLO Look who's fucking talking!

AMY I'm going to start screaming.

MARSHALL Guys, come on. Amy's gonna start screaming.

CAROLINE I'm going to the bathroom. And then I will be happy to wait outside, in the freezing cold, alone, while I wait for the man I love to take me away from all of you. Forever. Sayonara. Farewell. Arrivederci Roma.

MARSHALL Bon voyage.

CAROLINE Oh, and by the way, Marshall, ever since your father died you've been acting like a moralistic snob.

[*She exits.*]

PABLO Now I remember why I threw the wine in her face.

AMY Was it worth it?

[*As he hobbles towards the back room:*]

PABLO Probably. I think I need to get some ice. Oh. Sorry. You wanted us to leave. Never mind, I'll just . . . hobble on out of here . . .

[*He hobbles to his coat.*]

AMY Wait. I'll get you ice.

PABLO No, no.

AMY Yes, yes. Come on. Hold on to me, intern.

PABLO I really do think it's broken.

AMY What can I say? That bitch packs a mean punch.

[*They exit into the back room.* MARSHALL *looks at some of the artwork that is still on the floor. He picks up a framed photograph. He sits and admires it.* AMY *re-enters.*]

MARSHALL [*About the photograph.*] Yours.

[*Beat.*]

Sorry, I'll go.

AMY Don't.

MARSHALL I thought you wanted me to.

AMY I wanted Caroline to go. I already got rid of her once tonight, I didn't think she'd come back.

[*She sits with him. They look at the photo.*]

Ugh. Put it away.

MARSHALL I like it.

AMY It's stupid.

MARSHALL Controversial move. Director of the gallery putting her own work in a show.

AMY The gallery's closing. Besides, I didn't put it on the wall to be controversial.

MARSHALL Then why did you? Because you think it's good?

AMY No, because I think it's stupid.

MARSHALL That doesn't make any sense.

AMY Neither does your . . .

MARSHALL My what?

AMY Nothing. My voice trailed off.

MARSHALL What were you going to say?

AMY You know.

MARSHALL I don't think I do.

AMY Neither does your . . .

MARSHALL Oh. My green thing.

AMY Your AstroTurf thing.

MARSHALL Right.

AMY Now you understand.

MARSHALL I'm a bit slow tonight.

AMY Drink more.

MARSHALL Nah.

AMY Drink more?

MARSHALL I mean, at this point, why the hell not, right?

AMY My thoughts exactly.

[She pours them wine.]

A toast. To my last opening. The very worst of my career.

MARSHALL To you, Amy. And your last opening. One for the record books.

AMY Chin-chin.

[Her phone dings. She mimics the sound:]

Chin-chin.

[AMY looks at her phone.]

MARSHALL Got a hot date tonight or something?

AMY Wouldn't you like to know?

MARSHALL Well . . . well, yeah, I would. If you want to tell me about it.

AMY I don't think I do.

MARSHALL Oh. Okay.

[Beat.]

Is it because of—

AMY It's not because of anything.

MARSHALL Why you're having a hot date or why you don't want to tell me about it?

AMY Both.

MARSHALL Oh. Yeah, that's understandable.

AMY It's . . . You seemed to have such an easy time meeting a man online, I thought, hey, why not try it myself?

[*Beat.*]

MARSHALL I'm sorry.

AMY It's just.

MARSHALL I know.

AMY We shouldn't have even.

MARSHALL Totally not. But it happened. I guess we were both in vulnerable places. I've been fucked up lately, you've been fucked up lately—

AMY I have?

MARSHALL I thought . . . because the gallery's closing and you lost your job?

AMY Oh, right, I've been a little fucked up lately. But shit happens. Galleries close. Friends accidentally sleep with friends.

MARSHALL It wasn't exactly accidental.

AMY And then accidentally don't return phone calls or text messages.

MARSHALL I know, I'm not good at talking about—

AMY The phone calls I understand, but who doesn't respond to text messages?

MARSHALL I have trouble discussing—

AMY How hard it is it? "Sorry I didn't write back sooner. Been busy fooling around with random men I met on the Internet."

MARSHALL I shouldn't have told you about that.

AMY The gay thing?

MARSHALL The casually bisexual thing, if you want to do something reductive like put a label on it.

AMY That's the last thing I want to do.

MARSHALL Labels are for cans.

AMY Don't get preachy.

MARSHALL I don't know what I want. And I met someone I really liked who didn't like me. I shouldn't have used that as an excuse to exploit our friendship and sleep with you and then not call you back.

AMY Or text.

[*Beat.*]

MARSHALL I'm sorry.

AMY It's to be expected. You're a painter.

MARSHALL What does that mean?

AMY Painters are very serious. And very horny.

MARSHALL More than other artists?

AMY I've encountered every kind of artist there is, working here. Print-makers are uptight. Video artists are eccentric, to say the least. Glitch artists have terrible personal hygiene, every single one. Computer artists are like Berlin DJs. Radical feminists are highly intellectual, even Caroline. Sculptors are either macho or queer (except for Pablo, who's neither). And painters. Painters are very serious. And very horny.

MARSHALL What about photographers?

AMY We're pretentious.

MARSHALL Don't say that.

AMY Doesn't bother me. After all, I sit on the other side of the desk.

[*Beat.*]

MARSHALL I never thought of photographers that way. I always thought they were just . . . searching for something. Something they haven't found yet.

AMY Sound familiar?

MARSHALL I shouldn't have even told you about that guy. I knew it would make things . . . complicated. Between us. More complicated than they already are.

AMY And that's fine. That's life. People lose their jobs and drink more than they should and sleep with their friends. Or they experiment with same-sex partnerships with strangers they meet on an iPhone app. And, maybe, eventually people like this become so unhinged that they—

MARSHALL Tear the artwork off the walls?

[*Beat.*]

AMY Did you see me?

MARSHALL Did I see you what?

AMY In the middle of all the hullabaloo. Earlier on.

[*Small beat.*]

While Valerie Solanas over there was hogging the spotlight . . . I took a picture off the wall and smashed it on the floor, too.

MARSHALL Yeah. I did see you. Why'd you do that?

AMY She looked like she was having such a good time.

[*Beat.*]

I've stood in this gallery eight hours a day for four years. Eight hours a day staring at this, mostly, inert art. Boring art. Eager-to-please art. Art from the next big thing. Art by snobs who are gonna change the way we see art.

MARSHALL And the world.

AMY Social justice art. Narrative-based art. LGBT art. Old-man-looking-wistful art. Children-on-the-subway art. Muslim-woman-on-the-ferry art. Trippy graphic-design art that doesn't even look appealing after you've smoked a little dope (and I have). Twee art. In-your-face art. My whole life, day in day out, is looking at fucking art. And maybe it's the gallery closing, maybe it's having my neck on the chopping block, but lately I've wondered what it would feel like to just . . . tear everything down.

MARSHALL Still. You could've tried to destroy something that didn't have any personal value.

[*Re: the photograph.*]

You didn't even break the frame.

AMY I never was much of an iconoclast.

MARSHALL You should try it sometime. Caroline makes it look like fun.

AMY Caroline could use a healthy dose of her own medicine.

MARSHALL Honestly, even if she got it, I don't think she'll ever change.

AMY Sometimes I envy her.

MARSHALL Why?

AMY Must be nice to be so . . . devil may care. I'm too stuck to be reckless. And her fiancé. She found someone who'll put up with her insanity. Who actually likes her insanity enough to put a ring on it!

MARSHALL Yeah, but would you really want to spend the rest of your life with someone that masochistic?

AMY The grass is always greener, I guess.

[*Pause.* MARSHALL *looks at her.*]

I really don't want to make out with you right now.

MARSHALL Who said anything about making out?

AMY This is the part where we're supposed to make out. Where I forgive you without forgiving you.

MARSHALL Oh, that part. Well, we don't have to make out and you can still forgive me.

AMY I know. I do. I think.

[*Her cell phone dings. She looks at it.*]

MARSHALL He's running late?

AMY I don't think he's even coming.

[*Pause.*]

MARSHALL   Did I ever tell you (I don't think I did), tell you why I wanted to play around with mixed-media this time around? I mean . . . I don't think I told you why I made—

[*The front door opens.* JOHN *enters.*]

JOHN   I'm sorry, is this . . . ?

MARSHALL   John.

JOHN   Oh. Oh man. Hi. Marshall.

MARSHALL   You're . . . you're not John? You're not . . . Caroline's John?

JOHN   I didn't know you were friends with Caroline.

MARSHALL   Only on rare occasions.

AMY   You two've met before?

MARSHALL   Actually I think we might have.

[CAROLINE *enters.*]

CAROLINE   John, thank God. You will not believe what I've been through tonight.

JOHN   What happened here?

MARSHALL   Caroline put on a bit of a show for everyone.

CAROLINE   I had to talk to the police.

JOHN   What? How come?

CAROLINE   It was really, really awful.

[*She starts to cry.*]

JOHN   Oh, Caroline. Oh, baby.

[*He holds her.*]

CAROLINE   You're cold.

JOHN   It's freezing outside. Warm in here, though, jeez.

[*He tries to take off his jacket while still holding* CAROLINE.]

AMY   How do you know John?

MARSHALL   We just met once.

AMY   Oh.

[*Beat, realization.*]

OH NO!

JOHN   Caroline, Caroline, let go for a second, honey. My glasses are fogging up.

CAROLINE   I have that effect on people.

[*They part.* JOHN *cleans his glasses.*]

MARSHALL   It's not, Amy. It's not what you think.

AMY   Yes, it is.

[*Beat.*]

MARSHALL   Okay, yes, it is.

[AMY *gasps. A bit crazed, a bit delighted.*]

AMY   Drink more! Drink more!

[*She pours more wine. Drinks the whole glass.*]

JOHN   Tell me what happened. Where is everybody?

CAROLINE   I did something terrible.

JOHN   Oh, baby . . .

CAROLINE   I'm so ashamed of myself.

AMY   Drink more!

[*She pours more wine. Drinks the whole glass.*]

MARSHALL   What are you doing?

AMY   I'd like to be drunk for this, I think. Wouldn't you?

MARSHALL   I think I'm already a little drunk.

JOHN   Maybe we should go.

AMY   No, you should stay!

MARSHALL   Amy, this isn't something I want to do right now.

AMY I wanna be an iconoclast!

JOHN Let's find a cab. I think my toes are gonna fall off.

CAROLINE You need to wear proper boots. He refuses to go shoe shopping. He's such a baby.

JOHN No, I'm not.

CAROLINE You are. You're a big baby with love handles a receding hairline.

JOHN I don't have love handles.

CAROLINE He totally does.

JOHN She thinks I don't like it when she makes fun of me, but I know it's really just her way of saying—well, anyway.

CAROLINE Can you believe it! The cerebral scientist is too shy to say, "I love you."

JOHN [*Blushing.*] Come on, Caroline.

AMY Aw, you two are so sweet. Aren't they just a picture-perfect couple?

MARSHALL Nice meeting you!

JOHN You too, Marshall.

AMY I thought you had already met. Once.

CAROLINE Have you?

JOHN Um . . . I don't . . .

MARSHALL You look . . . somewhat familiar.

AMY Drink more!

CAROLINE What's wrong with Amy?

[PABLO *re-enters.*]

PABLO You didn't break her toe, too, did you?

CAROLINE Stop whining, your toe's not broken.

JOHN You broke his toe?

CAROLINE He threw a glass of wine in my face, so I stomped on his foot.

PABLO Twice.

JOHN You threw wine in her face? In my fiancée's face?

PABLO She destroyed my sculpture.

JOHN Huh?

PABLO Look around. This is all your fiancée. All of her doing.

JOHN What is he talking about?

AMY Ugh. This wine is so cheap. I love it.

JOHN Baby, what is he talking about?

PABLO Someone bought Marshall's piece. And Caroline got upset.

JOHN I'm confused.

CAROLINE It's not because of Marshall.

AMY She's always been jealous of him.

CAROLINE That's completely ridiculous.

AMY Intimidated.

PABLO I've never really noticed that.

AMY We're all jealous of each other, Pablo. That's something you're gonna learn really quickly about the art world. Everyone's jealous of each other and none of us have a very good reason to be. Except for Caroline and Marshall!

JOHN Let's get outta here.

CAROLINE Is she okay?

AMY I'm great. I have a secret!

MARSHALL Amy, Amy. Why don't you have some water?

AMY I wanna tell her!

CAROLINE Tell me what?

AMY This is how it feels, Caroline. This is how it feels when you take something and wreck it.

CAROLINE Wreck what? What are you talking about?

AMY Drink more!

[*She drinks more wine.*]

PABLO What's going on?

AMY I wanna tell her!

JOHN Come on, Caroline, it's time to go.

CAROLINE I want to know what she's raving about.

AMY She *wants* me to tell her!

MARSHALL Please don't.

AMY It'll make me feel better!

MARSHALL No, it won't. I promise you, it won't.

JOHN Put on your coat, we're going.

AMY Caroline feels better. Caroline felt bad, and jealous, and she burned the bridges, sledgehammered the walls, and she feels better.

MARSHALL But Caroline's a bitch.

JOHN Hey!

PABLO It's true, John. She's sort of a bitch. Nice to meet you, by the way. I'm Pablo.

JOHN Hi. Caroline, are these your friends?

PABLO Not me. I'm just the intern.

CAROLINE We're colleagues. But we're friendly.

PABLO When have you ever been friendly?

CAROLINE I'M FRIENDLY WHEN I WANT TO BE!

AMY Marshall and John had sex last week!

[*Pause.*]

JOHN Fuck . . . Fuck . . .

AMY You're right, that didn't make me feel as good as I thought it would.

[*Pause.* AMY*'s cell phone dings. She looks at it. Pause.*]

MARSHALL I asked you not to say anything.

[*Pause.*]

AMY Excuse me.

[*She goes to the back room, retching. She vomits offstage.*]

PABLO I'll, uh . . . I'll go . . . see if she's . . .

[*He exits into the back room. Pause.*]

CAROLINE So. Who's going to speak first?

　　[*Pause.*]

　　Okay. Me, then. I assume, by your silence, that this is, in fact, true. Am I correct in this assumption?

JOHN Caroline.

CAROLINE Cool. Excellent. I'm correct. I like being correct. It makes me feel like I can still do something right, like I still have some neurons firing, some instincts, whatever, warning me not to run towards the fire.

JOHN It wasn't a big deal.

CAROLINE IT WASN'T A BIG DEAL?

MARSHALL You of all people should appreciate the fact that gender is, perhaps, a bit more dynamic than—

CAROLINE Marshall, don't make me kill you, you're in way over your head.

JOHN We only went out twice.

CAROLINE Oh my God.

JOHN And we only fooled around once.

CAROLINE I can't believe this is happening.

MARSHALL   And neither of us even finished.

CAROLINE   Oh. I'm sorry. I was overreacting. The man I'm going to marry just went out on two clandestine dates, just had one sexual encounter with another man behind my back four months before the wedding day, but it's all right because neither of them came in each other's faces. Great. Let's go home and make up.

JOHN   It was a minor indiscretion.

CAROLINE   There is no such thing.

MARSHALL   This coming from the woman who used to say that monogamy was only for people who read books by Dan Brown.

CAROLINE   That was before I was in a real relationship.

MARSHALL   You were in a real relationship with that art star, What's His Name?

CAROLINE   No.

MARSHALL   The year we moved to the city. It was around the same time you agreed to do that performance piece . . .

CAROLINE   John and I are completely different!

MARSHALL   . . . the one where the Russian abstractionist had sex with you in front of an audience while you were suspended from the ceiling.

CAROLINE   I'm not shacking up with an art star anymore, Marshall. I'm getting married to a real person. John's a goddamn scientist!

MARSHALL   [*To* JOHN.] Don't you work for the city?

CAROLINE   I didn't want another relationship where my very impressive forty-something-year-old boyfriend watches a man named Nikolai hang me up like a portrait and screw me in front of strangers. I wanted something normal.

[*To* JOHN.]

I wanted you. Why did you do this to me?

[*Beat.*]

JOHN It was something, something I thought should . . .

CAROLINE What, try on for size?

JOHN I can't explain it.

MARSHALL We met online.

CAROLINE Marshall. Leave us alone.

MARSHALL I want to tell you what happened.

CAROLINE And I want you to take it up the ass. Maybe I should leave the two of *you* alone.

MARSHALL It was one of those apps. The dating app thingy.

CAROLINE Oh my God.

MARSHALL We went to an art gallery together. It was John's suggestion, not mine.

JOHN Stop. Okay?

MARSHALL We seemed to really hit it off. And the next night he texted me and we went for beer.

JOHN I don't want to talk about this!

MARSHALL And we talked about our families, and I told him about my dad, and the last five months. The funeral. The, the . . . dealing with the estate. Trying to sell off the art that he'd kept in storage.

JOHN Caroline, I . . .

MARSHALL And he listened to me and he was nice to me.

JOHN I don't even know what to say.

MARSHALL And we laughed about nothing, and we seemed to really like each other, and John picked up the tab.

CAROLINE What a gentleman my fiancé is.

MARSHALL And we were walking in the same direction, and I didn't really know what was going to happen, the conversation slowed down.

JOHN You're not making this any easier.

MARSHALL He sort of leaned into me, as we were walking, sort of, sort of nudged me off the sidewalk.

CAROLINE And he kissed you. Right? That's his move. That's what our first kiss was like.

MARSHALL We went back to my place and—

CAROLINE Had gay sex?

MARSHALL But we stopped. John stopped. And he sat up in bed, and he put his legs over the edge and he cried.

JOHN Please . . .

MARSHALL And he told me he was in love with someone else. An artist. Someone he met when he was on a business trip, a conference in Chicago. That he'd fallen in love with an artist and couldn't ever love anyone else. And he left. He left. I tried texting him a few times, but he never wrote back. That was it. He left.

[*Pause.*]

CAROLINE We didn't meet in Chicago.

[*Pause.*]

JOHN Baby . . .

CAROLINE No.

JOHN Caroline.

CAROLINE I should've seen this coming. After all . . .

MARSHALL Don't say, "Men are scum."

CAROLINE Don't tell me what to say, and fuck you for knowing what I was going to say, and I hate you, and I'm glad he used you and then left you with no regard for how it'd make you feel because that's exactly what he's done to me.

JOHN You tore paintings off the walls, Caroline.

CAROLINE So?

JOHN That's just it. Sometimes it's exhausting to be around someone so . . . so . . .

CAROLINE What?

JOHN Reactionary.

CAROLINE Someone reactionary without a penis, is that it?

[PABLO *re-enters.*]

PABLO Amy's not feeling so great.

CAROLINE Who the hell is, Pablo?!

PABLO I'm sick and tired of you screaming at everyone, Caroline. Regardless of what your, you know, justification, given the circumstances, might be. I couldn't really hear what you were saying back there, but I figure it's probably true that Marshall and John did, in fact, like, hook up even if I couldn't necessarily . . . I mean, the volume of your voice carries even if the acoustics are, whatever, even if I couldn't hear every word you were . . . I mean . . . Damn it, I had everything I wanted to say planned out before I came over here and now it's not coming out right.

CAROLINE Pablo, Harold, whoever you are. Leave us alone.

PABLO Why are you always so dismissive of me? I know I'm not cool like other sculptors. I'm not suave. I'm not earthy and manly and don't, like, casually wear clothes that show off my big muscles, don't grow my hair down to my shoulders. But I'm still an artist, and I still have a right to talk, and I still think you need to know that even if you have just cause in this one particular instance, you need to learn that if you treat people like shit, of course no one's going to want to make a long-term romantic commitment to you.

JOHN Dude. Stay out of this.

PABLO No, I won't. Why should I? I know you all think of me as just the intern because I didn't graduate in the same year as you and because I'm . . . I dunno, I had a whole big speech sort of welling up back there and now that I'm out here I don't really think I'm making it sound convincing, but I want you to know that I think it's time someone took a stand and tried to make you nicer. Just be *nicer* to people. Why do you have to be mean? Because you're an artist? Picasso once said, and I'm paraphrasing . . .

CAROLINE   Pablo adores Picasso. It's why he changed his name.

PABLO   My family left Spain before World War Two.

CAROLINE   It used to be Harold.

PABLO   Pablo was my great-grandfather's name. Don't turn this on me. I'm trying to make you *see*.

MARSHALL   You can't make anyone. See. You can't change anybody. No matter how many times you say, "Look! Look!" we can't change people. Not with our words, not with our work, not with anything. We stay the same. And we pretend to learn, and we tuck things away, maybe, and try not to think about them, try not to let them affect us, but they don't go away, they don't transform, they stay the same. We do, too. We think about changing, we think about, "Oh, wouldn't it be wonderful to be different, to be a little more like this person, to be something I'm not, I'm really gonna fucking change," but we don't. We stay the same. We stay the same, and then we die.

[*Beat.*]

I think I'm drunk.

[CAROLINE *picks up a piece of sculpture from the floor. She throws it at the wall.*]

CAROLINE   How do you like that, Marshall? You're right.

[*She puts on her coat.*]

JOHN   Caroline . . . Can't I talk to you about this?

CAROLINE   Go ahead, John. Convince me. Change me.

[JOHN *doesn't know what to say.* MARSHALL *approaches* CAROLINE.]

MARSHALL   I'm sorry I did this to you. I didn't mean to.

CAROLINE   I know that, asshole.

MARSHALL   You try not to let people see it, when you're hurt, but I can.

CAROLINE Oh my God. You're such a snob.

[*She goes to the door with no ceremony.*]

Woohoo, hooray, we're finally getting rid of her.

[*She exits. Beat.*]

PABLO So I guess the gallery will send you guys a bill in the mail or something.

JOHN What's that?

PABLO A bill. For my sculpture. And the rest of the—

JOHN You expect me to pay for, for what?

PABLO Caroline destroyed my work. My sculpture, which was priced at twelve hundred dollars.

JOHN Twelve hundred dollars!?

PABLO For the materials alone. I wasn't going to make a profit on it. I was just happy to have it in a show.

JOHN You're telling me your, your art cost you . . .

PABLO Twelve hundred dollars. Caroline broke another sculpture priced at seventeen. I expect you guys will have to pay for that, too.

JOHN You can't be serious.

PABLO Believe it or not, some people still live by the philosophy that if you break it, you bought it. And Caroline happened to break, well . . .

JOHN What? What's the estimate? How much did she break?

PABLO Amy and her boss have to appraise the damage.

[AMY, *entering.*]

AMY If I had to guess, I'd value the total cost to be somewhere close to twenty-five thousand dollars. Give or take.

JOHN You must be insane.

PABLO No, your fiancée is.

JOHN I don't know if she's my fiancée anymore.

PABLO If you were having doubts, that price tag might be the last nail in the coffin.

MARSHALL Hey. Come on.

JOHN Doesn't the gallery have an insurance policy?

AMY Sometimes the artists that use the space insure their own work. But our regular policy only covers things like floods, fires, acts of God.

JOHN You would think Caroline could be considered all of the above.

AMY Honestly, John, I've never had to deal with anything like this before. But there's no damage to the space itself, only to the artwork. That's on her.

JOHN But, if the police know she was the one responsible . . .

AMY It's not like they're going to fine her, she didn't spray-paint the courthouse. They barely even gave her a slap on the wrist.

JOHN Well, why the hell not?

AMY Because I convinced them not to.

JOHN Why?

AMY Because I'm her friend!

JOHN That didn't stop you from telling her about me and Marshall! And how did you know about that anyway?

AMY Because we slept together, too!

JOHN Oh! Of course!

AMY Except whereas you used Marshall to forget, however momentarily, about Caroline, Marshall slept with me to forget about you. Right?

PABLO [*Beat.*] I'm confused.

JOHN Well, the engagement is off.

[*Beat.*]

Whoever thought art cost so much money?

PABLO When you purchase it or destroy it en masse, it really adds up.

JOHN   You spent twelve hundred dollars on materials for a sculpture?

PABLO   Marshall spent three hundred and fifty on pieces of AstroTurf.

MARSHALL   They're not just pieces of AstroTurf.

JOHN   It sounds so irresponsible. Spending money on your work when you're never going to be guaranteed a return. I couldn't afford to do it. I'm not an artist, but . . . I just bought a condo. I have a mortgage. I live paycheck to paycheck just like any of you. And twenty-five thousand dollars!? Our wedding wasn't even going to cost that much.

AMY   Good thing you're not getting married anymore.

JOHN   Because of you.

AMY   No, actually because of you.

JOHN   You didn't have to tell her!

AMY   She didn't have to wreck the gallery I work for!

JOHN   IT'S CLOSING ANYWAY!

AMY   THAT'S NOT THE POINT!

[*Pause.*]

JOHN   I'm sick of artists.

AMY   I know exactly how you feel.

[CAROLINE *re-enters.*]

PABLO   Speaking of which.

CAROLINE   One thing. And that's it.

AMY   Caroline.

CAROLINE   One thing.

[*To* MARSHALL.]

Who bought your piece? Your AstroTurf? Who'd you sell it to? What do you know about them?

MARSHALL   Why? You need validation so badly that . . .

CAROLINE I GUESS I DO, MARSHALL! I could give a shit about you and him over there, that one. I'm over it already. But I want to know who on earth would pay that much money for pieces of AstroTurf with no aesthetic value and no meaning. Who'd want something so goddamn green?

PABLO No one talks about your work this way. No one challenges you. What gives you the right to say what's art and what's valuable and what isn't?

CAROLINE The man hung three square feet of AstroTurf on a wall and charged someone three-hundred and fifty dollars for it.

PABLO Everything sounds absurd when you reduce it to its basics like that. You didn't even try to understand . . .

CAROLINE Understand what!? Real art shouldn't need explanation. It should just move you. I don't know a thing about Marshall that makes me understand why anyone would spend money on his new piece, let alone why he wanted to all of a sudden switch mediums and make it in the first place.

JOHN Caroline.

CAROLINE And on the topic of switching mediums out of the blue, my betrothed. Got something to say, baby?

JOHN As a matter of fact, I do.

CAROLINE Christ, it's so fucking hot in here.

[*She removes her coat.*]

JOHN Marshall, if it's okay with you. I'd like to explain it to her.

MARSHALL I really don't like talking about my work.

JOHN But you did. With me. The AstroTurf, right? The, uh, the grass they sold at auction. That's what someone bought tonight?

PABLO Yeah.

JOHN Did you tear that up, too, Caroline? I don't see it out here.

MARSHALL You can't tear AstroTurf.

AMY I put it away in the back. I knew it meant a lot to Marshall, so I tried to hide it.

MARSHALL Thanks.

AMY I guess it's what I'm here for.

MARSHALL You're the best, Amy.

AMY Yeah, it really feels that way right now.

JOHN Marshall, Marshall told me about this piece.

CAROLINE On your gay Internet date?

JOHN Yeah, exactly. I had this thing once, about a year ago, before I met you, I met an artist in Chicago. A man. I skipped my conference. I work for the municipal government, doing environmental . . . it doesn't matter. The point is while I was in the city, I met this artist. This man. And he . . . he took me to the gallery and we looked at that painting, that Seurat, the one in *Ferris Beuller's Day Off*. And I was only supposed to stay through the weekend but I, I met this man, this artist, and I . . . I ended up calling in sick to work, staying a whole week longer in Chicago to be with this artist. And as soon as I came home, I had this . . . I don't know if it was to get closer to him, or if because he opened my mind to something I hadn't . . . Anyway, that's when I started trying to educate myself a bit about art. I didn't study like you did, it wasn't part of my life growing up, but I felt moved, in that gallery, I felt like I'd changed. Like I was different somehow. And you appealed to that part of me, that new part, that changed part.

CAROLINE Because I reminded you of a man you fucked in Chicago?

JOHN Because you were passionate about something I didn't necessarily understand. Something that could make me more than I was. I'm not explaining it properly.

[*Beat.*]

I didn't know Marshall was an artist when we met.

CAROLINE On your iPhones.

JOHN How could I be certain I wanted to, to settle down with you if I still had this, this . . . unfulfilled . . .

AMY I understand.

JOHN We went to the gallery and I did most of the talking. It was an exhibit about the period between wars, in Europe. Kandinsky and Picasso and Chagall and, and . . .

MARSHALL Klimt.

JOHN Klimt! I like that guy. Although he was mostly active before the . . . Anyway. I talked about all the things I knew about that period, all those new things I started trying to teach myself about art since I came back from Chicago. And it wasn't until we were leaving the gallery, getting our coats at coat check, that Marshall told me he was an artist himself. I wasn't going to, to text him again or see him again because I felt, when we were together, that I'd much rather be with you, but there was something . . . I wanted to know more about him, and his work, and if it would . . . if *that* was what I was drawn to. Not him as a man, but him as an artist.

CAROLINE You weren't drawn to me as an artist?

JOHN I just needed to figure it out for myself. So we went for a drink, and I kept asking Marshall about his work, and he's really not lying when he says he doesn't like talking about it, it took a fair bit of coercing. But finally around our third beer, he told me about this piece he was working on.

[*To* MARSHALL.]

Do you mind if I talk about it?

MARSHALL I . . . I don't see what difference it'll make. You're not gonna change anyone's mind. . . .

JOHN Let me tell them. See, Marshall's dad was from Texas. He was a minor league baseball player. Right?

AMY I didn't know that.

JOHN Except an injury kept him, kept him from playing professionally. Do you wanna take over?

MARSHALL I, I really don't. . . . It makes me uncomfortable to have to . . .

JOHN He told me this thing his dad used to say. This non sequitur. See, we were talking about being disenchanted with our jobs (lately I've been feeling a bit dissatisfied at work, maybe it's the winter, this cold) and I was saying, "I wish I had the ability to create something like you do." And he said he wished he had something like my job. Something stable, something that (even though it hasn't felt this way to me in a while) something that makes a difference in our city. Something . . . satisfying. A reason to get out of bed in the morning and feel useful. It might seem perfect on the outside, but . . . But I haven't felt that way in a while.

AMY I know exactly what you mean.

JOHN And I said to Marshall, "I guess the grass is always greener on the other side of the fence." And Marshall said, he told me this thing his dad used to say, this old saying of his . . . And that was the title of Marshall's new piece. *The Grass Is Greenest at the Houston Astrodome*. I don't know if I can . . . It's like . . . No matter how, how badly you think you want something . . . I'm not really putting this well. The grass is greenest at the . . . It's like. Our dream of perfection is a dream of something that doesn't exist. It's fake. It's not real. It's made to fool us into thinking that there is actually something more . . . desirable than what we've got right now. And now this place (I looked it up in the news after you and I talked about it) this seemingly perfect place . . .

MARSHALL It's being demolished. They're tearing down the Astrodome. We found out pretty much for sure a couple of days before my dad died. And, and lately there are all these initiatives in place to try and save it. But they still sold off everything inside. Even the AstroTurf. Square foot by square foot.

JOHN The greenest grass is all gone. Like it never existed in the first place.

MARSHALL Because it wasn't real.

PABLO That sounds pretty bleak to me.

AMY His dad died.

PABLO I know that but . . . But are you saying we should just, like, stop aiming for something better? Be satisfied with being mediocre, or whatever, because even if we make something better for ourselves we won't be able to, what, appreciate it? Understand it?

MARSHALL Even if my dad got to play in the major leagues, that sadness he had, the way he . . .

[*Beat.*]

I don't think that would've ever gone away.

JOHN And, it's like . . . It's like, I had a, a vision of something, I guess you could say, when I was in Chicago . . .

CAROLINE But you'll settle for me. Right?

JOHN Maybe we could help each other get someplace closer to that, that perfect place. Where the fields couldn't possibly be any more . . .

PABLO Verdant.

JOHN But there is no such thing as perfect. Especially with love. That's what I took away from the piece. Unless I'm explaining it wrong.

AMY I thought you were sick of artists.

JOHN Yeah, but . . . I think I still like art? Or at least, I don't know enough about it yet. Was I wrong? Did I get it wrong?

MARSHALL I think you did a pretty good job.

CAROLINE You're telling me, you spent over three hundred dollars on found materials?

JOHN They sold off the original AstroTurf at auction. Marshall bought it online.

MARSHALL Cheaper than a last-minute flight to Texas and back.

CAROLINE Okay, but here's the thing. Here's what pisses me off. Marshall didn't tell anyone at this group show tonight what that piece meant. He doesn't like discussing his work (which is so obnoxious, by the way. You make everyone else look like a dick, and you make yourself look like a dick. "Look at me, I'm so special and talented I don't like discussing my work.")

PABLO You must be the most unhappy person in the world.

CAROLINE No, I'm not. Why would you say that?

AMY Guys, I don't have the energy to break up another fight. One argument at a time, please.

JOHN What's your point, Caroline?

CAROLINE My point, princess, is that no one, not in their right mind, no one off the street coming into a lame group show with all these lame pieces on the wall would look at Marshall's AstroTurf, out of all of the other art here, and whip out their checkbook and say, "I must have this, name your price!"

AMY Marshall bought the piece himself.

[*Beat.*]

CAROLINE What?

MARSHALL I didn't . . . I didn't want to think about anyone else having it. My dad (well, everyone really) used to call the Astrodome "The Eighth Wonder of the World."

[*Beat.*]

In retrospect I shouldn't have put anything up in this show at all.

AMY I coaxed him into it. I thought it'd make him feel better.

PABLO Now it's value's appreciated to twenty-five thousand dollars.

CAROLINE How do you figure that?

JOHN The damage. The damage you caused tonight.

CAROLINE Is that true?

AMY Give or take.

[*Beat.*]

CAROLINE You should've let me go to the mental institution.

PABLO Maybe there's still time.

CAROLINE How the hell am I supposed to pay twenty-five thousand dollars!?

PABLO Maybe you should've thought about that before you started screaming.

CAROLINE I scream, Pablo. I scream because I'm not satisfied. Okay? We're not meant to be satisfied. We have the capacity to dream big dreams. We're artists. Of course we're never going to be satisfied.

JOHN Then what makes you think you would've been satisfied with me?

[*Pause.*]

CAROLINE I just wanted to do something that meant something. Thanks for wrecking that.

JOHN You did your fair share of wrecking things, too, Caroline. And I don't want to think of you like this, like the way you are right now. It's ugly.

[*Pause.* CAROLINE *exits through the front door.* JOHN *realizes what he just said. Pause.*]

MARSHALL [*To* JOHN.] Are you going after her?

[*Pause.*]

Why?

[JOHN *exits. Pause.* MARSHALL *sits.*]

AMY Let's turn off the lights. Let's turn off the lights and sit in the dark. I don't work here anymore, the gallery's done. Someone else will chase Caroline down for the cash because I resign. I quit. No going down with this ship for Amy. Someone else can sweep up the mess, someone else figure out the damage. Let's just sit in silence, and in the dark. No more art. Let's look at nothing for a while. Together. How's that sound?

MARSHALL I'm sorry, Amy. I don't know why I . . .

AMY What?

[*Small beat.*]

MARSHALL I'll text you.

[*He exits, putting on his coat as he goes.*]

AMY Always after something better.

[*She starts turning off the lights.*]

PABLO Amy. Amy, I know this night, I know it didn't go well, and that's, that's a crime. Because you worked so hard for this place, and for us. You talked about opening your own gallery, having a space just for you, and maybe this, the gallery closing, maybe this is exactly what you need to get that going.

[AMY *exits into the back room.*]

I want you to know that I, that I appreciate . . . See, no one's ever taken a chance on me or my work before. And, yeah, my sculpture's been destroyed and a radical feminist broke my toe, but, but I want you to know that I like it here. That I'm gonna miss this space. I've been trying to do everything right. Pay my dues. Sweep the floors, wash the windows, clean the bathrooms in the basement. Try and get my stuff out there and have people take me seriously, and it's hard. And we need to help each other, don't we? Because it's hard. And I want to help you now, if I can. The way you tried to help me.

[AMY *re-enters holding* MARSHALL's *artwork. Hangs it on the wall.*]

I know you're hurt, and I know that you guys are all involved in this, this, triangle or whatever it is, of emotions and unfulfilled, like, whatever. And I don't really know how to fix that. I don't know how to show you something that'll change your perspective about, about people and art and our friends, but I think if you listen to me, just for a second—

[AMY's *cell phone dings. She looks at it. Blank.*]

What's wrong? What's the matter?

[AMY *cries.*]

Amy? What is it?

AMY He's not coming.

[*She cries. She curls into herself.*]

PABLO I can't keep up with you guys. I don't understand, I don't know who's sleeping with who.

AMY [*Referring to her phone.*] I don't even like this guy. I just wanted . . . I just wanted something.

PABLO I know.

AMY I feel like smashing my cell phone, but then . . . I wouldn't have a cell phone!

PABLO Shh . . .

AMY I sound pathetic.

PABLO No, you don't. Everyone wants to break their cell phone.

AMY I didn't think it'd be like this. My life.

PABLO Aw . . . You're great, Amy. You're the best. And I'm not just patronizing you, even though I think it's important we say that to one another, as fellow artists, because, because, you know, if we don't say it to one another, who will? You're gonna be fine, and, and, maybe you'll open a gallery one day—

AMY Fuck art.

PABLO Sure. Or that. Or fuck art.

AMY Why couldn't I have been good at math? Marshall Downstairs.

PABLO You're good at something better than math.

AMY Math is perfect.

PABLO Perfect doesn't exist. Hey? Look. Look at this.

[*He finds her photograph on the ground.*]

It's yours. I was admiring it earlier.

AMY You changed your name. You didn't have to do that. Just to be an artist.

PABLO Hey. Hey, look at this. Look how good you did.

AMY I tried to break it.

PABLO I'm glad you didn't. Someone else might be, too. Someone who's also looking for something and also doesn't know what that something is yet. They'll come across this photograph and they'll think to themselves . . . "Wow. That person understands." And it'll change them a little bit. Or it'll change them a lot. I think it's great. It *is* great. Look at it.

[*She does. They do. Blackout.*]

• • •

Sword Play

Inspired by
Charles Hartley—
Nürnberg Cathedral

Charlene A. Donaghy

Charlene A. Donaghy

Playwright Charlene A. Donaghy's plays have been produced in New York, Boston, New Orleans, Memphis, Los Angeles, and around the United States, with recognition in Great Britain and Canada. Madison Square Productions holds the Broadway option for Donaghy's full-length play *The Quadroon and the Dove*, with expected production in 2016/17. Hansen Publishing Group released *Bones of Home and Other Plays*, a collection of Donaghy's plays, in fall 2015. Other publications include *Best American Short Plays*, *25 10-Minute Plays for Teens*, and *Estrogenius, a Celebration of Female Voices*. Donaghy is Festival Director/Warner International Playwrights Festival and Producing Director/Tennessee Williams Theater Festival. She teaches playwriting/theater at the University of Nebraska, is a founding member of Boston's Proscenium Playwrights, a core member of NYC's 9th Floor Playwrights, a member of the Playwrights Center, and Connecticut Regional Representative of the Dramatists Guild of America.

···production history···

Sword Play was inspired by *Nürnberg Cathedral*, oil on panel by Charles Hartley, for Know Theatre's Artists and Playwrights Festival. Directed by Tim Gleason.

MAEVE   Katie Barlow

AARON/AMARA   Alfie Massey

FATHER DOLAN   Rich Bocek

characters

MAEVE   23 years old. Irish American, no accent. Dressed in white blouse covered by a simple, bibbed, long black dress with a wimple on her head. In her first postulancy, perhaps on her way to becoming a nun but not yet fully committed to the vocation. Hopeful of the good in the world.

AARON   7 years old. African American. Dressed in simple, hand-me-down play-clothes of the era. Boisterous and not afraid to say what he thinks.

FATHER DOLAN   68 years old. Old-school, Irish-born Catholic priest. Dressed in severe black priest's clothing. He recently relocated from Virginia to New Orleans but longs for his home in Boston.

time

Hot August afternoon. 1962.

setting

The sanctuary of Mater Dolorosa Church, South Carrollton Avenue, New Orleans, Louisiana. A simple set of wooden benches can represent pews.

note

// = talking over. — = cutting off the line.

[*In darkness, the sound of a laughing child is heard, mingled with what sounds like a mother's laughter and a clashing of wood on wood. Lights wash onstage as a storm would brew: rising from black to purple to gray-blue. MAEVE, carrying a wooden sword, runs through the pews playing tag with AARON, who also carries a wooden sword.*]

AARON You'll never catch me.

MAEVE I will. I will.

AARON You're too slow, sister.

MAEVE I'm *not* a sister *yet*, but I *am* fleet of foot to do God's work.

AARON Ha. You're funny! Catch me if you can!

[AARON *is quick, but* MAEVE *sneaks a double-back, catching him.*]

MAEVE Who's funny now?

AARON [*Laughing.*] You ain't even.

[MAEVE *"noogies"* AARON. *He giggles.* FATHER DOLAN *enters with a box of Bibles.* AARON *spins from* MAEVE, *raises his sword.*]

I'm a pirate. On the guard.

MAEVE [*Silly, fake French accent.*] You mean *en garde*. A French expression.

AARON We ain't even French. We're Irish.

MAEVE Yes. We are. You'll always be my little Irish boy.

FATHER DOLAN Sister Maeve.

[AARON *turns sword at* FATHER DOLAN, *who raises the box as if to defend himself. Playfully.*]

Young pirate, do not point that sword at me.

[MAEVE *puts her sword on a pew. Pause. Then* AARON *bursts into laughter.*]

AARON Geez, Father, you look like you seen a ghost.

[FATHER DOLAN *puts the Bibles down.*]

FATHER DOLAN Only the Holy Ghost, my son.

AARON Anyways, we were just funning.

FATHER DOLAN I have fond memories of playing treasure hunt in the seminary sanctuary at St. John's in Boston.

AARON So you're kinda a pirate, too.

[FATHER DOLAN *chuckles.*]

MAEVE Actually we're celebrating, Father.

FATHER DOLAN Celebrating?

MAEVE Yes. Two years after New Orleans public schools, but the archdiocese has made a good decision. And you've joined us right at this turning point. How's your first week with us, Father? I'll bet New Orleans is a bit of a shock . . . I mean is it different from Virginia?

FATHER DOLAN Different. Yes. And a bit of a shock might be a good turn of a phrase. I had expected transfer to Boston, but Bishops sometimes have funny senses of humor.

AARON I like funny people.

FATHER DOLAN Silly pirates, perhaps. But not bishops who trade priests with no thought to my desires for home. First Virginia. Now New Orleans. They never send me to Boston. But I'll make Mater Delarosa a sanctuary for our people and then, perhaps . . .

[*Beat.*]

Please ignore this old pirate going on. What are we celebrating?

AARON Being Irish.

FATHER DOLAN You are not Irish, my son.

AARON I live here with a Irish nun and a wrinkled old . . . um, I mean a Irish priest. Don't that make me Irish? Ain't there Negro Irish in the world?

MAEVE [*Stifles a giggle.*] Of course there are.

AARON Let's go play swords in the choir loft.

FATHER DOLAN I am not sure that is a wise choice.

MAEVE We can take the swordplay to the playground, yes?

AARON But the choir loft is the mast of me *piiii-rate* ship.

[AARON *dashes offstage.*]

MAEVE [*Calling out.*] Be careful. Please.

[FATHER DOLAN *unpacks box, handling Bibles to* MAEVE, *who distributes them on the pews, on and off, throughout play.*]

FATHER DOLAN You did not answer my question. Celebrating?

MAEVE The decision by Archbishop Rummel. Aaron will get to go to school right here at Mater Dolorosa. Desegregation. The power of prayer, Father.

FATHER DOLAN I am not sure desegregation is the Lord's way.

[AARON *runs onstage with the sword, he trips, falls, and laughs boisterously.*]

AARON Catch me if you can!

[AARON *dashes offstage.*]

FATHER DOLAN Exactly why *this must* happen.

[MAEVE *hugs a Bible.*]

MAEVE I agree, Father. Of course. Two years since the public schools joined across race lines and, now, blessedly Aaron will have a fuller life than I had growing up here //

FATHER DOLAN Sister //

MAEVE Not that my life was . . . I mean . . . I've loved my life here, but now he'll go to school right where he's grown these months.

FATHER DOLAN Sister //

MAEVE We'll read together. I'll help with his homework. Guide his spiritual life. Make his projects together—

FATHER DOLAN [*With insistence.*] Sister!

MAEVE [*Takes a subservient stance.*] I'm so sorry, Father.

FATHER DOLAN Your enthusiasm for the young pirate and his well-being are commendable and will bear worthy for our next move.

MAEVE Our next move?

FATHER DOLAN St. Augustine Church is sending someone over this morning.

MAEVE For?

[*They distribute Bibles from box.*]

FATHER DOLAN Tell me, how is your formation process coming along?

MAEVE My formation?

FATHER DOLAN If I am to create a sanctuary for our people, then I should know more about you and the others who serve this parish. Don't you agree?

MAEVE Yes, Father. But forgive. I thought we were talking about Aaron. What does St. Augustine have to do with—

FATHER DOLAN [*With insistence.*] Formation. Now.

MAEVE I'm ending the first year of my postulancy.

FATHER DOLAN Good. So on to your novitiate.

MAEVE Well. Not. No. I mean. Mother Superior feels I need another postulancy year for transition. To truly feel the love and spirit of our Lord.

FATHER DOLAN I see. And where do you see your future, beyond swordplay in the sanctuary?

MAEVE Mother Superior says I like being in the community much more than my reflections and prayers. I've been guiding the children's spiritual life in Sunday school. I'm captain of the parish volleyball team, which can be challenging in my habit. It's been wonderful having Aaron in my life. Just getting out with him and other families. I know it's a sadness that his mother abandoned him on our doorstep, but he brings me such joy.

[AARON's *laughter fills the empty spaces.* AARON *crosses, sword slashing the air.*]

AARON Hey, sister, c'mon.

FATHER DOLAN She'll be along when we are finished.

AARON Let's do pirate hide-and-seek. You hide first.

[AARON *runs offstage. Muffled counting is heard.*]

FATHER DOLAN What do you mean by empty spaces?

MAEVE Perhaps I should go play with—

[FATHER DOLAN *holds up his hand, shakes his head "no." MAEVE hugs Bible.*]

I'm sorry I said anything, Father. I'm being silly. I love my life here. I do.

[*Pause as she hugs a Bible.*]

It's just . . . the days are long. Longer than I thought they'd be. I expected more sureness on my path towards devotion.

FATHER DOLAN   Yes. As I thought. You are early in your formation. Have not yet made your full commitment to our Lord.

MAEVE   I don't mean to have doubts. These questions between what I thought this life would be and what it is.

FATHER DOLAN   A life of servitude must have sacrifice.

MAEVE   Yes, Father. And New Orleans instead of Boston?

FATHER DOLAN   [*Nodding.*] Sacrifice. Which brings me to the young pirate.

MAEVE   At first Mother Superior wanted to put him in the dormitory, but we had no other children there six months ago. I offered the extra cot in my cell. It's a miracle how he's blossomed. He loves to read. We plant in the garden. Visit the neighborhoods. Have you been to Treme yet, Father? An amazing community full of history and architecture. I'm taking him to Myrtle Street playground to see what other mothers are doing. I can't believe our good blessings—

FATHER DOLAN   You came to this place as a child yourself. Also . . . left on the convent steps.

MAEVE   Raised and educated by the sisters. It seems natural for me to follow their path. I stayed mainly cloistered up until last year when I went to Albany.

FATHER DOLAN   Albany?

MAEVE   Georgia. With Southern Christian Leadership. Protest against segregation.

FATHER DOLAN   Oh, dear. I fear you are confused, and now you have grown all too fond of the boy.

MAEVE   Aaron brings me . . . we bring each other a sense of . . . belonging.

[AARON's *counting stops.*]

AARON [*Offstage voice.*] Ready or not. Here I come.

FATHER DOLAN Perhaps you tend to him with a zeal that speaks to your own desire for something outside the church.

MAEVE He needs a mother—

FATHER DOLAN Mother?

MAEVE Figure. A mother *figure.*

FATHER DOLAN But he is different.

[AARON *runs onstage with sword.*]

AARON You ain't even found no good hiding place! I can see you right here! My turn. Come find me.

[AARON *dashes offstage.* MAEVE *smiles towards* AARON, *anxious to join him.* FATHER DOLAN *stops her with his gaze.*]

FATHER DOLAN You are young. I can see how you might confuse your commitment to our Lord with your commitment to the boy. But you cannot allow one soul to override the good we must do for all souls. Our Father will fill your emptiness once the boy leaves.

MAEVE Leaves?

FATHER DOLAN St. Augustine will be sending someone for him.

MAEVE For him? Father. You're not taking him . . . away from me?

FATHER DOLAN It is not away from you. It is towards what is best for him. To a family with St. Augustine. A family . . . like the boy.

MAEVE But he has a chance for a life here. Please.

FATHER DOLAN And what would that life be?

MAEVE Growing up with love and devotion beyond measure. Having a spiritual life, which is also fun. Connecting with other children to learn.
[*Beat.*]
Being with me.

FATHER DOLAN Was your life growing in this orphanage as ideal as you describe it?

[*Pause as* MAEVE *considers this. She has the slightest shake of her head "no."*]

The family from St. Augustine are *his* people. They will give the boy more than we can within the confines of these walls. They will understand him. What society holds for him. Allows him. *Dictates* of him. He will be with his own people. I know this is difficult for you to understand but all things are not black and white.

MAEVE You're talking as if they are.

FATHER DOLAN You cannot care for him as his own kind can. You cannot hope to teach him what society demands of him. And making an example of him attending Mater Dolorosa next month—

MAEVE An example? Father, I'm not. He'll get the best education here—

FATHER DOLAN Among students and teachers who don't want him. Don't you see?

MAEVE We're all the same in the eyes of God.

FATHER DOLAN We're talking of society.

MAEVE God and society should be one.

FATHER DOLAN You will not preach to me.

MAEVE I didn't mean—

FATHER DOLAN Do you not think I have considered the best interests of the boy in this decision?

[MAEVE *slams down a Bible.*]

MAEVE No. I don't. I know what's best for him!

FATHER DOLAN I will allow your outburst because you are upset, Maeve, but you will remember your place in our Father's House. And in my parish. Do you understand?

MAEVE No. I don't understand. You just got here. You can't go changing everything. For over one hundred years the Sisters of St.

Mary have been serving this parish, caring for community, even taking in and raising abandoned children. I don't see how you can send Aaron to others just because of the color of his skin. This is 1962. We're integrating the schools. Aaron will have friends of all colors.

FATHER DOLAN   You are being naive.

MAEVE   Just because you believe in some archaic sense of separation doesn't mean I'm being naive.

FATHER DOLAN   Were you here when the public schools integrated?

MAEVE   [*Nods.*] I stood toe-to-toe with the protestors and I'd do it again.

FATHER DOLAN   Precisely my point, Maeve.

MAEVE   *Sister* Maeve.

FATHER DOLAN   Perhaps.

[*Beat.*]

If you do not think we will see the same reactions next month, then you are, indeed, being naive.

MAEVE   What do you know about it? You're not even from here.

FATHER DOLAN   New Orleans is not the only place with race issues. Prior to coming here I was priest at Sacred Heart Church in Meherrin, Virginia. I was under consideration for a Boston appointment. Then officials of Prince Edward County closed the public schools rather than integrate them and parishioners chose sides. Chose battles. Battles in my parish. I saw many people hurt: physically, emotionally, and most especially spiritually, and I will not allow that to happen here.

[*Beat.*]

You think me harsh but I am educated to the circumstances. I have a chance to create a safe haven for our people.

MAEVE   Our people? Stop saying that!

FATHER DOLAN   It is best. And *you*. Are *not*. His *mother*.

MAEVE   What?

FATHER DOLAN   You will *not* be going to Myrtle Street playground to see, as you put it, what other mothers are doing.

MAEVE   I didn't mean . . . for Christ's sake.

FATHER DOLAN   Maeve!

[*Beat.*]

I see the influences of the society around us changing the servitude of our sisters, our parishioners.

MAEVE   Of course society should change us. We can't live in the past anymore, cloistered off from the world. We're part of the world.

FATHER DOLAN   Is that what you think your life in service to our Lord will be? Caring for *those* people?

MAEVE   I always thought my life would be God *and* people. Together. Genesis says, "If as one people speaking the same language they have begun to do this, then nothing they plan to do will be impossible for them."

FATHER DOLAN   "I will make a distinction between my people and your people." Exodus. And if you feel as though you need to help those people, perhaps you would be best taking some time away from the church to figure your place. Choose your sacrifice.

MAEVE   "To do what is right and just is more acceptable to the Lord than sacrifice." Proverbs.

FATHER DOLAN   Enough! How dare you quote scriptures to me! You will lose that sanctimonious tone or I will see to it that your first postulancy is your last. This house will not be another Meherrin falling apart as race lines are drawn. This will be a place of sanctuary, and when the bishop sees so, I'll get to go home!

[AARON *bursts in, sword slashing.*]

AARON   You never found me. I win! Take that!

FATHER DOLAN   [*To* MAEVE.] You have no choice.

[*Beat.*]

Young pirate. Come here.

[AARON *stops slashing.*]

AARON Whatcha want, Father Pirate?

[MAEVE *steps between them.*]

FATHER DOLAN If you feel you must, I will allow you to tell him.
Then be in my office in one hour and we will discuss your future in
this parish. You will learn sacrifice.

[FATHER DOLAN *exits with authority, taking the empty box with him.* MAEVE
deflates. Pause.]

AARON What's he meanin', sister?

MAEVE Aaron.

AARON You ain't lookin' so happy.

MAEVE I'm always happy when you're around. My . . . my son.

AARON Ha! You're funny. You ain't even Negro.

MAEVE I ain't even.

[AARON *picks up* MAEVE's *sword from the pew.*]

AARON We can play pirates in the choir loft.

MAEVE Aaron—

AARON You ain't chicken, sister. You're one of the best fighters I know,
but you don't fool me. You'd never hurt a fly.

[MAEVE *touches his arm. Pause.*]

Why you look like you seen a ghost?

MAEVE Aaron. Father Dolan has made a decision about . . . about you.
You and your life. Your life here at the convent.

AARON I like livin' with you. I'd live with you anywheres.

[*Beat.*]

I don't wanna go to people at St. Augustine.

MAEVE You were listening?

[AARON *nods, points up to the choir loft.*]

MAEVE Hard not to hear the echoes from the choir loft. One of your favorite spots.

AARON We can go live in Treme right by the playground.

MAEVE But what if Father Dolan is right? Maybe the people from St. Augustine can teach you more than I can. And I should spend more time with the Lord.

AARON You ain't even gonna be no sister, anyways. You're too fun. Not all wrinkled up like the other sisters and that old father. Ain't nobody gonna teach me more than you. Can we play pirates now? Me and you, sister?

MAEVE I ain't even.

[*Beat.*]

Aaron, we're going to Myrtle Street playground, but first we should go pack some bags.

AARON Where we goin'?

MAEVE On a pirate adventure.

[AARON *hands* MAEVE *her sword, grabs his sword. They cross blades and smile.*]

[*Lights fade.*]

• • •

Dolor

Hal Corley

Hal Corley

Hal Corley has developed his plays with major companies (Seattle Rep, Syracuse Stage, Walnut Street, Premiere Stages, Atlanta's Alliance, Adirondack Theater Festival, Stageworks/Hudson). Three full-length scripts, *Easter Monday, Mama and Jack Carew*, and *ODD*, are published by Samuel French, excerpted in French's *Exceptional Monologues 2* and S&K's *Best Men's/Women's Stage Scenes and Monologues of 2011*. His *Treed* is published by *Playscripts in Great Short Plays Volume 10*, his adaptation of Wilder's *Fanny Otcott* by YouthPlays, and over thirty of his other one-acts have been produced in the US and Canada. He was twice a finalist for the Heideman Award and three times a semifinalist in the O'Neill Competition.

···production history···

A site-specific version of *Dolor* was staged in Flush Ink's Asphalt Jungle Shorts IX, Waterloo, Ontario, June 6–15, 2013; produced by Paddy Gillard-Bentley, directed by Terre Chartrand with the following cast:

MELINDA   Kalene Ticknor

TEDDY   Douglas Morton

The American premiere of the revised *Dolor* was on February 5, 2015, in Blue Box World's Sticky Series at the Beauty Bar, Brooklyn, New York; directed by Michele Travis with the following cast:

MELINDA   Nicole Greevy

TEDDY   Todd Faulkner

characters

TEDDY   20s/30s

MELINDA   20s/30s

time

A slow Monday evening. Summer.

setting

An empty bar. Rural or suburban.

note

A "/" in dialog indicates overlap.

"Any fool can be happy. It takes a man with real heart to make beauty out of the stuff that makes us weep." —Clive Barker

[*A nondescript tavern, only two people visible at nearby tables, each nursing a beer. Critically: Their backs are to one another.*]

MELINDA   Eighty-year-old woman. Bone-thin. White-headed. Hunched over. Unmarried.

TEDDY   A widow. Entirely on her own.

MELINDA In a restaurant. Small table. Burnt-down candle nobody bothered to change.

TEDDY Tablecloth all stained—

MELINDA With somethin' obviously *festive*. Big, sweet globs of—crème / brûlée—

TEDDY A table no one *else* would / take.

MELINDA Tiramisu . . . panna cotta . . . blancmange—

TEDDY An *unappealing* table the snotty maître d' wouldn't dare give another patron.

MELINDA By the kitchen. With three empty chairs.

TEDDY And she's unable to decide what to order.

MELINDA 'Cause she didn't know the place was Italian and she's had to eat at the Olive Garden—

TEDDY No, no, that just makes her a bitch.

MELINDA Then 'cause she can never make up her mind, after hearing the specials—

TEDDY *No*, everything on the menu—remember—is an emotional *trigger*.

MELINDA I get it, pushes her buttons. Then maybe associated with her dead husband?

TEDDY Or just associated with *her*. Her childhood. In the 1930s.

MELINDA A shrimp cocktail.

TEDDY *What?*

MELINDA She suddenly totally craves one.

TEDDY Shrimp cocktail during the Depression? She wouldn't have had *crackers* that go with it.

MELINDA Maybe she's remembering all that. Remembering, like, nothing but saltines for supper.

TEDDY But it gets complicated, the algebra to connect them to /
shrimp—

MELINDA Maybe she's allergic to shellfish.

TEDDY And wants it anyway, 'cause she's *suicidal*? No.

MELINDA She's unable to hold a fork in her hand.

TEDDY What, because it's wet? Greasy?

MELINDA 'Cause she's palsied.

TEDDY She shakes?

MELINDA Sure, the free crudité on her table, that stuffed olive she'd
love, falls off her damn / fork.

TEDDY Not an *ailment*, she's entirely *well*, but just alone. Alone and old
are *enough*.

MELINDA Unable to pay.

TEDDY That makes her a thief. A con artist.

MELINDA Not if she *thinks* she's got cash in her wallet but actually
doesn't have a cent.

TEDDY Then she's forgotten, and her failing mind takes us back to
Alzheimer's.

MELINDA Progressive subcortical dementia is pretty damned shitty—

TEDDY She's unable to get the waiter's attention.

MELINDA *And* the young server reminds her of her cute husband at that
age.

TEDDY Maybe. But we don't need it, just her feeling alone and—

MELINDA Ignored, entirely—neglected.

TEDDY Good.

MELINDA And she watches a family at the next table, little twin boys
ordering from the kids' menu.

TEDDY And one of them glances over at her and gives her that look—

MELINDA The missing-front-tooth, *I-Heart-Grandma* smile.

TEDDY Excellent.

MELINDA And an elderly couple is at the table by the window, and it's—Valentine's Day night.

TEDDY But if it's also a holiday it kinda / gilds the—

MELINDA No, her birthday! *And* the birthday of the old lady by the window / too—

TEDDY Wait—

MELINDA 'Cause *that* lady gets a cake—a Sachertorte! Totally authentic, flown in on Lufthansa, like, packed in dry ice like a donated organ, brought over as a surprise by the waiter!

TEDDY Whoa, whoa, whoa, suddenly it's about European baked goods, a Viennese heritage. Lufthansa is German by the way. Austria's got its own airline.

MELINDA I know for a fact Lufthansa's got international flights outta / Salzburg—

TEDDY Whatever! That stuff makes it all a coincidence. Another lady a table away born the same day? That's almost, like, *uplifting*, not melancholy.

MELINDA But if the waiter sings "Happy Birthday" to the other lady, "Alles Gute zum Geburtstag."

TEDDY No, *no*, we don't need a damn *singing* wait staff. The *aloneness* for a solitary meal is what makes it so *wrenching*. Aim for some restraint, think minimalism.

MELINDA Less can be more, yeah, awesome. *Hey*, can't I come to your table / now—

TEDDY God, *no*! *Ruins* it! No eye contact! Don't even turn around!

[*Regroups, perhaps propping his feet on another chair.*]

Okay, then. Whole new image: A *child*.

MELINDA Lost.

TEDDY Well, that's always—no, too disturbing, no, a child—celebrating Christmas in July.

MELINDA 'Cause he likes the holidays so much?

TEDDY 'Cause he'll be *dead* by December.

MELINDA Oh God, Ted, no.

TEDDY Wears pajamas twenty-four seven now, in a motorized wheelchair.

MELINDA Oh my God, no—wait—*hey*—disease is involved in *that*.

TEDDY But it's way different in this case . . . 'cause his being terminal *creates* the circumstance.

MELINDA A kid getting his final Christmas in the summer. Stab me in the damn heart.

TEDDY The family's *tree* up, with presents, everybody *else* with a tan, going to the beach.

MELINDA 'Course in Florida that's how it is when you celebrate at the regular / time—

TEDDY Then Minnesota. A balmy eighty-four, only in July, Christmases always white.

MELINDA Near the tree is this miniature lit-up Ye Olde Dickensian Village, a beloved / heirloom.

TEDDY Other kids are all taking off that week for sleep-away camp.

MELINDA Maine, the Adirondacks. Some are *fat*, headin' off to deal with childhood obesity—

TEDDY Irrelevant, they're leaving *him* for *good*. Even the best bud he'll never see again.

MELINDA Shit, man. And the mom baking, like, reindeer and elf cookies.

TEDDY The dad telling the boy Santa *himself* insisted the holiday be moved up this year.

MELINDA Shit, you're getting to me. You knew that would do it.

TEDDY 'Cause Santa's bringing summer toys and wanted him to have 'em when it's warm.

MELINDA Those fancy slalom water skis! You can ski with only one and make razor / sharp turns!

TEDDY And *so*, so, they write a final letter to Santa, father and son.

MELINDA And Santa sends a quick reply *back* that explains the need to move it up to July.

TEDDY Gettin' a little baroque, Santa Claus doesn't *write* / letters—

MELINDA They decorate outside, icicle lights, a massive inflated snowman that glows in the dark.

TEDDY And freak the neighbors out? No, a single lit tree in an AC'd house is plenty.

MELINDA And the kid has no hair left, from chemo injected directly into the cerebrospinal fluid.

TEDDY *TMI*, Melinda! Jesus! You get off on ugly details! *No*. It's all a question of *situation*.

MELINDA [*Had it, wheeling around to face him; rising.*] Says *who*. I don't like this game.

TEDDY *Game*—turn back arou—get back to your table!

MELINDA I hate the way you make up new rules as you go.

TEDDY *Rules?* We're free-associating about the emotional weight of conditions that spark our sadness. When it gets too visually *textured*, it doesn't get to us.

MELINDA *Us?* You edit me, so it's only about whatever pulls feelings out of *your* tight ass.

TEDDY Excuse me.

MELINDA You have to be the person with the biggest goddamn woe in the room.

TEDDY Honey, this so-called game brought you n'me / together—

MELINDA Well, I happen to think an eighty-five-year-old babe ordering a shrimp cocktail—whether it reminds her of bread lines *or* makes her lips swell from the anaphylaxis—is *miserable.*

TEDDY Maybe in some circles, allergist conventions, New England states where fisherman layoffs are pandemic, but it's not the sorta everyday incident / we first—

MELINDA Maybe the idea of Saint Nick writing back to a kid with a brain tumor is shattering!

TEDDY Again, except that the fat man in red / *wouldn't*—

MELINDA Not just any tumor, a craniopharyngioma.

TEDDY The big guy with the sleigh has never *corresponded* with a *child*, / anywhere—

MELINDA A juvenile pilocytic astrocytoma.

TEDDY If ya have to *reinvent* the mythology to hold on to your trigger—

MELINDA Maybe I'm just more imaginative than you! Deep down more creative? Maybe my sadness triggers are more complex and more colorful because *I* am!

[MELINDA *moves away from him again.*]

TEDDY I'm beginning to wonder if the saddest thing ever might be two cum laude grads having to play mind games in a for-shit bar, pissin' distance from the roar of I-94—

[*Spitting it out.*]

Because both of us still live with our fucking parents.

[*They exchange a brief look of shame.*]

Trying to treasure a new relationship, only to find it might not *be* there. To seemingly be so close to another person, yet the proverbial million miles away. To learn your heart has been unfairly judged, your empathy misconstrued as / self-serving—

MELINDA Still all about *you*! Your inklings, your wounds, your agony, your excruciating *story* always has to be the most tragic fucking one on the planet!

[MELINDA *grabs her jeans jacket;* TEDDY *goes to her.*]

TEDDY And where are you going? To an all-night diner for a tuna melt? Only to find yourself the only single woman in the place, surrounded by *couples* celebrating anniversaries?

MELINDA An anniversary in a damn *diner?*

TEDDY Or maybe a pediatric ward? The kids not comatose still wide awake? Waiting for friends that couldn't be bothered to show during visiting hours? Maybe some even have tiny, blinking evergreens next to their mechanized hospital beds. Or music boxes playing *"Up on the rooftop, click click click, down through the chim—"*

MELINDA Stop it, damn it! I'm so done here!

[MELINDA *pulls out her cell phone to check for messages.*]

TEDDY Before you go to sleep for the night, call me. When I'm back home. Alone.

[MELINDA *cocks her heads slightly; a dare.*]

Let me tell you what my little *cell* looks like at 3 a.m. As I lie there on my cot, sprawled across the wrinkled Woody-in-*Toy Story*-themed bedspread. The one I was actually way too old for when my mom bought it but would never admit.

[MELINDA *sneaks a covert peek at him.*]

A single lamp lit, 'cause the dark still reminds me of my blackened boyhood room. . . .

[*Distant thunder rumbles.*]

And *rain*. Droplets on the window panes. In perfect sync, my cheeks grow wet as well, not from revisiting my wretched youth, but *tonight*. The blunders. Strategic errors made trying to get to you. The myriad ways my ego ruined my shot with—

MELINDA Leave the lamp out. Instead of sad, it's just wimpy.

TEDDY   But if the lamp is just a tiny thing? No? Too much? Will you call me?

MELINDA   Know what will *really* make it sad? This middle-of-the-night abyss of yours?

TEDDY   What? Melinda, *what?* Tell me! Say it! Do it! Lay the final straw on me!

MELINDA   A deafening click. On your end. When I hang up on you. For good, asshole.

[*She's gone.* TED *flops back in his chair, takes a pull on his beer. He readjusts. Almost posing, he creates a calculatingly pitiful image and holds it a moment. He then gets an idea and reaches down into his jeans pocket, fumbling to find his cell. He readjusts himself with a pietà-worthy look of abject melancholy. Then strategically snaps a picture of himself. Blackout.*]

• • •

Gonna Need to See Some ID

Donna Latham

Donna Latham

Donna Latham is an award-winning playwright whose plays have been produced coast to coast and across the pond. *And We Will Share the Sky* was a regional finalist for the Kennedy Center's David Mark Cohen Playwriting Award and is the recipient of the National Theatre for Young Audiences Playwriting Award. *Grievances and Whirligigs* was part of the Biscuit Tin Series in Belfast and the EstroGenius Festival, Manhattan Theatre Source. *Coyote's Moon* went up at the La MaMa Theatre 50 Block Party in New York. *A Midnight Clear: The Christmas Truce of 1914* and *The Haunted Widow Lincoln* were produced at the Batavia Arts Council in the Chicago area. *The Haunted Widow Lincoln* is a semi-finalist for the Playwrights First Award. Latham is a proud member of the Dramatist Guild.

···production history···

Vero Voce Theatre, St. Charles, Illinois, March 2015. Directed by David M. Rodriguez.

JASON David M. Rodriguez

TIGGY Jennifer Torchia

SECURITY GUARD Tony Pellegrino

LOUIE Brian Downing

CRAZY-ASS PERSON Paul Cepysnky

Theatre Unchained, Milwaukee, Wisconsin, August 2014.

characters

JASON M 20s. Suspicious and inappropriate cashier.

TIGGY F 20s–40s. Harried mom fighting a cold.

SECURITY GUARD M 20s–30s. Guard—suffers from delusional badass syndrome.

LOUIE M middle-aged. Curmudgeon landlord.

CRAZY-ASS PERSON Any age. Scary-ass, mask-wearing, weapon nut.

synopsis

Sizzurup? Bombs? A suspicious cashier interrogates customers as they attempt to make purchases.

[*At rise,* JASON, *who wears aviator shades, slips into his employee vest and puts on his ID badge.*]

JASON Another day on the job in Chi-Town. Wrangling the bad guys like Rootin'-Tootin' Shirtless Putin on a steed.

[TIGGY *enters with shopping cart and loads purchases on counter, and* JASON *rings them up.*]

Welcome to All-Get, yo.

TIGGY Hi there.

JASON I'm supposed to say that to everyone. Annoying, right? All those lame rules and regs? So, how ya doin'?

TIGGY Another day, another zillion errands. Plus I'm fighting a summer cold, hacking up a lung.

JASON The worst! Hate summer colds with the heat of a thousand suns.

TIGGY How about you?

JASON I'm not usually up before the butt crack of noon. This working-stiff stuff sucks the big wazoo. Know what I mean? Way to harsh my summer-break mellow. But, whatevs. Scan your customer loyalty card. Please and thank you.

TIGGY Oh, I'm not a regular customer. I live near Devon and California.

JASON My condolences.

TIGGY All-Get's so close to my daughter's tumbling class. I figured why not sneak out for a minute.

JASON No problem-o. Just hoist your stuff on the belt. Cold-B-Gone, tissues, honey spice tea, cough drops. Diet Coke? Nasty.

TIGGY I know, I know. It's all chemicals, but I just can't quit my favorite poison.

JASON Go for the straight-up sugar bomb. Co-Cola. The real thang, sweet thang.

TIGGY Awk, these huge bottles weigh a ton. Can I count this as a bicep workout?

JASON Hell to the yes! Sprite, huh? Jason likey.

TIGGY So refreshing on a summer day, right? Here—more bottles.

JASON Mountain Dew? Seriously?

TIGGY Styrofoam cups. Aaaand—last bottle.

JASON You don't look like the Mountain Dew type. Doesn't jive with the yoga pants.

TIGGY It's for my daughter's fourth-birthday party. I only allow Lainey to drink it once a year.

JASON I can't even. You'll peel that tot off the ceiling in a hot minute. Jolly Ranchers?

TIGGY Lainey's daughter's favorite.

JASON A likely story.

TIGGY Talk about peeling! Jolly Ranchers clamp onto my veneers like bloodsuckers.

JASON You think I'm stupid?

TIGGY Why do you ask? Noisemakers, pretty princess tiaras, glitter soap. All the trappings of an awesome shindig, right?

JASON What you got stashed in that cart?

TIGGY Oops, almost forgot to pop this in my purse. Cough syrup. I already paid for it in the pharmacy. See? Here's my receipt stapled to the bag.

JASON Knew it! Codeine Queen! You're brewing sizzurup!

TIGGY Scissor what?

JASON Purple Stuff. Oil. Sweet Tea. G6.

TIGGY I have absolutely no clue what you're gabbering about. Can you finish ringing me up? My to-do list is three miles long.

JASON Gonna need to see some ID.

TIGGY What is your problem?

JASON Whip it out.

TIGGY You're carding me because—?

JASON Prove your identity. Now.

TIGGY Oh, all right. Here, see? Tiggy Baines—me.

JASON I know your type, Tigs. Hiding behind the Mom Mask. Security!

TIGGY You're out of your mind. I'm a perfectly normal human being, not some crazy criminal. Get a life.

JASON Security! Got us a sizzurup guzzler on Lane Two!

TIGGY Shhh, everyone's staring.

JASON Wait 'til they ogle the pat-down.

TIGGY Never mind. I'll hit another store where the cashiers aren't off their meds.

JASON Get back here. You're not faking another prescription somewhere else. Security, move it!

[SECURITY GUARD *enters, panting.*]

SECURITY GUARD Hauling tail as fast as I can. Got a hitch in my giddyup.

JASON The suspect is attempting to flee.

TIGGY Suspect?

SECURITY GUARD Hold it right there, little missy. Reach for the sky, nice and high.

TIGGY Help, someone, help!

SECURITY GUARD Pipe down, little missy. I know me a guzzler when I see one.

TIGGY I have to pick up my daughter!

SECURITY GUARD All in good time. Shit howdy, Jason, you are badass!

JASON Preach!

SECURITY GUARD Stash the evidence in a bag for me, pardner.

JASON Hell to the yah-hah! Nabbed her like a boss!

SECURITY GUARD Now you? Hustle your badonkadonk to the pat-down area.

TIGGY Let me go, skeevy creeper! Police! Someone, call 911!

[SECURITY GUARD *hauls* TIGGY *off, and* LOUIE *enters and begins to pile purchases on the counter.*]

JASON Hey, bruh. Hot enough for ya?

LOUIE Oy, don't even ask. My fakakta tenant gobbed up the damned toilet in 3B again.

JASON Hell to the foul.

LOUIE What that little pisher does in there? I don't wanna know.

JASON Lentils. Sounds like lentils.

LOUIE Here you go, kid. Plunger. Replacement flapper. Beer and a shot for afterward. You don't need my ID, do you?

JASON We only card under forty. No offense, old-timer.

LOUIE None taken, wisenheimer. Okay, rubber gloves, auger.

JASON That thing's creeping me out. Do you need a safe word with it?

LOUIE Snake it down the crapper, one, two, three. Unclog that disaster like a pro.

JASON That everything?

LOUIE One more item. Drano. If all else fails.

JASON Knew it! Try to play me with your feeble geezer routine, huh?

LOUIE Play you?

JASON You're building a bomb!

LOUIE Bite your tongue! The way everyone's so paranoid already. You wanna get us killed?

JASON You can't bamboozle me. Drano for a clogged toilet? My ass! It's an explosive!

LOUIE Listen, punk. That's no way to talk to your elders.

JASON Gonna need to see some ID.

LOUIE For what already? You cleared me on the PBR and Jack.

JASON I need to scan you into the system.

LOUIE Here, take it. Do what you gotta do. Now ring me up already. I got work to do.

JASON Stare straight ahead. Don't look away until the flashing light goes out.

LOUIE The hell you say?

JASON Retinal scan. And three, two, one. Done. Okay, grab this and step behind that curtain. It's private, I promise. No one wants to see your droopy old balls. Just sayin'.

LOUIE What's this container?

JASON It's for the sperm specimen. No biggie. Coupla squirts will do.

LOUIE Over my dead carcass.

JASON You know the drill, am I right? Yank your auger, if you catch my drift. Afterwards, screw the lid on tight, got me? Write your name, date of birth, and time of collection on the label. Tuck the specimen close to your body until the hazmat team arrives to pick it up.

LOUIE Enough already with the cockamamie prattle. Keep your crappy auger. I'm outta here.

JASON Not so fast, dude.

LOUIE This city's going to hell in a handbasket. Go back to Wicker Park, you little pisher.

JASON Security! Security! We got us a bomber codger in Lane Two!

[SECURITY GUARD *enters, snaps rubber glove gleefully.*]

SECURITY GUARD Jason, you da man! You're cleaning up!

JASON Just keeping this joint safe for democracy.

LOUIE Lemme go, you big lummox!

SECURITY GUARD Shut your yap. Don't make me taze you.

LOUIE Help! Somebody, call my daughter the lawyer!

[SECURITY GUARD *hauls* LOUIE *off.* CRAZY-ASS PERSON *slinks in.*]

JASON Whew, what a morning. Break time can't get here fast enough. Hey, how you doing? You're rocking the balaclava.

[CRAZY-ASS PERSON *grunts and mutters.*]

Full Mutant Ninja, right? Hell to the oh-yeah!

[CRAZY-ASS PERSON *grunts and mutters.*]

No offense, but aren't you roasting in there? I'd keel over from heat prostration.

[CRAZY-ASS PERSON *grunts and mutters.*]

Just scan your customer loyalty card. Rack up those loyalty points for a free hot dog and fries!

[CRAZY-ASS PERSON *curses and glances furtively about. Places a gun on the counter.*]

Ruh-roh. Hold it right there. We got ourselves a problem. Don't we, buddy?

[CRAZY-ASS PERSON *grunts quizzically. Glances furtively about.*]

A big honking problem. HUGE.

[CRAZY-ASS PERSON *tenses, grumbles, reaches hand under hoodie.*]

The register didn't take your card. No worries, my man. Do-over. Try, try again. Go on, scan again. Presto, got it! Pile your stuff on the counter. Please and thank you.

[CRAZY-ASS PERSON *piles guns, ammunition, and other weapons on counter. Glances furtively about.*]

Credit or debit?

[CRAZY-ASS PERSON *mutters. Glances furtively about with increased agitation.*]

Need any help hauling that stuff to your car? Okay, then. You're all set. Thanks for stopping in. Have a kick-ass day!

• • •

There's
No Here
Here

Craig Pospisil

Craig Pospisil

Craig Pospisil is the author of *Months On End*, *Somewhere in Between*, *The Dunes*, *Life Is Short*, and *Choosing Sides*, published by Dramatists Play Service. His short film *January* was an official selection at the 2015 Big Apple, Black Bear, and Laughlin International Film Festivals. His plays have been seen at EST, Purple Rose, Barrington Stage, Bay Street, Detroit Rep, New World Stages, around the US, in two dozen countries, and translated into Dutch, French, Greek, Mandarin, and Spanish. He has written over sixty short plays, including *It's Not You* (*theAtrainplays, Vol. 1*), *On the Edge* (*The Best Ten-Minute Plays 2005*), *Perchance* (*The Best Ten-Minute Plays 2006*), and *Dissonance* (*The Best American Short Plays 2010–2011*). His newest play is a full-length comedy called *The Poles of Inaccessibility*. Visit www.CraigPospisil.com.

··· **production history** ···

There's No Here Here had its professional premiere at Barrington Stage Company (Julianne Boyd, Artistic Director; Triston Wilson, Managing Director) in Pittsfield, Massachusetts, as part of the 10X10 Upstreet Arts Festival in February 2014. It was directed by Christopher Innvar, and the cast was as follows:

JULIETTE   Emily Taplin Boyd

WAITER   Scott Drummond

STRANGER   Peggy Pharr Wilson

LANCE   Dustin Charles

[*A Parisian café. Spring. French music, perhaps something by Serge Gainsbourg, plays in the background.* JULIETTE, *beautiful and chic, sits at a café table, reading Camus's* L'Etranger. *A menu lies on the table. A* STRANGER, *who we will come to learn is named* GERTRUDE, *in frumpy clothes, sits at another table with her back to the audience. She does not turn around until indicated. She has a glass of rosé wine, which she sips from time to time. A bored French* WAITER, *who we will come to learn is named* JEAN-LUC, *enters and sets a cup of coffee down on* JULIETTE's *table. He gestures to the menu to ask, "Anything else?" She shakes her head, "No." The* WAITER *shrugs, a little put out, but it means less work. He starts to exit, when* LANCE *comes barreling in, carrying a notebook.* JULIETTE *looks up as he stops in front of her.*]

LANCE   You can't touch someone's life like that and then just be done with them!

[JULIETTE *stares at* LANCE, *confused. She looks at the* WAITER, *who shrugs. They look at* LANCE, *who turns to the audience.*]

LANCE   [*To audience.*] At least, that's what I wanted to say. There's a lot of things I want to say. I don't actually say most of them. Or anything like them really. It comes out wrong.

[*Slight pause.*]

So, that's what I wanted to say, but I think what I actually said was:

[*Turning back to* JULIETTE, *plaintively.*]

Why won't you answer my calls?

JULIETTE   Lance . . . *chérie, cette chose entre nous, c'est fini.*

[LANCE *winces and holds up his hand to her to say "wait." He turns back to the audience.*]

LANCE [*To audience.*] Sorry. Uh, we're in France. Paris, actually. Left Bank, not far from the Seine. Does everyone speak French? No?
[*Turning back to the others.*]
You've got to speak in English.

JULIETTE Quoi?

LANCE *Parlez en anglais.*

JULIETTE *Pourquoi?*

LANCE [*Pointing to the audience.*] *Parce que.*

JULIETTE [*Sighs and shrugs.*] Okay.

[LANCE *looks at the* WAITER, *who shakes his head.*]

WAITER *Non.*

LANCE Please?

WAITER *Non.*

LANCE They won't understand. That's rude.

WAITER *Oui.*

[WAITER *exits.* JULIETTE *goes back to her book.*]

LANCE Juliette—

JULIETTE I have nothing to say to you.

LANCE You're being unreasonable.

JULIETTE I am a French woman.

LANCE But this is why I'm here.

JULIETTE Oh, yes, you saved, for years you saved so you could come to Paris and write, just to write.

LANCE Yes! But now there's also you.

JULIETTE Hmmmpf.

[*She goes back to her book again, but* LANCE *takes it.*]

LANCE Juliette—

JULIETTE *Donnez-moi ce livre!*

LANCE In English.

JULIETTE Give me my book!

[*He gives her the book.*]

You want to write, fine. Go be with your words. I have words too, and my words are "Good-bye."

LANCE All I said was that I needed to work this afternoon.

JULIETTE Yes, one afternoon after another. Hmmmpf.

LANCE Why can't we just talk about this?

JULIETTE You talk and you talk and you talk until the talking is over.

STRANGER [*Turning around.*] Oh, I like that.

[LANCE *and* JULIETTE *look at her.*]

STRANGER Don't mind me, I'm just listening in.

LANCE Um . . . we're having a private conversation.

STRANGER In a public place.

LANCE Do you mind?

STRANGER All right. I'm sorry.

LANCE That's okay.

STRANGER You don't mean that.

LANCE Sure, I do.

STRANGER No, you're just being polite.

JULIETTE Who is this person?

LANCE I have no idea.

STRANGER Yes, you do.

LANCE No. I don't.

STRANGER You're never going to write something true if you keep that up.

[LANCE *stares at her. He recognizes her on some level, but he's unable to place her.*]

LANCE Wait, are . . . who are you?

STRANGER *Garçon?*

[*The* WAITER *enters, full of ennui.*]

WAITER *Oui, madame?*

STRANGER Another glass of rosé, please.

WAITER *Certainement.*

[*The* WAITER *exits, bored.*]

LANCE You already have a glass.

STRANGER It won't last forever.

JULIETTE Ooo! You come here, you interrupt my reading, saying you must talk to me, why won't I talk to you . . . and then you stand and talk with this, this stranger, meanwhile my café crème has gone cold, and my temper is hot.

STRANGER She's a spitfire.

LANCE Just hold on, there's something . . .

JULIETTE There is something, yes, there is something! This is how it always is with you. You see only what is right in front of you and the rest just fades away. You expect me—me, a beautiful French woman!— to be here when you want me, but even when you are here, you are not here.

STRANGER There's no here here.

[*The* WAITER *returns with a glass of wine, which he sets on her table.*]

WAITER *Voila, madame.*

[*As he leaves again,* GERTRUDE *swirls the wine in her glass and takes a sniff of its bouquet.*]

STRANGER A rosé is a rosé is a rosé.

LANCE Oh my God!

JULIETTE What?

LANCE She's Gertrude Stein!

JULIETTE Who?

LANCE An American writer who lived in Paris in the 1920s and '30s.

JULIETTE That's impossible.

GERTRUDE I prefer it that way. If it can be done, why do it?

LANCE No, no, no . . .

[*Turning to the audience.*]

I'm sorry, I don't know why she's here.

[*Back to* GERTRUDE.]

You can't be here. You're dead.

[*Back to the audience.*]

She's dead.

GERTRUDE Who are you talking to?

LANCE Them.

GERTRUDE So, it's all right for you to have a fight with your girlfriend in a café in Paris while this audience somewhere else watches you, but talking to a woman who's been dead since 1946 . . . *that's* going too far?

LANCE Okay, this is . . . this is . . .

GERTRUDE This is your story.

LANCE My story?

JULIETTE Wait, you are writing this?

LANCE Oh my God, I think I am.

JULIETTE You! You come to make this big scene here at the café, to talk, to make me take you back . . . but you are somewhere *still* writing?!

LANCE . . . Yes?

JULIETTE You are a bad writer.

LANCE Juliette—

JULIETTE And! You are a bad lover.

GERTRUDE Bam, said the lady.

LANCE Do you mind?!

GERTRUDE Hey, this is your imagination. You don't want me here, say the word.

LANCE Go!

GERTRUDE That's not the word.

LANCE Look, please just . . . go back to your table and finish your wine.

GERTRUDE Sorry, Lance. I aim to misbehave.

[*Hearing wine mentioned, the* WAITER *returns.*]

WAITER *Un peu plus de vin?*

LANCE Juliette, please this is—

JULIETTE Don't bother speaking. I hear the lies already.

LANCE No. I'm here to write. This could be my last chance. Either something happens this year or . . . I've been doing this since I was twenty-two, and all I've got to show are a couple of short stories in an anthology and an agent who won't take my calls. I'm divorced. I don't have any kids. I have a cat. I found her in an alley around the corner from here, and I call her Elle. I saved her life, but she only pays attention to me when it's time to eat. I just want to get something down on the page that's alive. But I haven't been able to. Then I met you, and I feel something. And it inspires me and—

[JULIETTE *slaps him.*]

GERTRUDE Affection can be so dangerous.

WAITER *Pardon, monsieur, mais—*

LANCE Would you go away? Can't you just ignore us like most Parisian waiters?!

WAITER No. I will not. I have, as you say, a bone to pick. My role in this story of yours is nothing more than an insulting cliché. A rude French waiter? Oo-la-la! So clever. How ever did you come up with an idea such as that? Feh! No wonder you have no success. You have the imagination of a cow. I don't even have a name in this scenario of yours.

[*Waving a hand toward the audience.*]

To them, I am just the French waiter, full of ennui, saying only "*oui*" and "*non*" because your French is too poor to allow me to truly give voice to all that is inside me. And I'm supposed to just go in and out bringing you wine and coffee while you play out this ridiculous scene with this woman, telling her you "feel something," instead of telling her you love her. If you love her, you take action. You don't plead and moan about writing words. What are words? Will they love you anymore than your cat? But like all Americans all you think of is yourself and you miss the point completely. In love you should act and act decisively! A woman like this needs to be grabbed hard, and then held tenderly.

[*He takes hold of* JULIETTE *and pulls her to him in a flash, then holds her tenderly in his arms. He caresses her face with one hand.*]

Darling, your cool beauty overwhelms me. You are like a tonic to a man lying in bed with malaria and a high fever, on the knife's edge between life and death. You are water in the desert. You give me life, you give me breath.

JULIETTE Oh, Jean-Luc.

JEAN-LUC Yes . . .

[*Then looking to* LANCE.]

That is my name.

JULIETTE Jean-Luc, will you take me away from here?

JEAN-LUC Yes, my darling. We'll leave this behind. Come with me to the casbah.

JULIETTE Yes, yes, I will. If we go now we can still catch the night plane.

[JEAN-LUC *and* JULIETTE *kiss passionately. When they break apart,* JEAN-LUC *turns dismissively to* LANCE.]

JEAN-LUC   That is how you keep a woman like Juliette.

JULIETTE   *Oui, c'est vrai.*

[*Then remembering the audience.*]

I mean—

LANCE   No, it's okay. I think they get it.

JULIETTE   [*Kissing him on both cheeks.*] *Au revoir, chérie.*

LANCE   *Au revoir.*

[JEAN-LUC *takes* JULIETTE's *hand and they hurry offstage.* LANCE *watches them go.*]

GERTRUDE   That's what happens when you ignore minor characters. They come back and bite you in the ass.

LANCE   I'm starting to wonder who the minor character here really is.

GERTRUDE   You don't understand what you don't understand.

LANCE   What?

GERTRUDE   Think about it.

LANCE   [*Pause, thinks.*] I'm blind to the parts of myself that I don't want to hear.

GERTRUDE   Oh, I like that.

LANCE   Yeah.

[LANCE *sits and begins to write in his notebook.* GERTRUDE *gets the glass of rosé from her table and sets it down by* LANCE.]

GERTRUDE   To write is to write is to write is to write . . . but you might get thirsty.

[LANCE *continues to write.* GERTRUDE *smiles and gently pats the back of his head.*]

Good man, Lance. You keep working.

[GERTRUDE *makes her way down the boulevard, as the lights fade on* LANCE, *who keeps writing.*]

• • •

Vertical Constellation with Bomb

Gwydion Suilebhan

Gwydion Suilebhan

Gwydion Suilebhan is the author of *The Butcher, Reals, Abstract Nude, The Constellation, Let X, The Faithkiller, Cracked,* and *Anthem*. His work has been commissioned, produced, and developed by Centerstage, Ensemble Studio Theatre, the National New Play Network, Gulfshore Playhouse, Forum Theatre, Theater J, Theater Alliance, and the Source Theater Festival. A founding member of the Welders, Gwydion serves as DC's representative to the Dramatists Guild. In addition, Gwydion speaks on the intersection between theater, the arts, and technology. Recent engagements include South by Southwest, TCG, LMDA, the Dramatists Guild, CityWrights, APASO, TEDxMichiganAve, and TEDxWDC. His commentary appears on HowlRound, 2am Theatre, and at www.suilebhan.com. He has consulted for Ford's Theatre, the Playwrights Center, and the Dramatists Guild, among others. He is currently serving as director of brand and marketing for Woolly Mammoth Theatre Company and project director of the New Play Exchange for the National New Play Network.

··· production history ···

Vertical Constellation with Bomb was commissioned by the Welders (Washington, DC). Produced by New Theatre (Miami, FL). Directed by Philip Church and Anton Church.

VERNELL   Adele Robinson

ALEXANDER CALDER   Charles Sothers

NUN   Margaret Ricke

[*Evening. New York. The latter days of World War II. A young mother,* VERNELL, *sits on the front stoop of her house, fretting over a crushed scrap of aluminum. Beside her stands* ALEXANDER CALDER, *a sculptor. His gaze is fixed upward toward the sky. On her other side stands a* NUN, *an old empty wheelbarrow set awkwardly at her feet.*]

VERNELL   [*To the audience.*] The first one to approach me was the artist.

CALDER   I'm a sculptor.

VERNELL   This is my story. Now be quiet.

[*To the audience.*]

Like I said . . . the first one to approach me was the sculptor. He was walking around the neighborhood stargazing, and I . . .

CALDER   I wasn't stargazing.

VERNELL   He says he wasn't stargazing, but he was looking up at something. And whatever it was, he was so distracted by it he almost tripped over me. And the thing is . . . if it was stars he was looking for, he was wasting his time. You can't see any stars here in the city. There's too much light pollution from all the office buildings and houses and whatnot.

CALDER   Excuse me?

VERNELL   People think it's clouds when you can't see any stars, but it's really just all this artificial light drowning out the constellations.

CALDER   Well, I wasn't stargazing anyway.

VERNELL   Right.

[*To the audience.*]

You're gonna love this.

CALDER   I was trying to figure out whether, if there were bombs falling—you know, from the Germans—they would be visible in the night sky.

[*To the audience.*]

See?

[*To* VERNELL.]

Do you think we would see them coming from down here or not?

[*A dubious look from* VERNELL.]

I'm not crazy. It's a genuine question. Do you think that if somehow the Germans could get their U-boats all the way here to the coastline to launch rockets at us, we would see them before they . . . ?

[*He makes an "explosion" gesture.*]

I need to know.

VERNELL   Why?

CALDER   For a new sculpture I'm working on. I want to understand what it would look like. Or *feel* like.

VERNELL   What do you think it would feel like? Like a bomb. Like . . . death coming right at you! And you can't move in time! You're completely helpless! You're about to get run over!

[*A beat.*]

CALDER   Sorry. I . . .

VERNELL   Just hush.

[*He does. She collects herself. To the audience.*]

He did not make a good first impression. But really, to be fair . . .

[*Indicating the* NUN.]

. . . neither did she.

NUN   Excuse me?

VERNELL   So it's dark out. And I'm out here all alone, just sitting on my stoop, trying to get some time by myself, when this nun with . . .

NUN   Oh, no. No, no. Nobody sits outside, in public, if they really want to be left all alone. And besides, you *weren't* alone.

[*Indicating* CALDER.]

He was here.

CALDER   Don't bring me into this.

VERNELL   [*To the audience.*] What would you think if you were me and a nun, with a full habit on, comes walking right up to you, out of the darkness, at night, pushing a wheelbarrow?

NUN   I meant you no harm.

VERNELL   I know that now.

NUN   [*To the audience.*] The sisters and I were all out patrolling the neighborhood collecting scrap metal for the war effort.

VERNELL   At night?

NUN   We're the Sisters of Mercy, not the Sisters of Letting Other People Do All the Hard Stuff. If all those young men we sent overseas can endure watching their fellow soldiers being run over by Panzer tanks and still . . .

VERNELL   Stop! Please.

[*A beat.*]

NUN   Sorry, dear.

[*A beat.*]

VERNELL   [*To the audience.*] To be fair, they were both hitting a lot closer to home than they could have possibly realized.

NUN   [*To the audience.*] I was just trying to do my part for the war effort, that's all. I have a nephew over there. Not even twenty-one years old, and he's fighting when he should be doing anything else. And I would absolutely take a bullet for him, if I could, without reservation. But I can only . . . collect scrap metal.

VERNELL What's his name?

NUN Stephen.

VERNELL I'll pray for him.

NUN Thank you. You know, even a thin strip of tin can protect a soldier. It can become part of an artillery shell. Deflect a stray bullet. It can make a real difference.

CALDER No, it can't.

NUN What do you know?

CALDER I know scrap metal drives don't do anything. Not really. They're only for show.

NUN So you say.

CALDER They get people excited, that's all. Keep morale up. But the metal just ends up in trash heaps, rusting away, under armed guard, at military depots. It's of no use to anyone.

NUN I hope you'll forgive me for saying that still strikes me as nonsense.

VERNELL He's right, though. My cousin Vincent did a hitch looking over a big scrap pile down at Fort Bragg. Nobody knows what to do with it all. Or how to sort through it.

NUN So maybe they haven't used it all yet, but I believe they will.

VERNELL I know you want to believe that. And you want other people to believe that, too.

NUN Yes.

VERNELL [*Noting the empty wheelbarrow.*] But it's not so easy to get some people to believe, is it?

NUN It's getting more difficult the longer the war goes on.

VERNELL I bet it is.

NUN And all the easy scraps have been gathered up already.

CALDER They have, yes. There's no new metal to be found anywhere any more.

[*To the audience.*]

I use metal in my work. I make mobiles. Bright scraps of metal balanced across thin wires so that even the slightest current of air sets them rotating, almost imperceptibly. The way planets move through the night sky.

NUN You make toys.

CALDER No, I do not.

NUN You would rather use metal to make toys than to fight Nazis.

CALDER They're mobiles, but they're not toys. They're art. I have work on display all over the world.

NUN Including in Germany?

CALDER I don't like what you're suggesting.

NUN I'm sure you don't.

CALDER I'll have you know: I offered to help the Marines as a *camoufleur*. To make camouflage to protect soldiers. I tried to do my part.

NUN So instead you make playthings for children.

CALDER I make *mobiles* because they remind us of how we're all part of the same solar system. Connected by gravity, by the forces of nature. So if you move, I move, and if I move, she moves. So when a constellation rises here in New York, and a German bomb sails through the sky over in London, in both places everybody's eyes look up toward Heaven. During war time, we need that.

NUN During wartime, we need soldiers. How can you possibly defend keeping scrap metal for yourself when boys, young boys, are dying over in Europe? You don't need it the way they do.

CALDER I need metal. I speak in metal. I don't know who I am without metal.

NUN Oh, you are just . . . ugh.

[*To* VERNELL.]

I'm sorry. I don't mean to press or anything, but . . . I *was* wondering whether you wouldn't mind parting with that . . . whatever it is you're holding there. That scrap. If you haven't already given it . . .

VERNELL Look! Shooting star!

[*They all look up.*]

CALDER Where?

VERNELL You missed it.

CALDER How do you know it wasn't a bomb? Or a bomber?

VERNELL It wasn't either.

NUN You don't know. You just said yourself we can't see any stars around here.

VERNELL A shooting star isn't an actual star. It's a meteor. A big hunk of rock and metal burning up in the atmosphere. And it's bright enough to see even here.

NUN Oh.

CALDER [*To* VERNELL.] Where was it again?

VERNELL [*Pointing.*] Right over there. Above that gray building. I saw one there earlier, too. It's the right night for them.

[*For a beat, they all look.*]

CALDER I would sure like to see another one.

NUN I don't mind saying: I would, too.

VERNELL Keep your eyes open, both of you. They come in bunches.

[CALDER *and the* NUN *stare hopefully into the night sky. Silence.*]

VERNELL [*To the audience.*] And at that moment, with the sculptor and the Sister of Mercy both standing there communing with the night, I almost left, but . . . something said *stay*, so I did. And the three of us all just sat there, right on my stoop, and before long it was like we were all surrounded by a deep calm that, being strangers, we really had no right to expect.

[*Silence. To the audience.*]

And then came the breeze.

[*A small wind passes by them. To the audience.*]

And the brief balance we had, in all that quiet, began to shift.

[*A beat.*]

CALDER I'm sorry, but do you mind if I ask you something personal? It's about your scrap. And I understand you don't want to part with it. That's just fine. I . . . probably need to explore new materials anyway. I'm just curious.

VERNELL Go on.

CALDER Well, I was just wondering . . . what is it? Or was it?

VERNELL A toy plane. My son's. It . . . got crushed in the accident. He was pretending to be an Allied soldier, fighting off a Panzer division, and he jumped off this stoop and just ran out into the street without . . .

[*She need not say more.* CALDER *and the* NUN *exchange a look. They understand. The* NUN *takes* VERNELL's *hand.*]

NUN Your son's with God now, dear. He's in Heaven. And he wants you to remember him as the bright boy he was, not as . . . a crushed scrap.

[*She touches* VERNELL's *scrap.*]

You can't hold on to your pain forever.

[*The* NUN *looks at* CALDER.]

Let it become something beautiful.

[VERNELL *takes a last look at the scrap, then hands it to* CALDER.]

VERNELL Make it mean something.

CALDER I'll try.

VERNELL [*To the audience.*] And I hope he did.

• • •

With a Bullet (Or, Surprise Me)

John Patrick Bray

John Patrick Bray

John Patrick Bray (MFA, PhD) has written plays under grants from the National Endowment for the Arts and the Acadiana Center for the Arts (Louisiana). He has earned commissions from organizations in Louisiana, Minnesota, North Carolina, Virginia, and New York City (Off-Off-Broadway). He is a resident playwright with Rising Sun Performance Company (Off-Off-Broadway) and a member and moderator of the Athens Playwrights' Workshop. His plays include *Friendly's Fire, Liner Notes, Hound, Donkey, Goodnight Lovin' Trail*, and *Erik: A Play About a Puppet*. His plays and monologues are published with Applause, Next Stage Press, Original Works Publishing, Smith and Kraus, JACPublishing, the Riant Theatre, Heartland Plays, and Indie Theatre Now. Bray is an assistant professor at the University of Georgia and a member of the Dramatists Guild of America, Inc.

···production history···

With a Bullet (Or, Surprise Me) premiered at the GOOD Works Theatre Festival in Marietta, Georgia, in November 2014. It was directed by Suehyla El-Attar and featured the following cast:

> **BIG J**   Andrew Sweeny
>
> **DR. LEE**   Kevin Stillwell
>
> **PIDGE**   Ronalda Thomas
>
> **DONNY**   Dylan Easley

characters

> **BIG J**   late 30s, a libertarian
>
> **PIDGE**   30s, a priest (Episcopalian)
>
> **DONNY**   30s, a spiritually wounded man
>
> **DOCTOR LEE**   40s, a karaoke host who only has songs he wrote himself

setting

A bar in the Hudson Valley, New York. New Year's Eve, 1999.

synopsis

Refusing to surrender control of their lives, a staunch libertarian, a female Episcopal priest, and a wounded liberal walk into a bar on New Year's Eve in 1999 to debate love and loss; however, they learn that anyone can succumb to the phrase "it looks like rain."

[Lights up. Sounds of a bar. Some activity. A sign reads "DOCTOR LEE'S KARA-OKE NIGHT—HAPPY 2000!" DOCTOR LEE, dressed in tight jeans and very tucked-in shirt, stands on a small stage getting his gear—microphone, CDs, books, etc.—ready. BIG J, in an un-ironic John Deere webbed ball cap, equally un-ironic work boots, and scraggly, libertarian beard, enters. He carries a small plate covered in foil with him. He places the plate on the table and sits with arms folded—the posture of a man who has an answer for everything. DOCTOR LEE approaches him and plops a large book of songs down in front of him. DOCTOR LEE regards him.]

DOCTOR LEE [*Recognizing him.*] Hey!

BIG J Hey.

DOCTOR LEE I thought I recognized you. Holy cow!

BIG J Yeah.

DOCTOR LEE Big J, right?

BIG J Yeah.

DOCTOR LEE Well.

[DOCTOR LEE *sticks out his hand.* BIG J *shakes it.*]
What brings you back to town? I haven't seen you since . . .

BIG J Eleven years. When we graduated.

DOCTOR LEE Right. What's been going on? Where are you these days?

BIG J I'm here. Next town over.

DOCTOR LEE Huh. I never see you.

BIG J Well, life stuff.

DOCTOR LEE Right. But you had a couple of friends, right? The girl and the skinny guy.

BIG J Yeah. They're coming tonight.

DOCTOR LEE Reunion?

BIG J Not at the college. Just us three.

DOCTOR LEE I'll have to make sure you guys go first. Here's a book.
[*Hands him a karaoke book.* BIG J *flips through.*]
Things are a little different. I started writing songs.

BIG J I heard you started writing.

DOCTOR LEE So, you can do . . . anything, really.

[BIG J *flips. Pauses.*]

BIG J You wrote all of them?

DOCTOR LEE All of them.

BIG J So . . . I'm supposed to sing karaoke to songs I don't know.

DOCTOR LEE Think of it as the ultimate kamikaze karaoke.

BIG J Okay.

[*Beat.*]

DOCTOR LEE Don't get all—

BIG J I'm not.

DOCTOR LEE —upset.

BIG J I'm not!

DOCTOR LEE You can't argue with originality, right?

   [*Beat.*]

   RIGHT?

BIG J Yeah, right, of course.

DOCTOR LEE Good.

   [*Beat.*]

   Your friend. The skinny guy. The guy whose . . . you know.

BIG J Yeah.

DOCTOR LEE Yeah. I knew *he* stayed local. I saw him talking to a girl.

BIG J A girl?

DOCTOR LEE Woman. Last week. You know. He might be dating.

BIG J Wow. Huh.

DOCTOR LEE So, him I see. But not you. Never see you around.

BIG J Nope. Never. But it's a new millennium starting tonight. So. We'll see.

   [*Awkward beat.*]

DOCTOR LEE Song?

BIG J You know what? Surprise me.

   [DOCTOR LEE *grins widely, and nods.* DOCTOR LEE *leaves the book and exits.* BIG J *to himself:*]

Dating.

[*There's a sense that* DOCTOR LEE *continues to distribute books around the bar. NOTE: the rest of the bar can be offstage. There should be a sense that a few folks are milling around, but it's nothing like crowded.* PIDGE, *a plucky woman in her early 30s, enters.* BIG J *regards her, and greets her warmly.*]

PIDGE Big J!

[*They hold. It's a second too long for* PIDGE. *Okay, two seconds two long. Really, he can stop now. They finally part.*]

BIG J How's China? They all Christian yet?

PIDGE We'll keep trying.

BIG J When do you go back?

PIDGE Don't know. We'll see. Donny here?

BIG J Not yet. But he's gotta be pissed.

PIDGE ?

BIG J For wasting his tax money. Didn't you hear?

PIDGE No.

BIG J So, last storm, they're picking up branches. And it turns out, the guy in charge—whose salary is being paid by *Donny's* taxes—he stops and helps a friend. Cleans up the friend's yard. Hell, if he can't do it for everybody, he shouldn't . . .

PIDGE You complain?

BIG J Hell yeah.

PIDGE Even though it's not your money. Not your taxes.

BIG J A concerned citizen.

PIDGE Even though Donny probably doesn't care.

BIG J Someone should, it's his pockets. He needs it.

PIDGE And this has nothing to do with your running a tree-removal business.

BIG J Hey. I'm a workingman. And, yeah, okay, that might've been a job my crew could've had. It might've. But the bigger picture is if the government can only do for one, then it shouldn't do at all.

PIDGE Okay.

BIG J And I'm gonna tell him tonight.

PIDGE Tonight?

[*Beat.*]

You don't want to, I don't know. Do it tonight. We haven't seen him since . . .

BIG J You mean *you* haven't seen him. You're out changing the world. *I've* seen him, but not lately. Probably because he's dating again.

PIDGE [*Disappointed.*] Is he?

BIG J Yeah. Some girl. Or something. I don't know.

PIDGE Oh.

BIG J Good for him, though, right? It's been, what, a year?

PIDGE Yeah. Has it already?

BIG J Few days before Christmas. And here he is.

[DONNY *enters. He wears a buttoned-up winter coat that might have looked ritzy a few years ago. But now it is starting to fade, and stains have not been attended to. He is noticeably missing a button. His wash-and-go haircut has not seen many washes. He smiles at* PIDGE *and* BIG J. *He hugs* PIDGE. *He and* BIG J *hug each other, but they pat each other hard. Harder. Real hard.* DONNY *stops.* BIG J *regards* DONNY.]

What's cooking?

DONNY Nothing.

BIG J Nothing, huh?

[*Confidentially.*]

I baked brownies.

DONNY Did you?

[BIG J *takes a plate from under the table. He removes foil. Perfect, moist brownies.* PIDGE *reacts.* BIG J *notices.*]

PIDGE What? It's fine, go ahead.

BIG J Donny, I know you don't drink but weed is okay, right? / I mean, is it? If not, I'm so sorry man, I just thought—

DONNY Weed's fine. / No, it's fine. / I'm fine with weed.

PIDGE / You are?

DONNY Yeah.

BIG J Good.

> [*Sits. Each takes a brownie.* PIDGE *puts hers down.* BIG J *takes a little bite.* DONNY *scarfs his like an animal, leaving crumbs.* BIG J *and* PIDGE *watch* DONNY.]

Yes! Y'see, I want it to be like it was when we first met, you know? Fifteen years ago. Brownies. Doctor Lee. Fifteen years. Can you believe it?

DONNY Yeah. Fewer people, though.

BIG J Across the street. The Apple Bar. They got karaoke there tonight.

PIDGE But they have it here, too.

BIG J Yeah, but. Doctor Lee's writing his own songs.

DONNY I know.

PIDGE So, you guess the lyrics?

BIG J They're on the screen. It's the tune.

DONNY They're actually pretty good. You know he's a real doctor, right? PhD in music? When we were undergrads he got his doctorate here. The college paid for his tuition.

BIG J You mean the taxpayer. The taxpayer paid for it. But I guess you should be used to your tax money getting wasted.

DONNY [*To* PIDGE.] What's this now?

PIDGE Tree-removal service. Town of Rosedale is cutting into private business.

BIG J   And wasting your taxes.

DONNY   You mean Mrs. Middleton?

BIG J   That her name?

DONNY   Yeah. Those guys are in big trouble, but Mrs. Middleton is ninety-three. She lives alone, and the only joy she gets is walking down to her mailbox every day. With the tree down . . . I dunno. Made her house look abandoned. So. It's a shame they're in trouble. I get her milk whenever I go shopping. Sometimes, eggs or bread. Depends on what I think she needs. I mean, she won't tell me. So. I try to figure it out. Anyway, yeah, it's a shame. Some asshole phoned them in. Big trouble. Know anything about that?

BIG J   You look at the book yet? Let's choose some songs.

[Regards table.]

DONNY   Who do I gotta screw around here to get a pencil?

PIDGE   [*To* BIG J.] Bend over.

BIG J   Ha. This from a minister.

DONNY   Priest. Episcopalians are priests, right?

PIDGE   Right.

DONNY   So. How's God?

PIDGE   Still there.

DONNY   Right. Right. See him lately?

PIDGE   Every day.

DONNY   Good. Glad he can do that for you. And Big J, how's . . . how's Little J?

BIG J   Good. His mom's got him tonight. That's working out pretty well. We don't even fight no more. Just pass the kid. Last weekend she barely stopped the car. So. Things are, you know. Good.

DONNY   Good. Good.

BIG J   Plus! I'm out!

[*Looks around the bar.*]

Good to be out.

[*Awkward moment.*]

PIDGE [*Beat*]. Can I tell you what God looks like?

BIG J and **DONNY** No.

PIDGE I was sitting with my mentor, Father George Condor. We're in California at a retreat. Now, Father George, he knows he's dying, right? So, he spends his days watering marigolds and talking to God, talking to the world. Just talking. So, I see him sitting out there on a bench, it's this old, curved stone bench. It's supposed to look Roman. And I walk around and see him. And he has this little face, like a Santa Claus cherub. And he says, "Hi there." He stops talking, smiles, and I watch this gold beam of light . . . the Holy Spirit come down and embrace him. He smiles, closes his eyes, and lets out an "Mmmm." Then he looks at me. And that . . . that is God. For me, that's what he is.

DONNY Sunny in California. Must be God.

BIG J Come on, Donny. Let's leave the big conversations to smarter people.

[DOCTOR LEE *approaches.*]

DONNY Hey, Doc.

DOCTOR LEE Same as last time?

BIG J Last time?

DONNY You know what? Surprise me.

[DOCTOR LEE *nods.*]

BIG J That's what I said!

[DOCTOR LEE *regards* PIDGE.]

PIDGE Surprise me.

[DOCTOR LEE *looks around the table.*]

DOCTOR LEE Let's do one together tonight. To start. Okay? Like we used to.

BIG J It used to be Hall and Oats.

DONNY Don McLean.

DOCTOR LEE Yeah, yeah, you want that? You can go across the street.

[*Beat.*]

Have I ever steered you wrong?

PIDGE REO Speedwagon.

DONNY I like REO Speedwagon.

BIG J [*To* DOCTOR LEE.] Brownie?

[DOCTOR LEE *takes a brownie. He nods. He returns to the mini-stage, setting up his gear, etc. As the conversation continues, music starts to play softly.*]

PIDGE Wow. And some people just worry about singing off-key.

DONNY Okay. I changed my mind. I'm talking about God. See, for me, God is not something we see, it is something we do. God is a verb.

BIG J I don't believe in God. Sorry, Pidge.

DONNY Okay, but, let's talk about it. God being a verb, I mean.

BIG J A verb. Sure. What's something God does? I got it—God gets our soldiers killed. Every day. Tells me what I can't put in my brownies. Tells grown men and women they can't love who they want to love. And God is now in politics. He's federal. He's after *your* vagina, Pidge, and your sanity, Donny. It's all part of His plan.

PIDGE You either believe in God, or you don't. Either way you have no access to His mind, you don't know what His plan is.

BIG J It's what preachers say.

PIDGE Any preacher who says random death and destruction is part of His plan is spiritually wounded and should not be in front of his congregation.

BIG J It's all part of His plan or there is no plan. It's black and white . . .

PIDGE It's *not* black and white, nothing is black and white . . .

BIG J Fine, then let's take a tragedy for a moment. Let's take . . .

DONNY My wife and son. I get it. You guys aren't very subtle.

BIG J Sorry.

PIDGE No, I'm sorry.

BIG J What, you're sorrier?

PIDGE We weren't going to talk about it. But. It's just . . . I won't believe it's part of His plan, Donny. I won't. I don't.

[*A moment. DONNY reaches into his coat, and takes out a couple of buttons.*]

DONNY If God is a verb, then. If God is doing, like doing good. Then.

[*Beat.*]

These are kind of small.

[*He takes off coat, and he is wearing a T-shirt, which has a rifle and a red circle with a line through a gun. To BIG J.*]

I want you to get rid of your guns.

BIG J Whatever you say, Donny.

DONNY I want you to take your son somewhere else instead of hunting—a bike trail, fishing.

BIG J Killing fish is okay?

DONNY I want you to show him that guns only have one purpose—to kill each other.

BIG J And how am I going to show him that?

DONNY The thing about guns, you know, you can never lock them up tight enough. Never. So. Destroy them. All of them. If my son were here . . .

BIG J Okay. Okay. Have another brownie.

DONNY I have been drinking for the past seven days straight.

PIDGE But? No . . .

DONNY Your brownies won't touch me. You think I can just come in here and say, "Hey, I'm fighting to get guns off the street." To you? Without taking a week to get myself good and ready? You think I have the nerve to look at you, Pidge, because when I see you, I'm reminded . . . can there really be a God?

[*Beat.*]

Had to fortify my courage. I'm here by the grace of Old Grandad rot-gut.

BIG J   Great.

DONNY   Tomorrow is the new millennium. Y2K. We've been climbing God's pop charts, all of us, through our performative . . . what do you call it . . . humanity . . . only to reach this. This is the last night on earth. And I want . . . I want it all to be over. *All. Of. It.* There is no healing, no vigil. I'm tired of waiting for politicians, so-called world and religious leaders to solve this. They won't. We can. Big J: get rid of your guns. Do it in front of your son, and let him know he should be proud of his old man. Tell him . . . tell him . . . promise me here, tonight, on the last night on earth that tomorrow you will look him in the eyes . . . you will look at him . . . and . . . tell him . . .

BIG J   You were going to let Archie come hunting with me.

PIDGE   Wait . . .

BIG J   You said he could come with. Your wife said he could come with. So, this new political stance of yours . . . it's grief, man. So. Let's talk about something else. You, me. Some songs. Brownies. Look at Pidge's ass, you ever know a minister could be so hot?

PIDGE   Priest.

BIG J   Whatever.

PIDGE   [*Beat.*] I hear you're dating.

[*A moment. DONNY looks away.*]

DONNY   Yeah, well. Date. It was *a* date.

PIDGE   So. Will there be . . . you know, another?

BIG J   Yeah, let's talk about that, Donny.

[*A beat. He regards the buttons.*]

DONNY If you're my friends, you'll wear these. Wherever you go. If you're not my friends, you can leave.

[*Pause.* PIDGE *looks at hers. Looks at* BIG J.]

BIG J I don't do ultimatums. Tomorrow we start the new millennium. You know what that means? It means more of the same. It doesn't mean new beginnings. It doesn't mean I'm suddenly wearing a button. It doesn't mean anything. It means more of the same. Tonight is *not* the last night on earth.

[*Beat.*]

Go home, Donny. Sleep it off. I'm gonna check on Doctor Lee.

[BIG J *approaches* DOCTOR LEE *on the small stage.*]

PIDGE How can Big J do something tomorrow if tonight's the last night on earth? You said tonight's the last night on earth, and you said tomorrow you want him to get rid of his guns. So. Which is it? Is there a tomorrow or isn't there?

DONNY I dunno . . . guess we find out on midnight.

PIDGE Our midnight? Other side of the world already had its midnights. Nothing yet.

DONNY . . .

PIDGE Can I get you anything?

DONNY No.

PIDGE You by yourself?

DONNY What do you think?

[*Beat.*]

I'm sorry. Yes.

PIDGE [*Beat.*] You can stay at my room tonight. You know? I mean . . . I don't mean . . . what I mean is . . . you can shower. You can have the bed.

DONNY I think I need to be alone. You know?

PIDGE Yeah.

[*Beat.*]

No, I don't know.

DONNY Pidge. Okay. Don't tell Big J. But. I am dating.

PIDGE Oh.

DONNY His ex.

PIDGE Gina?

DONNY Yeah.

PIDGE You're dating Big Gina?

DONNY Yeah. And she's not that big.

[*Beat.*]

Yeah.

PIDGE Holy shit, Donny!

DONNY I know, I know.

PIDGE How the . . . why?

DONNY I stopped at Tantillo's for gas. About a month ago. And I saw her there. Little J in the back. We start talking. I tell her that I like Tantillo's. It's friendly. Familiar. Best buttered hard rolls in the valley. Don't know what they do to those rolls. So. I buy her one and Little J one. We talk for a while. You know, Gina didn't know Archie had autism? Big J never told her. He doesn't believe in things like that. Thinks it has to do with label-happy liberals. Bad parenting. I don't know. So, I tell her about how when we'd ask Archie where he was going if he left a room, he'd say "to get answers." Or, if we asked him how he was feeling, he'd say "looks like rain." Even when we were inside, he'd say, "looks like rain." It took me two years to figure out that he did that because he liked the control. If you say "looks like rain," folks invariably look up. They can't help it. And I'm thinking these things and saying these things to Gina, looking at Little J, who's sitting on my trunk looking bored. Archie never looked bored, so it's new to me. And we keep talking. And I'm eating this hard roll, and for the first time in a while, I'm not thinking about . . . but what I am thinking about is Little J and Gina. Being on their own. About me being on my own. So, the next night, I take Gina out. We hit the diner on the other side of town, I know Big J likes the one that's on this side. And we've done that three times. Came here last week.

[*Beat.*]

So, yeah. It's good. She knows what happened. I don't have to talk about it. A friend of mine had wanted to set me up, you know? On a date? But, with a blind date, I'd have to talk about it. With Gina? There's nothing to talk about.

PIDGE Big J is going to skin you.

DONNY Probably. Yeah.

[*Beat.*]

I am really sorry about. You know. Not taking you up on the invite. I do really appreciate . . .

PIDGE I think I'm in love with him.

DONNY . . . ?!

PIDGE Yeah.

DONNY Big J?

PIDGE Yeah.

DONNY Oh.

PIDGE So. I really meant, you know. If you wanted to come over. It would just be for a shower. And crash on the . . . you know. Sober up. Nothing. You know. Like. Goodness. No. Blech! You're . . . you know, Donny. I mean—DONNY! Right?

DONNY Yeah.

PIDGE So.

DONNY Right. "Blech!"

PIDGE [*Forces a shudder.*] Yeah. We'd have too much to . . . I don't know. Talk about or something. Yeah. Big J, though. Challenge. I like a challenge.

DONNY   Right. He's an atheist!

PIDGE   There you go!

DONNY   Plenty of challenges ahead.

PIDGE   Right.

DONNY   And he's divorced!

PIDGE   He is!

DONNY   So. No one to interfere with.

PIDGE   Right.

DONNY   You know.

PIDGE   No one there.

DONNY   Right. No one there.
   [*Beat.*]
   He is a little grabby, though.

PIDGE   Yeah. Just a bit. But.

[*Pause.*]

DONNY   I . . . I'm gonna go. Okay? You two should have /

PIDGE   / No, don't /

DONNY   / a chance to talk. Catch up. I'm . . . I'm not good at talking tonight.

PIDGE   [*Beat.*] You gonna tell him?

DONNY   [*Chuckles.*] No, that's your business.

PIDGE   I mean about the other thing?

[BIG J *comes back holding an enormous drink with a carrot stuck in it.*]

BIG J   Okay, no more politics tonight. No more buttons, no more shirts. No more Mrs. Middleton and tree service talk. Just singing, okay? Let's have our brownies, drink, sing, and find something to laugh about.

[*He sits. A moment.*]

DONNY I'm dating Gina.

[*Beat.*]

I'm . . . I'm sorry.

[*Pause. They all look at each other.* BIG J *is completely still. Then, he bursts into laughing.*]

BIG J Jesus. She's gonna eat you alive!

DONNY Yeah.

[BIG J *laughs some more.* DONNY *picks up one of the anti-gun buttons. Puts it away in his coat. Goes to pick up the other one.* BIG J *grabs his hand. Takes the button and holds it up.*]

BIG J Is that . . . what this is about?

DONNY ?

BIG J You gonna start telling me what I can and cannot do with my son?

DONNY No, I . . .

BIG J Gina put you up to this? The shirt, the buttons?

DONNY No, this is me . . .

BIG J This is *not* you . . .

DONNY Of course it is!

BIG J I knew she was going soft. Jesus. And you. You friggin' weenie, letting the system think for you! That *woman* think for you!

DONNY I think for me, you self-righteous piece of shit!

[*Pause.*]

BIG J I'm the self-righteous one?

[*Points at* PIDGE.]

YOU come in here with Jesus Humping Christ telling me how to run my life, and YOU

[*Points at* DONNY.]

come in here wearing bullshit propaganda telling me how to raise my son? And I'm the righteous one?

DONNY You're the one who doesn't want to help.

BIG J I'm the one who doesn't want to BOTHER or BE BOTHERED.

DONNY Right. Like you didn't bother with Mrs. Middleton's tree. That wasn't you sticking your nose in someone else's shit.

BIG J I have a business!

DONNY That had NOTHING to do with your business!

BIG J The workingman suffers at the hands . . .

DONNY You got your BA in English RIGHT HERE! At a state school! You DON'T get to play that card!

BIG J Who the hell do you think you are, Donny?! The two of you! FUCK YOUR CASE, FUCK YOUR GOD, AND FUCK THAT USED-UP, UGLY-ASS WOMAN YOU'RE LETTING BULLY YOU!

[BIG J *turns.* DONNY *grabs him.* BIG J *backhands him.* DONNY *stumbles. He stands up. Looks around.*]

DONNY Did . . . did you just bitch-slap me?

BIG J That wasn't a bitch-slap.

PIDGE It was a bitch-slap.

DONNY Dude!

BIG J A warning. A . . . "snap out of it" kind of thing.

[DOCTOR LEE *enters, eating a brownie.*]

DOCTOR LEE Well. Someone ordered a bitch-slap.

DONNY I just fell, Doctor Lee. It's fine.

DOCTOR LEE Jesus Christ. I should have known. You're like the rest of them. The fratties, the assholes. You guys used to let me sing with you. Harmony. The guys in town since? Nope. It's like I'm an embarrassment. I bring the party, and I'm an embarrassment. They told me here that I'm out. End of the year. This is my last night. So, man . . . what happened? I decide to start sharing my songs. I got thousands. I program them in, boom. And you're supposed to sing with me tonight. We're supposed to have one more moment.

[*Looks at* DONNY.]

Before reality really sets in. Get it together, guys. Look, I'll get the song going. Okay? Just . . . I'll get it going. Fuck everybody else. Just wait, okay?

[DOCTOR LEE *runs back to the stage and hurries. As the following conversation happens,* DOCTOR LEE *continues testing mikes, etc.* DONNY *shakes his head and turns to exit.*]

PIDGE Donny . . .

BIG J Wait a sec . . .

PIDGE Come on, it's freezing. Where you gonna go?

DONNY [*Beat.*] To get answers.

[DONNY *exits.* BIG J *stands for a minute, not sure what to say.* PIDGE *looks at* BIG J. DOCTOR LEE *puts the brownie on the table. Gives* BIG J *a devastating look. And exits.*]

BIG J That was too far. I know. Okay. But. Nobody tells me how to raise my son. Nobody.

PIDGE His whole family was murdered, Big J.

BIG J Not by my son. Not by me. It was a nut. A random nut.

PIDGE We're all nuts.

BIG J Exactly.

PIDGE Exactly.

BIG J [*Beat.*] That doesn't give him the . . . what the hell is Gina doing with such a weenie?

PIDGE Big J . . .

BIG J He knows what he is.

[*Beat.*]

What?

PIDGE Nothing, I . . .

BIG J What?

PIDGE I should go. Check on him.

BIG J Fine. Go. I don't need all the judgment.

PIDGE You think . . . do you think I judge you?

BIG J I can feel it. Looking at me. Staring. I can feel the judgment. Maybe you don't mean to, but it's there. I'm sure you can't help it, just like he can't help his button addiction. Jesus. Don't you have church people to be with? Obligations or something?

PIDGE If I'm looking at you, it's because . . . this was the first time we've seen each other in years.

BIG J Right.

PIDGE The first time I've seen Donny since . . .

BIG J Right.

PIDGE There might not be a next year.

BIG J Of course there will. More of the same.

PIDGE No. Nothing will be the same.

[*Pause. She looks toward the exit. She gets upset.*]

BIG J Ah, shit. Pidge. Hey.

[*He approaches her.*]

Hey. Hey.

[*He holds her. She cries into his jacket.*]

I'm really sorry, all right? Really sorry.

[*Beat.*]

Guess. Guess I should have let it go tonight. Let him say what he needed to. It doesn't change anything, right? I mean, he can say whatever. It doesn't change the world. Right?

[*Beat.*]

I just don't want anyone to think that they can control me.

[PIDGE *steps back.*]

PIDGE [*Beat.*] Looks like rain.

[BIG J *looks up. Big, slow synthesized notes start to play. Think 1980s.* PIDGE *moves to* BIG J. *She takes his hands. They slowly start dancing. Not romantic, just dancing.* DOCTOR LEE *enters, striking poses that are, in his mind, majestic. He starts singing. It's loud. Unapologetic. It actually fits the music. His motions are deliberate. He is singing the end-credit song to the end of the universe. And he knows it.*]

DOCTOR LEE You know what? Surpriiiiiiiiiiiiiiiiiiiiiise meeeeeeeeeeeeeeeee.

You know what? Surpriiiiiiiiiiiiiiiiiiiiiiiise meeeeeeeeeeeeeeeee.

[DOCTOR LEE *continues singing the same words. The tune continues repeat.* PIDGE *and* BIG J *hold each other close.* DONNIE *re-enters. The clock starts to toll. He slowly puts his arms around the two. They welcome him in. They all start crying, holding each other close;* DONNY *carefully places a button of a rifle with a circle and a line through it on each of their backs without them noticing, while* DOCTOR LEE *continues striking poses; at some point, he hands a microphone to* DONNY, *which he shares with* BIG J *and* PIDGE, *and they're all singing until the twelfth toll, until the end of the world; singing until blackout.*]

• • •

acknowledgments

Thanks go out to everyone who submitted their work for consideration, making my job both a pleasure and a challenge. I continue to welcome submissions from all walks of life. My e-mail inbox is always open.

Thanks especially go out to all the contributors that have made this volume the special collection that it is. Thanks to Jim Price and John Fleming at Texas State University for tracking me down and making several very good recommendations. Keep on the lookout for good work! And a big thanks goes out to John Patrick Bray at the University of Georgia. His connections with the vast playwriting community is impressively expansive. He has used his connections to help me locate talent in the past, and this year he sent me no fewer than seven submissions that are included in this volume, from all over the United States. Thanks, JP.

Needless to say, without the great editorial help of Applause Theatre & Cinema Books, this book would never come to press, especially not in its current excellent form. Thanks, Bernadette Malavarca, Carol Flannery, and John Cerullo. I also want to thank June Clark, friend and agent, for all her advice and assistance. And as always, thanks to Jean and Erin.